346

Dear Jacqueline,
perhaps this is of some
interest / use. Alas it is
written more for a lay
audience so probably
doesn't have anything in
it that you have not
seen before.

See you soon,

Anna

Meritocracy and the University

Also available from Bloomsbury

Rethinking Knowledge within Higher Education: Adorno and Social Justice,
Jan McArthur
Academic Working Lives, Experience, Practice and Change,
edited by Lynne Gornall, Caryn Cook, Lyn Daunton,
Jane Salisbury and Brychan Thomas
Academic Identities in Higher Education: The Changing European Landscape,
edited by Linda Evans and Jon Nixon
Learning Communities in Imagined Social Capital: Learning to Belong,
Jocey Quinn
*Interpretative Pedagogies for Higher Education: Arendt, Berger, Said, Nussbaum
and their Legacies,* Jon Nixon
Towards Teaching in Public: Reshaping the Modern University,
edited by Mike Neary
Acts of Knowing: Critical Pedagogy in, Against and Beyond the University,
Stephen Cowden

Meritocracy and the University

Selective Admission in England and the United States

Anna Mountford Zimdars

Bloomsbury Academic
An imprint of Bloomsbury Publishing Plc

B L O O M S B U R Y

LONDON · OXFORD · NEW YORK · NEW DELHI · SYDNEY

Bloomsbury Academic

An imprint of Bloomsbury Publishing Plc

50 Bedford Square	1385 Broadway
London	New York
WC1B 3DP	NY 10018
UK	USA

www.bloomsbury.com

BLOOMSBURY and the Diana logo are trademarks of Bloomsbury Publishing Plc

First published 2016

British Library Cataloguing-in-Publication Data
A catalogue record for this book is available from the British Library.

ISBN: HB: 978-1-8496-6522-3
ePDF: 978-1-8496-6549-0
ePub: 978-1-8496-6548-3

Library of Congress Cataloging-in-Publication Data
A catalog record for this book is available from the Library of Congress.

Typeset by Deanta Global Publishing Services, Chennai, India

Contents

Acknowledgements

No book of this sort is ever the work of just one individual and many people share the credit for the completion of this project. I am grateful to all who have generously contributed through participating in interviews and informal conversations. I would like to thank the respondents who participated in this project for generously giving their time and sharing their experiences. I am grateful for your contributions – and I am sorry I cannot give you all named credit due to research confidentiality.

I would also like to thank the following named people for their particular contributions: Special thanks to William R. Fitzsimmons, Dean of Admissions and Financial Aid at Harvard, for hosting me at the Harvard Summer Institute on College Admissions and to all attendees at the event who have explained aspects of US college admission. Special thanks also to the Sutton Trust for inviting me to attend an event that discussed elite higher education in England and the United States. Professor Mitchell Stevens generously facilitated and mentored me through a research visit to New York University, and shared his insights into how college admission works. Special thanks also to Janet Graham, Director of Supporting Professionalism in Admissions, Dr Samina Khan, Director of Admissions, University of Oxford, Dean Fitzsimmons and Barbara Geier for their comments and corrections on the first draft of the book, and Professor Michael Bastedo for some factual clarifications. The work of the editors at Bloomsbury, Caroline Wintersgill and Alison Baker, is also gratefully acknowledged.

Last but not least, I am grateful for the opportunities for formal and informal exchange and discussion provided by the conferences in my field, namely SRHE, BERA and ECER as well as events organized by HEFCE and SPA and the Higher Education Study Group at King's College and discussions with friends and colleagues. Funding from the SRHE and the ESRC is gratefully acknowledged. All errors and omissions are my own.

Introduction

If we get admissions right, the rest looks after itself.
(Ivy League admissions professional)

This is a book about undergraduate admission to renowned highly selective universities in the United States and England. Admission to one of the leading universities – including Cambridge and Oxford in England and Harvard, Princeton, and Stanford in the United States – carries kudos, social cache and the promise to open doors for some career entries. There is great public and media interest in who is admitted to these institutions. As one admissions professional working for a US Ivy League (see glossary) institution noted, this fascination is due to admission being a 'high stake game, because it is a mystery, and it is a ritual that is great to watch'.

But how does selection to these universities actually work? What are the ideas that underlie their admission decisions and processes? What are these institutions looking for in students? Making sense of the aims and processes of selective admissions through a comparative perspective is the aim of this book: the book offers an insight into the curious world of university admissions.

Applying for post-secondary education and enrolling at university can be an emotional phase in the lives of students and their families. Especially for those going to university straight after school, it can mean, for the first time in their lives, moving away from a known social environment and from their circles of friends. This might also entail geographic moves and the formation of new identities for students and their families, as well as a new journey of learning and discovery. Indeed, the highly selective universities in this book are built around a residential student experience model, which sees students live and dine together while pursuing full-time undergraduate study. Many of us will either have experienced a transition from school to university or know someone who has gone through the university admissions process (or someone who is considering joining a university). Moreover, just as sporting competitions like the Olympics, the US Open or Wimbledon offer a moment for reflecting on the state of sport in a nation, university admissions can provide an annual focal point for national debates on the state of the education system in a country. It is a time when new statistics comparing universities emerge, when applicants reflect on their experiences of navigating the admissions process, when recent graduates share their stories about entering or trying to enter the world of work, and it can be a time to think of the things that work well and to reflect on potential flaws within the current system.

Not surprisingly then, admissions decisions, and especially those involving selective universities, feature prominently in public life. Admissions decisions are discussed by students, parents, families and schools as well as in the media; they are subject to judicial reviews in the courts, and are debated by politicians in parliament. They are part of our national consciousness.

In England, disagreement with an individual admissions decision was commented on in the highest echelons of politics: In 1999, Laura Spence's unsuccessful application to study medicine at the University of Oxford led the then Chancellor of the Exchequer (and later prime minister) Gordon Brown to accuse Oxford of 'elitism'. In his words, Laura Spence's rejection was an 'absolute scandal' (BBC 2000). Incidentally, Laura went on to pursue her undergraduate studies at Harvard in the United States. In the United States, cases involving the unsuccessful application of students for university places have repeatedly progressed through the judicial appeals system all the way to the Supreme Court. Recent cases in the United States considered the legitimacy of Barbara Grutter's rejection by Michigan Law School in 1996 as well as Jennifer Gratz and Patrick Hamacher's unsuccessful applications to the same university's undergraduate programme in 1995 and 1997 respectively (Grutter v Bollinger 2003). In 2013, the Supreme Court ruled on the rejection of Abigail Fisher's application to the University of Texas (Fisher v University of Texas at Austin et al. 2013). The most powerful court in the world has thus repeatedly decided whether students had been wrongly denied admission by a particular university. Most recently, in 2014, the Supreme Court upheld the ban on affirmative action in higher education in the state of Michigan, a decision affecting seven further states with similar bans. In England, cases of non-admission very rarely get as far as the law courts as the Higher Education Act 2004 has laid down that university admissions in the UK is the responsibility of individual universities and should be based on academic judgement.

It is not only the political and legal debates surrounding admission that are fierce. The competition involved in admission to some of the best-known universities in the world is also becoming fiercer every year, with more students applying for a limited number of undergraduate places. Every year, many applicants – often with an array of the highest possible scores in their prior schooling – fail to gain admission to their first-choice university. Selective universities admit only a few for undergraduate study, about one in fourteen at the most selective US universities and about one in five of highly self-selected candidates at Cambridge and Oxford in England are successful. There are even lower success rates at some other institutions and for specific courses. Some admissions decisions take teachers, parents and career advisers by surprise: Josh might not be admitted to his first-choice university this year although Amy, from the same school, had been admitted with a similar schooling record in the previous year. Such stories can make what happens in the admissions process appear like the functioning of a black box.

When a selective university admits one applicant and rejects another one, it inadvertently makes a statement about what it considers to be a fair way to choose among applicants. The values apparent in the process of university admission also align with the purpose and education models of the respective institutions and are embedded in widely held ideas about what fairness generally means and the sort of attributes a successful individual should have. Through the lens of university admissions, we can thus learn about what English and American societies value, even beyond the university gates, as virtuous, deserving characteristics. This book uses a comparative approach to look at admission in both England and the United States. In doing so, it shows which admissions considerations are unique features of either the English or the US system and national context and which ideas are shared across the two countries and thus transcend specific national contexts.

This book then is written to provide a glimpse, an insight into the curious world of university admissions. The description and discussion of admissions processes are based on interviews and observations I undertook with admissions professionals and academic selectors responsible for admitting students to highly selective universities. To explain how I researched this book, I respond to some typical questions about what the research for this book project has involved and lay out the structure of the book. Readers not interested in this aspect of the work can skip this section and jump straight into the actual description of the admissions world in Chapter 1.

Who is this book written for?

The book is written for anyone interested in admissions to higher education or with an interest in 'how society and organizations work'. It is written as an introduction to admissions and the world of higher education. Therefore, you do not need to know anything about admissions or higher education to read this book. The book introduces readers to those working in admission, the purpose of and ideas and values in the university admissions process as well as offering a look inside the actual process of admitting students to selective universities. References for further reading are provided for those who wish to delve deeper into particular aspects of admissions.

Readers will gain a greater understanding of admissions processes as a result of reading this book. However, this is not a guidebook on 'how to get into a top university'. Instead, it is a book that explains the hows and whys of admissions processes in the United States and England. Along the way, the book seeks to solve the question of why Laura Spence and Barbara Grutter were not admitted to their first-choice university.

Why do you look at elite universities in England and the United States?

There are many ways to approach the subject of university admissions and universities. One way is to think about the world rankings of universities (certain US and English universities consistently occupy the top places). Graduates from these universities enjoy a high level of representation in public offices – this is evident when one looks at the education of politicians and judges – and occupy leading positions in the private sector. Parents, schools and applicants are voting with their feet on institutions, with demand for places far outstripping supply in the most prestigious institutions. What goes on inside the world of admissions at highly selective institutions thus has potentially considerable impact on the world around us. It is those universities' admissions world that this book is about.

Hopefully, this book will provide some new insights to readers with a range of interests and to those who have prior knowledge of the admissions process. Because this book uses insights from both the United States and England, readers who are somewhat familiar with either of these countries as well as readers who do not know either system will find out something new about the admissions process in selective institutions. But this comparative approach also has limitations – what is presented is not a like-for-like comparison. The English institutions described in this book are public institutions. The US institutions in this book are non-profit private institutions. This difference has implications for the mission of and admission to these institutions as well as for who these institutions are accountable to.

Which universities are represented in this book?

Most of the US universities in this project are part of the Ivy League (see glossary), a group of eight selective private universities in Northeastern United States. I interviewed current and some past admissions professionals at Harvard, Yale and Princeton and at two further Ivy League institutions. I also talked to selectors at two selective liberal arts colleges (see glossary) and at two further highly selective private four-year institutions that were not part of the Ivy League. Liberal arts colleges have traditionally been renowned for their focus on teaching and the student experience and they tend to be smaller and less focused on graduate study (see glossary) than the Ivy League. I also interviewed admissions professionals in less selective US institutions and public institutions but these findings are not part of the present book.

As regards England, I interviewed academics and admissions professionals at Oxford and Cambridge and at eight other Russell Group institutions (see glossary). The Russell Group is a membership organization of public universities with a focus on research excellence. Oxford and Cambridge are members of the Russell Group but are often considered separate from the other universities in the group by the media and in scholarly analysis. Together, Oxford and Cambridge are referred to as 'Oxbridge'.

For most institutions in both the United States and England, several interviews with different people took place; in several instances, I interviewed the same person more than once.

Where and when did you undertake your research?

I conducted interviews in both the United States and the four regions of the UK (England, Northern Ireland, Wales and Scotland) for this project. But because higher education policy in the four regions of the UK has increasingly been diverging, I have only included findings from my interviews in England in this book. The English universities that are included in this book, however, recruit nationally and have students from the devolved UK regions in them. As regards the United States, most interviews took place at institutions broadly located in Northeastern United States, some interviews were held at institutions located in the West Coast.

In addition to the interviews with academics and admissions professionals, I attended the annual Harvard Summer Institutes on College Admissions in the United States in 2013, various campus tours at US universities, two UCAS conferences in England, a Sutton Trust summit on admission (Sutton Trust 2013) as well as academic conferences, including an event on the selection of elites organized by Sciences Po in Paris and a conference I co-organized on fair admission at the University of Manchester. I also observed several selection meetings at Oxbridge.

Most of the research data presented here was collected between 2011 and 2013 but some quotations are drawn from earlier work. Such earlier quotations were only included when the factual information it related to was judged to still be accurate and up to date.

Do you say who you have talked to for this project?

Participants in both the United States and England were assured anonymity and also that the name of their institution would be kept confidential. In England, the universities of Oxford and Cambridge are referred to as 'Oxbridge', while other universities are referred to as 'Russell Group' (excluding Oxbridge). The term 'Big Three' or 'HYP' is used to identify the Big Three Ivies in the United States, namely Harvard, Yale and Princeton. Other institutions are referred to as 'Ivy League' (excluding HYP), 'liberal arts college' and 'non-Ivy selective university'.

In order to keep information confidential, direct quotations were sometimes modified. When a respondent referred to his or her institution by name, this was replaced with saying [this university]. So, instead of 'Princeton does this', my quotation would read '[This institution] does this'. In some cases, further identifying information was deleted. For example, during a research interview, a selector might make a comparison between the percentage of accepted applicants at a particular university and the acceptance rates at their own institutions. Because it is possible to trace such information back to particular institutions and thus to identify the institutions, such comments were not included in direct quotations. However, I have also used quotations that are in the public domain; in such cases, the source is attributed and the institution is identified. For example, a director for admission might write something for a website or give a public interview or speech. When such quotations are clearly in the public domain and accessible, for example, via internet websites, news archives or conference recordings, they are attributed directly to a particular respondent as well as being referenced to the publicly available source.

Did you have permission to undertake the research?

All participants gave informed consent to be part of confidential one-to-one interviews and had a right to withdraw participation at any point. The research project has received ethics approval from the universities of Oxford, New York University and King's College London.

What sorts of questions did you ask the selectors?

For the one-to-one interviews, I used a semi-structured interview schedule. This means that I had thought about some of the sorts of questions I wished to cover, but there was flexibility in terms of taking the conversation wherever participants wished to take it. The interviews covered why someone had chosen to work in admissions (if they had), the purpose of admission, what they were looking for in the admissions process, the process of how admissions was undertaken, and the challenges they faced in selection. Participants generally elaborated on these topic areas and often provided some critical analysis and reflection on selective admissions as well as raising additional issues they felt were relevant.

In addition to the interviews, I observed some admissions meetings at Oxbridge and attended some development events for selectors in the US and the UK.

Who paid for the research? Has the funding or anyone else influenced what you found in this project?

I was fortunate to have received funding and other support from various sources. Funding for the overseas research visits and transcription was awarded through the Society for Research into Higher Education newer researcher award. Several interviews also took place as part of an ESRC funded studentship at the University of Oxford (2004–7) which also supported a three-month visiting scholarship to New York University. Because of the time lag between the time the interviews took place and the publication of this book, the information used from this time was double-checked. Attendance at the Harvard Summer School for College Admissions in 2011 was supported through funds from Manchester University. The funding and support from all these sources is gratefully acknowledged.

None of the funders have influenced the research findings or retained any rights to alter findings prior to publication. I have sent some interview scripts to selected participants when I wanted to ask further clarification questions about what they had said or when participants had chosen to view their interview scripts.

Why did you write this book? Do you have a personal interest in the topic that may have influenced your writing?

My interest in university admissions stems from my own life experiences and my academic interests. I am originally from Hamburg, Germany, but I have lived in England for almost twenty years. I work as a senior lecturer (roughly equivalent to an associate professor in the United States) in higher education at King's College London. I have also spent some time visiting the United States.

I had been schooled in a country with a 'flat' higher education structure – until recently, Germany did not have 'elite' universities. In Germany, the question of which university one studies in continues to be more about where a student wishes to matriculate and not so much about which institution would give one a place. For most subjects, enrolment at a university only requires passing the school-leaving examination. University matriculation (see glossary) happens after students know their grades in the school-leaving examinations – it is a post-qualification enrolment system. Furthermore, higher education in Germany is usually free or subject to nominal charges.

Against this background, I was fascinated to experience and learn about education systems in England and the United States, which have steep institutional hierarchies. The result of these systems being in place seemed to be a fierce competition for places at high-status universities with some parents, teachers and potential applicants starting to build their college admissions files from early childhood. The different funding and student support models in the Anglo–Saxon world also raise interesting questions about the relationship of the state and the individual and to what extent higher education serves individuals, communities or both and how private and public universities react to policies and shape this space. A key point in this world of higher education, a point that powerfully focuses national debates, is who is admitted to which university and why. I thus became curious about the curious world of university admissions.

Because of my background, I am once or twice removed from the subject matter of this book. I am an academic sociologist writing about admissions professionals and admission, and I am a German living in England writing about England and the United States. Writing from this perspective has inescapable drawbacks. Inevitably, I will have missed details and overlooked nuances. On the flipside, I have no obvious axe to grind and I can potentially help see the familiar as strange and in doing so describe some of the implicit, unarticulated assumptions underlying the two different admissions systems. I thus hope that the insights gained may excuse the inevitable flaws.

How confident can your readers be in the accuracy of your description of the admissions process?

I have attempted to reproduce all materials accurately to the best of my knowledge and to be faithful to the original sources. I have not interviewed every single person who works in admissions at the institutions that participated in this project. In most universities, I had an opportunity to speak with more than one admissions professional with both senior responsibility for admissions and with someone newer to the admissions world. As far as academic faculty interviews were concerned, I tried talking to people from a wide range of academic disciplines and, again, to those with significant experience and to those newer to undergraduate admissions. There were only rare instances when the professionals or academics whom I approached did not participate in the project. This was due to being unable to align schedules, especially in the case of my somewhat briefer US fieldwork visits, or academic staff being on sabbatical or fieldwork. Only in one instance in the United States and one instance in England did admissions professionals or academic selectors not agree to be interviewed because they thought all admissions information was on their website and because they did not wish to talk about the admissions aspect of their role.

In other words, I have not interviewed everyone in university admissions – however, I have interviewed a range of people representing different institutions and sometimes slightly different roles within university admissions. Therefore, a different study, interviewing completely different people would have been based on different quotations to tell the story of university admissions. However, it is unlikely that such a project would have arrived at fundamentally different descriptions of the admissions processes for selective institutions.

Finally, university admissions are a constantly evolving context and aspects have been changing quickly in the past few years. In England, the introduction of tuition fees and formal agreements to increase the number of students from under-represented groups in higher education and related policies about student numbers have created year-on-year changes in admissions. The United States had several significant recent court rulings regarding university admissions and especially selective universities have been facing ever-increasing numbers of applicants. In the present book I have tried to include information up to May 2014.

Structure of the book

The chapters in this book are written as to serve as stand-alone pieces of writing that can be read on their own as well as forming part of the book.

The Introduction introduces the context of selective universities and answers some of the questions about how the research for the book was conducted. Chapter 1, entitled 'Meet the Selectors', introduces the people who work in admissions, those who work in admissions offices as full-time professionals as well as academics who occasionally undertake admissions work as part of their role. Chapter 2 discusses the aims of the admissions process in different contexts. Chapter 3, entitled 'Selecting for Academic Success', describes how selectors in England and the United States go about finding the academically best qualified applicants. Chapter 4 describes 'Special Interest Cases' in admissions. The discussion spans admission for athletes, those with a link with the institution, those belonging to certain ethnic groups as well as those from different geographic areas, socio-economic groups and from different types of secondary schools such as private and publicly funded ones.

Chapters 5 and 6 are about the 'nuts and bolts' of application to universities (Chapter 5) and selection work (Chapter 6). Chapter 7 discusses 'Challenges in Decision-Making'. Perhaps surprisingly, one of the challenges described here is that, despite the fierce competition for places, institutions might not be selective enough. Next, in Chapter 8, the challenge of 'Fair admission in the context of inequality' is described as well as some strategies universities use for seeking to admit fairly. Finally, Chapter 9 asks 'So what?' as it evaluates not only what this book has shown and not shown but also how and whether elite higher education matters.

1

Meet the Selectors

The purpose of this chapter is to introduce readers to the people working in university admissions and to examine some of the differences in the admissions systems in the United States and England. After reading this chapter, readers will find it easier to understand both the purpose and the process of admission, which are explained in more detail in the following chapters. In particular, the chapter explains why some of the quotations in the subsequent chapters are based on interviews with academic faculty while others are taken from conversations with full-time admissions professionals.

United States

To recap, all the US institutions that participated in this project were private not-for-profit institutions. Most were drawn from the Ivy League, but two liberal arts colleges and two private non-Ivy League universities also participated. All these US institutions had centralized offices for undergraduate admissions.

A centralized system means that there is one central place that answers questions from prospective applicants, organizes recruitment and information visits to schools within the United States and abroad, decides which applicants for admission will receive an offer and liaises with admitted students after offers have been made. Admissions offices are generally no longer directly involved with students as soon as they enrol and become current students. In exceptional circumstances – usually when a student runs into academic or social problems – admissions files might be revisited to see whether there were any 'red flags' in the application that might have been overlooked.

The admissions offices discussed in this study have between fifteen and forty full-time staff – the difference in range is partly due to whether or not financial aid staff are included in the headcount. At busy times, additional part-time staff are sometimes employed, usually to help with reading applications or to help with campus visits.

This undergraduate admissions model can be described as an admissions professional-led model and, as we shall see, it contrasts with the academic-led model in some of the English institutions in this study. In US undergraduate admission, academic faculty play only a minor role – although this scenario changes for postgraduate admissions. The academic role for undergraduate admissions can entail being part of selection panels and strategic admissions practice and policy groups, and in exceptional circumstances, evaluating the submissions from applicants with unusual talents in a particular subject specialism. However, by and large, it is the full-time admissions professionals who are in charge of engaging with prospective applicants up to the point of enrolling new students.

The admissions professionals

A respondent for this project who works as a full-time admissions professional in a selective liberal arts college (see glossary) explained the structure of the admissions profession in the United States as follows:

> I'm 24 and I've been doing this [working in admissions] for three years and it is amazing to me how many admissions are done by 23-year-olds in their first job. At least in North American admissions offices you have two kinds of people. You have the 22-year-old that is doing this as his first job that typically only does it for two years. There is a two to three year turnover rate in admissions, it is about 90 per cent – 90 per cent of people that starting admissions leave after two or three years … they go off and do something or go to law school or grad school [see glossary 'graduate study'] or go into consulting or do something completely different. The other half is – you have the career people, the people who are usually in their 30s or 40s who have been doing this from the beginning. That's the way my office is. There are those of us in our early 20s and those of us in our late 30s and that's it.

Another experienced full-time admissions professional working for one of the Big Three institutions (Harvard, Yale, Princeton) also described how there were recent graduates from the institution as well as more experienced admissions professionals in her team, but also some people who had been doing different things outside admissions.

> A lot of the people hired here [in the admissions office] are actually recent graduates from [this institution], so there's kind of a mix … of people who

graduated last year and then people who've been out of college for a while and doing other things, and then … come back. … So there's a whole mix. And I think the recent graduates they bring in, of course, because they have the real, most current experiences, and can talk about [this institution] in a very fresh way … [but we also] like … an outside perspective, as well, I think, is very important. So it's about half and half.

Returning to the recent liberal arts college graduate from the previous quotation, the respondent elaborated further on how and why he had started his employment in higher education admissions:

Well I worked in the admissions office at [liberal arts college where he got his first degree] the whole time I was a student as a tour guide. That's the primary things students do in the American admissions offices. I don't know how familiar you are with the whole thing but primarily when you visit an American college the thing you do is get a tour from current students so students take you around and show you the campus. That's what I did for two years and in my senior year, my final year I interviewed prospective students for the college. Where I work now we don't do this but where I have worked they want to interview everyone who is applying and they have so many kids applying … so then they use students. So I did that, it seemed interesting and it seemed like something I could get hired in.

The sentiment that admissions work was a reasonable option for a first job especially for humanities graduates was also observed elsewhere. This more experienced selector from one of the Big Three institutions noted that

for somebody with a degree in English or history, who isn't going to law school right away, and isn't sure what they want to do, and maybe the job market's not that good … You know, it's a good generalist job. You get a lot of general skills. You get public speaking skills, you get the writing skills. You know, but … there's a lot of turnover, because you work really hard during certain times of the year, and you have to travel a lot.

Returning yet again to the story of our liberal art graduate's journey into admissions work, he recalled how after deciding to work in admissions, the choice of where he would work was then largely taken out of his hands:

You know, I applied to about 50 different colleges and I got job offers from two. And [liberal arts college that employs him now] was the more selected of the two colleges, it was the primary thing that made the decision. … Typically with admissions even if you go to other jobs you try not to go down, you trade up and be at a more selective place each time. The type of admissions that I do is sort of different than a lot of other admissions because if you're at a selective place you're really dealing with admissions but if you're at a place where they are accepting more than 50 per cent [of your applicants] and your job is primarily recruitment, it's actually getting kids to apply and convince kids to come. I don't have to convince kids to come; I am mostly selecting the ones I want. ... [Big Three Ivy] of course is the extreme of that.

Readers familiar with university rankings will see how the selectivity of the institution is clearly not something that only the *US News and World Report* or parents and applicants consider when deciding where to apply for undergraduate study. It is also something that the admission practitioners themselves (or at least some of them) consider in their career options and choices.

Another still relatively recent graduate with just over three years' experience of admissions work explained how he ended up working at the particular Ivy League institution. Like the previous respondent, he had started off helping out at the admissions office as a student and then moved into full-time employment in admissions upon graduating:

I lived [near this Ivy] on campus at [another non-Ivy League university where he got his first degree], a very residential experience, like here, where all of our students live on campus for four years essentially. I got very involved in a lot of volunteering, just at the admissions office. So I was tour guide, I was speaking on panels at different houses for prospective students, and there's ... a lot of what admission officers do, ... and it wasn't paid work really, until my senior year, where I was an intern. So that's where I was exposed to the admissions office, but I also debated through college. And I thought I wanted to go to law school, because that's what debaters do, and that sounds more prestigious and more scholarly; and I had done law as an undergrad, so had worked for a law firm ... for a year and a half. I absolutely despised the experience. Just ... it was not for me, the work, I didn't feel like I was helping anyone, and I really enjoyed what I did as ... in the administrative type of work I was doing in higher education. So there was an opportunity, because there was an opening in [degree awarding] admission office, maybe it has 15, 16 full-time staff members, including a dean and a director. And there was an opening, and it was the right time and towards the end of that summer, it was after working at the law firm for a year. So, this is one year after I graduated. ... So I was hired, fortunately, and spent two years there. It was fantastic, and I just got promoted, when on a Listserv in higher ed, I found out that [Ivy League institution where he works now] had a couple of openings.

As in the previous narrative, when given a choice, this admissions professional moved to a more selective institution when the opportunity presented itself. At the point that he participated in this research project, it seemed like he was now seriously considering joining the group of those who work in admissions as their long-term career.

Another selector from the Big Three had more fallen into her admissions role rather than making a conscious decision to go into this role:

> I did a master's degree at [Big Three Ivy] in education, and then we moved to [other Big Three Ivy] because my husband wanted to pursue his PhD. And I got the job [in the admissions office] because ... when they get very busy, they hire what they call part time tutors and readers ... and you do a first read on the application, and you write your comments on it. ... They were very happy with my work and offered me a job afterwards, and I found it very interesting, so I said, yes, great.

Some other, more senior respondents had career trajectories that included working their way up from entry level to a senior level, coming to admissions after a stint as an academic social science faculty member, and moving their way up across seniorities and institutions to be a leading Ivy League admissions professionals.

Overall, diversity in terms of age and life experiences within admissions offices was valued, but all admissions staff were themselves university graduates and many had master's level degrees in education. This Ivy League selector explained how such a policy of diversity among staff was designed to counter potential biases in the admissions process:

> I think your own subjective bias does come in, but ... we try to be very aware of it through socially engineering, even our own Committees. ... [dean of admission] lived an incredibly different life than I have. And you have that all throughout the office. We're not an elite office, in terms of not everybody went to [Ivy League institutions], some went to [names of other four year institutions]. All sorts of schools, all sorts of perspectives, gender balances, sexuality balances, age balances, race balances, first generation students (see glossary), when they went to college, people in this office who's, you know, they went to [a particular Ivy] and their father went to [the same Ivy]. So, it's a very diverse mix, even here. I mean, we're practising what we preach in terms of our own office.

Diversity was valued among admissions staff and among incoming students. However, one Ivy League respondent also observed that 'there's a lot of women at the lower levels, but at the top levels, they tend to be males. ... I think it has a lot to do with, just, the lifestyle and the travel. I mean, it's very hard to leave your children.' We will revisit the idea of how diversity plays a role in selection decisions in the coming chapters.

There was some general consensus among practitioners that working in admissions aligned with some of their deeply held values, as well as offering a fun job that allowed opportunities for honing a range of skills. Several admissions professionals explained how they had chosen to work in education and one selector commented how he thought it 'would be hard for me to work for a company where all you're concerned about is the bottom line' and that he wanted to 'do something good for the world'. Another Ivy League selector elaborated on further aspects of the role he found intrinsically rewarding:

> I think it's fascinating. I interview lots of people in our office and you find that people ... don't do it for the pay cheques, certainly. It's the ... you feel like you're, for the most part, helping in the social grid because you are fighting for people, you're fighting for policies that do include ... and you're changing people's lives by the admission decisions you make, by how you recruit, by ... what high schools you visit, by how they find out about [this Ivy] and who's the face of [this Ivy] that they see? So, they meet me first, or they meet a student first, that's their impression of [this Ivy].

In particular, the young admissions professionals also enjoyed the professional skills they were developing through on-the-job training, professional development and sometimes staff retreats. They thought it was 'fun because you get to travel', and offered an 'unbelievable amount of autonomy and responsibility for being 22'.

There is some movement and connection between the different highly selective institutions and respondents seemed to know each other. Occasionally, I was even asked whether I had spoken to a particular person and whether they would agree with this sort of statement. For research confidentiality reasons, I could affirm neither whom I had spoken with nor what had been said, but the question itself showed familiarity with colleagues and their specific roles. Respondents commented on career moves of colleagues, for example, one Ivy League respondent remarked that someone from their office had moved to a highly selective West Coast institution. In other instances, selectors looked forward to travelling with colleagues from other institutions, in particular for overseas recruitment visits, and were knowledgeable about their personal life and circumstances. One Big Three selector explained how such joint overseas visits were

> very friendly. I'm doing a talk at Eton (prestigious private school in England) next Monday, and I'm doing it with [other Big Three Ivy] and it's probably with [colleague]. … We often do that. Schools will do, … yes, kind of, double-bill, sort of thing. Yes, so I'm probably going to be doing it with her. Yes. So she'll, … she'll talk about [Big Three] and I'll talk about [other Big Three].

The admissions office

In terms of how the admissions office and their processes work, a Big Three selector explained the structure of her office as follows:

> You have the dean, then you have a director, and then you have what they call assistant and associate deans, and they are all the team leaders. And what that means is, essentially, they have a region, and they do the second reading. They make the decisions about which students are going to come to committee. And then you have … admissions officers at the bottom, and they're usually entry level, right out of school.

Another Ivy selector elaborated on the structure of his office as follows:

> We are 19 now, with two officers having dual appointments. They're both admission and financial aid, because otherwise financial aid is separate. … We have 18 full-time or 19, who are on the Committee who are reading and evaluating candidates for admission, and that includes our executive director which, in other schools, would be called the dean. Every school, kind of, has a different formula for it. And then we have our support staff. We have two main support liaisons who work behind that front desk, and then two who sit at the front desk all day, who answer phones here. We also have a visitors' centre in the library, and there's support staff that's based there. And then we have student employees … and we have a whole lot of student volunteers.

In terms of how work was split, this Big Three selector explained her role this way:

> Basically, the way it works … each of the admissions officers is responsible for a different area. So, for example, I have [two US states] and [five international territories]. And I read all of the applications that come from those areas first. Then I will … send off some of the applications to other readers to have a look

at, so there's two readers on a lot of the applications, and then those are sent back; those evaluations are sent back to me, and I will then decide on who I feel should be presented for a committee (committees make admissions decisions). And the committee is made up of admissions officers, usually the dean or the director of admissions, if not one of them, probably two associate directors, the, sort of, next level down from dean or director. And then, also, sometimes faculty, deans of residential colleges, but usually a committee is made up of about five people, and there has to be a majority vote for someone to be admitted to [this Ivy].

The admissions office also had relations with various other offices and departments such as 'the development office, the athletics department and the music department' (Big Three selector). Another Ivy selector elaborated further on how the various parts of the university were involved in the admissions endeavour:

We [the admissions office] are constantly feeding all that information in, so our deans [names] who are probably the two most senior people in the office, and a couple of other people who have been here for a very long time, are constantly meeting with deans and faculty members, and everyone has an opinion and everyone's involved. And so we have to constantly funnel all that information in. Then the alumni office is involved. And in American universities, because it's all private … money is very important and a lot of the institutions pride themselves on being as accessible as possible … like, [the money] has to come from somewhere. So, there's all of these larger issues that weigh on the admission office.

The respondent describes a close link between US admissions offices and other university offices, such as the alumni office, that are not usually part of the admissions process in England. We will also see in the subsequent chapters that relations with the sports and some academic and music departments are also part of the US admissions process. In England, admissions offices may have input from recruitment and marketing, widening participation and planning and finance.

To summarize, admissions at selective universities in the United States is run out of professional, centralized admissions offices. The admissions work is mostly undertaken by full-time admissions professionals who were either relatively recent graduates or career admission professionals. Occasionally, additional staff was hired for key peak work times. Many of those working in admissions are motivated by some underlying values about doing something good for society. In addition, especially the newer staff valued the experiences and skills they could gain in the post. The staff was trained through professional development, on-the-job training and retreats. The admissions offices had strong links with high schools, geographic regions, other offices within their institution, and previous graduates.

In the next section, this model of how university admissions is organized in the United States is compared and contrasted with how admissions is done in English universities.

England

In England, there are three different models for organizing the admission of undergraduate students. Today, the most frequently used model is centralized admission, where selection is undertaken by admissions professionals. Next are decentralized or devolved admissions systems, where the admissions decisions are made by academic faculty and not by the central admissions team. And the final one is a mixed model. This means that for some courses and subjects, admissions is centralized, and for others, it is devolved.

In recent years, there has been a trend across the higher education sector towards centralizing admissions processes and functions as found by surveys conducted by the organization Supporting Professionalism in Admissions. Between 2010 and 2013, the percentage of higher education institutions with devolved admissions systems decreased from over 40 per cent of the sector to just over 10 per cent, and centralized admissions systems are now over two-thirds of the sector, with a quarter of institutions operating mixed models (SPA 2014).

In practice, the centralized admissions offices in England share many ways they operate with US admissions offices. They are staffed by full-time admissions professionals. Some, but not all, English admissions offices also look after outreach and recruitment into schools and coordinate open days and campus visits. In other cases, outreach and recruitment is undertaken by separate departments. The admissions professionals are in charge of admissions decisions. This can be as straightforward as applying academic grade cut-off points to admission to particular subjects, but can also involve a more detailed reading of the entire application dossiers and looking at non-academic factors. Just as their US counterparts, some English admissions offices hire temporary additional staff for working through application forms. Some centralized systems have committee decisions for particular applicants such as those coming through an outreach scheme.

One Russell Group respondent at a centralized institution explained what he valued about being in a centralized admissions role compared with his previous position in a devolved institution:

> We have a very centralized system, which means we can be much more consistent in the way we approach [admissions] and ensure that every student is treated exactly the same way if they're from one group or another. ... So for me, it was quite freeing to be able to come [to this institution] and say, here's a policy ... we have the operational wherewithal to be able to implement this pretty much immediately, we've got senior management buy-in, let's go for it.

In this central model, staff in admissions offices and senior university teams including academics have input in deciding admissions aims and criteria but policies are implemented by the central admissions offices. In mixed models, some of the admissions decisions are made centrally and some are made by academics in their departments, as this Russell Group respondent explained:

> Mostly, those decisions are made within the [institution admissions] offices by professional admissions staff, so they will have their criteria and they'll apply them. Exceptions tend to be professional and vocational courses, where academics or clinicians or whoever might be involved and there might be another stage of selection, ... in a very few cases, we interview, and we have portfolios for art and design and that kind of thing. But the vast majority of decisions are made by professional staff.

In devolved systems, all admissions decisions for undergraduate study are made by academic faculty in their academic departments. Academics, usually working in teams or small groups, make decisions and the admissions process can involve academic-led interviews as part of the selection process. The actual admissions decisions are then processed centrally. Those familiar with graduate or professional school admissions process in the United States may see similarities here. Devolved admissions systems also have admissions offices. The function of these offices is primarily an administrative co-ordinating function in processing and preparing applications for academics to read and ensuring that the process is compliant with guidelines and quality assurance, and that there is consistency across processes. Admissions offices also increasingly add some information to the application files from other sources with an aim to give selectors as much information as possible about the applicants. As one admissions professional in a devolved system explained his role:

> And our responsibility is basically the running of the admissions process; so the handling of applications from UCAS (see glossary) and dissemination of that information across the colleges and departments for them to make their decisions.

The admissions professionals facilitate the admissions process, and often there are additional staff who work in outreach, but these professionals do not make admissions decisions. The Universities of Oxford and Cambridge both operate devolved admissions system. Overall, just over 10 per cent of English universities operate devolved admission (SPA 2014).

At Oxford and Cambridge, admissions is not only undertaken by devolved departments but also coordinated through the colleges that constitute the university. In fact, one of the respondents in this study noted how someone not familiar with the working of a collegiate university would find the decision-making process rather complex at first glance. He observed how 'the collegiate universities have this incredibly convoluted ways of making decisions'. The then director of admissions to Oxford elaborated how his professional role sat within the collegiate university:

> My main responsibility is trying to keep the university honest, would probably be the best way to describe it. So we've got 30 undergraduate colleges plus … private halls who are the admitting authorities. We've got 29 different subject areas who also have a hand in the admissions process, and we're trying to get them to work in a common fashion. (Nicholson 2013)[1]

The organization of admissions in a devolved system then requires solid co-ordination processes as explained by another Oxbridge admissions professional:

> Each college has an admissions tutor and then each subject within the college has their own committee. … Many colleges would split [the committee], Arts and Sciences or something even finer grain than that. Some only have the one [committee]. Some colleges would have an admissions committee that might bring together the senior admissions tutor, the admissions tutor or some of the senior fellows, most colleges don't. But the decision taking is taken between the admissions tutor or tutors and the specialists who have done the selecting

that year in a given subject who would oversee that subject. It's the admissions tutor that plays the coordinating and oversight role and at the margins, says to a subject, 'don't be greedy', or to another subject, 'yes, you can have a bit more this year, you've got a strong field' ... [furthermore] in each admission subject there is an [intercollegiate] subject convener.

Collegiate universities like Oxbridge then have various ways to co-ordinate admission to individual colleges and to different subjects, for example through 'agreed intercollegiate policy' or a 'common framework for admission'. There is also compulsory training for academics who are new to admissions. At the same time, decisions continue to be made at a local subject level by academics. The then director of admission to Oxford explained who the academics are, who make selection decisions and also how his role worked in relation to the academics:

> Thirty, forty, fifty years ago, many of the people who would be doing the selecting were themselves products of the system. And, probably, the biggest shift at Oxford has been the change in the tutorial staff at the university. So, almost 50 per cent of our tutors are not themselves UK educated and most of those who come to work in the university have not studied at the university [Oxford] or at Cambridge. And, I think that's is actually a helpful thing because it opens up debate. People bring their experiences from elsewhere and they question why we do things constantly. Which is a healthy thing – I think if everybody accepted that everything is set in stone and perfect, than that's where the weakness would be.
>
> The biggest change ... in my time at Oxford compared with my previous roles in admissions, is actually, as far as I am concerned, I would rather have a highly engaged tutorial body who want to do admissions well and all think that they are my boss. Because with all 1600 bosses, then actually, I am always under scrutiny, and the process is always under scrutiny. In previous institutions were I have experience, I might've been the only person ... who actually cares about who gets in ... so it is important to recognize that there is a lot of engagement and this is a very very positive element of how Oxford approaches its selection. (Nicholson 2013)

So, while selective admissions offices in the United States might have as many as forty professional staff, the collegiate English universities can have potentially more than 1,500 people involved in admissions. In addition to the staff in colleges and departments, doctoral students might sometimes be involved in interviewing processes as co-interviewers, thus further increasing the number of people involved. While diversity is not a formal criterion for hiring at Oxford, the quotation highlights that there is diversity in terms of prior educational experiences and geographic origin among the academic staff. This diversity is valued as a constant source of discussion, ideas for enhancement, and feedback on the process.

Senior academic admissions leads in subjects and colleges then support all those involved in selection and promote awareness and knowledge of the context and processes in admission. Individual subjects have their published admissions criteria, although it was partly the job of senior admissions leads to promote awareness and to safeguard consistency across admissions decisions for the same subject.

The vast number of people involved in academic-led admissions systems and the room for discussion and debate about admissions can also mean that not all academic selectors agree on whether they should or wished to undertake the selecting or someone else should select on their behalf. Such views could be strongly held. Faculty also had ongoing detailed discussion about aspects of the selection process and the relative weight of different parts of the application. As noted in the previous quotation from the former director of admissions at Oxford, such debates and discussions were viewed as strengths of the process as they provided constant scrutiny.

An example of an academic strongly in favour of selecting his own students was an Oxbridge science selector, who was originally from the United States, where he had undertaken his own undergraduate studies. He highlighted how he considered, in particular, the academic admissions interview to be a useful part of the admissions process. This was because of how closely the interview related to the subsequent educational experience at Oxbridge and teaching in small tutorials. He noted:

> If I'm going to sit in a tutorial with these two people I need … to interview them myself. I need to find out what they're like myself. I'm not going to take a student that I haven't seen. … This is a very unique system: the tutorial system is very unique. In the States everything's done with classes and big classes. I was never in a class of fewer than twenty people until I was, there in the fourth year in a very specialist area … So I would much rather have colleagues who do this tutorial teaching, interviewing candidates, assessing whether they think these candidates can handle a system like the tutorial system based on their own experience, 'right? I'd be much more confident in that than have some bureaucrats in central administration trying to determine it on the basis of targets.

Other selectors were not so enamoured with the interview process and the idea of academics selecting their own students. An Oxbridge social science academic who had also experienced selection systems that were led by professional admissions staff stated how this alternative system had worked well for him previously:

> My own general view about admissions is that I have … no commitment to picking my own students. … I have taught at other places where I had absolutely no role in picking the students. And I was very comfortable with that. And, maybe there are people in [this university] who are not comfortable with that. But my own view is that I would be … it would make no bit of difference at all if someone else picked the students, … I have no commitment at present to picking my own students.

These two quotations are illustrative of the range of opinions and views concerning academic selection for undergraduate admissions in a devolved system. The diversity of academic selectors at Oxbridge, many without prior experience of collegiate systems, has played part in the emphasis on subject choice rather than college choice in admissions – selectors wish to admit the best academic students regardless of the college that provides their residential home and social life. The fact that lawyers have successfully argued that admissions is a matter for the subjects and not the colleges to decide, and that it would be of concern if different colleges had different evaluation processes for the same subject has also been part of the push for change. Intercollegiate meetings, a pool system and college 'blind' applications now aim to ensure consistency in admission for applicants to the same subject.

In some other English universities, a college or house system only maintains nominal meaning, and allocation to a college or house occurs only after the academic decisions have been made. This is more similar to the way house or college membership is assigned in some US universities.

Unlike the US respondents, who often volunteered information about why they were working in admissions without prompts, English respondents only infrequently drew on their personal motivations for their jobs as part of a discussion of admissions.

Academics are primarily driven by interest in research and teaching to choose their profession, although for some academics, their profession is also a way to make a difference in the world. For many academic selectors, undergraduate admissions is thus just one of many aspects of their academic role.

However, for academic leads in admission, there is often an element of self-selection in having applied for such a position in the first place. Several academic leads recalled personal histories or other values as the reason why they had been motivated to lead on admissions. For some, this was because of an interest in society and schooling. For example, during the observation of a science admissions meeting at a devolved university, the chair was clearly motivated to promote social justice concerns and to make a particularly strong case for students who had not been able to fully develop their educational potential. He later explained that this was part of his personal experience of educational inequality and his deep-seated view of the role of admission in addressing the shortcomings of previous education. Only one admissions lead voiced a more career-oriented motivation for taking on a senior admission role as a stepping stone for moving further into university management and away from being a full-time academic.

While US admissions professionals viewed their own personal histories as an integral part of why they were in their role and how the backgrounds of others contributed to diversity, English admissions professionals tended to discuss their own backgrounds either not at all or as part of the informal, unrecorded 'warm up' or closing parts of a conversation. Those working in outreach and recruitment rather than admissions were most open in talking about their personal experience and social justice motivation for having chosen their roles. However, while US admissions professionals were undertaking recruitment and school visits as part of their role, in England outreach and recruitment are usually undertaken by different staff than those making admissions decisions.

Among the personal histories shared by admissions and outreach professionals in England were examples of growing up in mining communities with the mines closed, resulting in few opportunities, having gone to a particularly poor performing primary school, having to be geographically mobile in order to participate in higher education and to undertake their current role. For many, participating in higher education had had a profound impact on their own lives. Several respondents mentioned being the first in their family to have gone to university, one mentioned being the only one from their school to have progressed into higher education. Respondents mentioned initially lacking experience or an understanding of how higher education worked: 'I did not have all this cultural capital. I didn't even know what questions to ask or how to ask for support.' Another outreach professional noted:

> No one in my family had ever gone to university. I got involved in working in outreach as a student ambassador. After graduation, I worked in the voluntary sector but then went back to working in higher education, I am now back at the university where I graduated – but with a fresh pair of eyes.

There are similarities here to the accounts from the younger US admissions professionals who had often also acted as student volunteers and were sometimes working for the university from which they had originally graduated.

Chapter summary

The way in which admissions works is organized in the United States is different from that in England. In the United States, all the institutions represented in this book had central offices staffed with full-time admissions professionals, who make the admissions decisions. Some, but not all, English universities also have centralized admissions offices where admissions decisions are made. In Oxbridge and some other universities, devolved, academic-led systems mean that admissions decisions are made by academic faculty as part of their academic role. The centralized offices in such devolved systems have an administrative but not a decision-making function. The current chapter has thus set the scene for why some of the voices we hear in the next chapters are from academic selectors, who undertake admissions as part of their wider academic roles, and why other voices are from full-time admissions professionals.

With this in mind, we can now consider the key question in admission: What is the goal of the admission process? What are institutions and selectors trying to achieve in offering places to some and not to other applicants? What are they looking for and why?

2

The Aims of Admission

Asking about the purpose of admission is the most fundamental question about admissions

(Big Three selector)

'Why are you doing what you are doing?' seems like a good way to start a conversation about the admissions process. What do institutions and selectors aim to achieve in their admissions processes? How does 'why, how and whom' they admit for undergraduate study relate to the core ideas and vision of the university?

Answering what is the purpose of admission is at the same time at the heart of admissions and a difficult question. As this chapter will explore, ways of thinking about the purpose of admission are closely linked to the general aim and mission of universities. Depending on the answer, work supporting the ideas of university admissions can span from working with young children to enhance their attainment in school all the way to supporting students through university and seeing what graduates from the institution choose to do with their lives decades after they graduate. The process of turning applications for study into some enrolled new undergraduate students then might be the core of the actual admissions process, but it does not fully explain what the aim of the admissions process is.

In a well-designed admissions system, all activities and processes for admission align with the underlying purpose of admission as well as the purpose and mission of the institution. Respondents with greater experience in admission thus tended to have an overview concerning how all sorts of different aspects, processes and activities linked together to support such an overarching purpose of admissions. Some respondents also had over-time insights, sometimes spanning decades, of how both the purpose and the process of admissions had already changed. This could include detailed discussions of how and why an institution had changed or revised aspects of admissions or introduced new values.

This overview from experienced admissions professionals contrasted with the responses from some of the respondents who were newer to admissions or only undertook admissions activities as part of their role. Those newer to admissions had perhaps initially focused on making their area of responsibility in admissions work and found it easier to describe the activities they undertook as part of their admissions role rather than discussing the more abstract, conceptual and strategic goals of 'the aim of admission'. Indeed, a surprising number of respondents did not have a ready-made answer to the question of what the admissions process aimed to achieve. One Oxbridge respondent remarked: *'Well it's, it's difficult isn't it?'*.

After describing one particular aspect of how admissions worked, one US respondent with two years' experience in admissions stated:

> I don't know why we are doing this; I don't understand this aspect of admissions and have never understood why this is important to institutions.[1]

An academic selector for Oxbridge echoed this sentiment. He was not only new to the Oxbridge selection process but also new to living in England after having previously lived, studied and worked in continental Europe. He observed, 'I learnt a lot about English secondary schools as a result of the admissions process.'[2] This shows that even those who are part of admissions decisions can take a while not only to learn the techniques and practices, the nuts and bolts of admitting students in their context but also to learn about the purpose of admission, what is important and why. Indeed, later in this book, we will see selectors describing how explaining admission to newer colleagues and having new voices challenging admissions practices is part of ongoing efforts of enhancing processes.

This chapter then summarizes the different voices and comments from selectors in England and the United States regarding the following questions: 'What is the aim of university admission?', 'What are the aims you are wishing to achieve through your admissions process?' and 'Is there an underlying institutional philosophy that drives these aims?'. These questions naturally intertwine with questions about the purpose of universities and the way in which these institutions think about teaching and learning and the student experience.

The purpose of the university

Admissions is one part of the wider mission and purpose of the institution. The following quotation from a Big Three selector illustrates how some respondents used their overarching institutional mission to explain the aims of admission:

> It is important to have a mission and to refer back to it. For example [this institution] was founded for the betterment of mankind, to produce leaders in every field. [the founder] had consciously rejected fees to avoid the stratification of society. Our founding documents call for a multi-dimensional approach to achieve this

The dean of admissions from another selective private US institution simply stated the mission of his institution as thus: 'We want our students to solve the world's problems.'

The key to evaluating whether an admissions process works is to see how it supports such greater institutional mission and vision. Another senior admissions professional from a Big Three institution explained this link:

> The value of our admissions operation, recruitment, which is the key, and the selection process is the way you'd decide whether you were doing the job is who shows up in September and then 25 years later … starting 25 years later, have they done great things with their lives? … These fat books here [pointing at books on her bookshelf] … are 25th reunion reports which [our institution's] alumni give. … I always say to my new staff when I hire someone: 'I'll give you one of these books to keep for a year and you can keep it in your office somewhere you can see it to remember that the first marker of whether we've done a good job comes then; not how they do in the classroom.'

For this Big Three selector, the outcome of a university education, and whether the purpose of the institution had been achieved, was not something that can be evaluated at the point of graduation or even a few years after graduation. It is something bigger than that: it is related to what people are doing with their lives. If a mistake is made in admissions 'this person will be a graduate from [this Big Three Ivy] for 50, 70, or 100 years in the future'. Another Big Three selector remarked: 'We are in the future business.'

Judging the potential for worthy life outcomes rather than academic accomplishments is how the admission process is evaluated; as this senior Big Three selector elaborated:

> We know how to judge people who've been in a class, in front of a classroom. That's a fine thing but it's not … the worthy main goal of the office. The main goal

of the office is something else, and a means to an end is all those other things between here and there. So we want to keep our eye on the ball ... the horizon. So in order to think that way we try to think big. We try to look for people who would bring us diverse talents and interests – all, we hope, with energy and ambition.

The sentiment that the overarching goal of the university was something more than academic accomplishment was echoed by another much more junior selector in the Ivy League:

> You really feel like we're training the next leaders of the world here. That what we're going to offer is so powerful that it's going to not just change their lives, but it's going to change the world. ... And you could question that, and think, 'oh, that's very lofty', or, 'oh, that's way overblown'. ... What that student does here is still going to be up to them, but ... we try to predict that they might do some great things.

Another Big Three selector also commented that one way to evaluate the success of the admissions operation was to

> look at the Fortune 500 or something, there's a list of CEOs, Chief Executives of ... big companies and some disproportionate number of them have some [name of university] association. That's a convergence of a lot of things.

Therefore, the overarching goal in the US admissions endeavour was to have alumni who contribute to society. In some ways, this was broadly defined, but the institutions were keen to have some measure of this success in terms of being able to quantify their share of leading business people.

In the book *The Shape of the River* (2000) the former presidents of Princeton and Harvard universities, William Bowen and Derek Bok, evaluate the effect of admissions policies in the United States that gave preferential admission to under-represented students from racial minority groups. In their evaluation of whether these affirmative action admissions policies had worked, their aim was to look at what alumni were contributing to society after leaving college.

Another book written from the perspective of a Harvard alumnus, *Privilege* (2006) by Ross Douthat, also observes that the academic part and graduating was the 'easy part' of the Harvard experience. The tougher part was navigating the social experience and life of the institution, the bits that made it a Harvard experience rather than just an experience of mastering new academic material.

The US approach to measuring the success of admission and a university education in terms of life accomplishments contrasted with the views about the purpose of admission voiced in England. Here, selectors are more likely to comment and pay attention to the immediate impact that graduating from university might have on individuals' life and employment prospects. A senior Oxbridge admissions professional observed:

> Even from this university, these days, unless you graduate with a 2:1 [see degree classification in glossary] or a First [see glossary], your appointment prospects are not great. So anyone we take in who doesn't get a 2:1 or a First, we have to interrogate that decision and say, what did we get wrong?

Perhaps contrary to common perception, the English selectors thought that the degree from Oxbridge or another selective university alone would be insufficient for securing entry into a highly competitive labour market and there was no reference to business entrepreneurs akin to the Fortune 500 list in the English interviews.

There was evidence in the US interviews that the lived experience of recent US graduates reflected the English concern that even degrees from the most prestigious universities were no guarantee for superior employability. Two relatively newly appointed admissions professionals with two to four years' experience in the United States reflected on their own experiences of graduating from selective liberal arts institutions:

> Graduating in the middle of a recession there aren't a lot of options for a 22-year-old with a BA in history and admissions seemed like something I could do.

And a colleague at another institution reflected:

> I mean there are no jobs for somebody like me looking ... no one is hiring and there are no jobs. Yesterday I said keep going (in admissions work) as long as you can. You do not want to try to find a job today.

Employability might thus be a real issue for graduates on both sides of the Atlantic. However, in the United States, admissions professionals were a lot more positive about the long-term career opportunities for their graduates than about short-term employability concerns as voiced by the selectors at Oxbridge and the Russell Group.

The quotations from England also show a somewhat different point of view regarding the relationship between graduates and their institution and a different time frame for thinking about the future of their alumni. While the US institutions tended to think about the general life outcomes and the leadership potential of their graduates, priding themselves when their students achieved economic successes or became leaders in some form, the English selectors saw their primary duty to select and admit students who would do well academically. Some selectors and those working in strategic institutional positions saw it as part of their role to help students graduate, so that these graduates could reasonably expect to secure employment afterwards. The fact that some of the research was undertaken during a time of economic downturn and general concerns about prosperity may have had something to do with this concern about employment prospects for graduates in England.

The English concerns with immediate employability might also mirror how the nationwide survey conducted by the Higher Education Statistical Agency collates information on what graduates do six months as well as three years after graduation (e.g. HESA 2015). This information, in turn, is crucial for marketing and recruitment departments in highlighting career outcomes to prospective students.

While some US universities contemplated how they were serving the nation and the world in the medium and long term in educating future leaders, their counterparts in England were more focused on the individual and immediate impact the qualifications gained at university had on their graduates.

Admitting 'the best'

All universities try to do the same, to admit the best from diverse backgrounds.
(Ivy League selector)

The Ivy League selector quoted above later qualified this statement by noting that there were still individual differences between institutions in terms of their nuances and strategies of admitting the best. But the key message here is that there is an uncontroversial consensus among all selective institutions that they all wish to achieve the same goal, admitting the best.

In the US, this goal is twofold: the first aim is 'admitting the best' and the second aim is admission 'from diverse backgrounds'. Admitting the best is a shared value in selective admissions in both the United States and England, although the definitions of what 'the best' means differ. The aim of admitting 'from diverse backgrounds' is a clear part of admitting the best in the United States. English selectors are aware of their duties under the Equalities Act 2010 not to discriminate, however, diversity is not part of the formal criteria for admission akin to the United States. It thus turns out that understanding a potentially simple statement like 'admitting the best' can hide a variety of further assumptions and additional aims of the admissions process. Indeed, there are different interpretations in England and the United States of what it means to admit the best.

Here is an example of how an experienced senior selector for one of the US Big Three universities elaborates on the idea of admitting the best:

> We have interestingly had reconfirmation repeatedly by the [university] president that the highest priority … [this institution] has been … the people part … recruiting and attracting the best faculty; recruiting and attracting the best students. The thinking has been if you do that right, if you really are indisputably the best in those categories, whatever silly measure you use for that, the rest of it will take care of itself. So … if you need buildings, you'll get the buildings … the theory is that if you have the best place, the best brains as it were, that the rest of it really will draw the kind of support from those who admire excellence or medicine or whatever it is they want to support.

As this senior selector noted, the aim of admission is, therefore, to admit 'the best'. However, the idea of admitting the best is expanded and linked to another institutional aim: the ability to attract funding. This is funding for buildings and for research such as medical research. Getting admissions right is part of getting the overall funding and the economics of the institution right.

Another aspect comes into the question of 'admitting the best': recruitment. This Big Three institution admits fewer than one in thirteen of those who apply, yet recruitment is clearly an integral part of what this institution is doing when thinking about admission. This institution does not rest on its laurels to simply admit the best from those who apply, it actively recruits 'the best'.

In England, those making admissions decisions also shared the idea of 'selecting the best'. An Oxbridge admissions official stated that '[this institution] wants to select the best students academically'. This sentiment was echoed by academic selectors across different academic disciplines: 'A lot of the tutors … do think that admissions is trying to get the best students, best being varyingly defined by different tutors, but somehow trying to get the best candidates.'

Unlike the two US quotations, there was no unprompted discourse in the UK of how 'admitting the best' served other institutional objectives such as diversity or the ability to attract funding. Recruitment was mentioned by full-time admissions professionals as being part of admission, which was not usually mentioned by academic selectors. Some academic selectors were involved in activities that helped young people from various backgrounds without histories of higher education find out about universities. Many academic selectors considered such activities as distinct from their admissions work.

What academic selectors did do, however, was elaborate on their understanding of 'the best', where their aims were, for example, to look for 'academic grounds' (Oxbridge selector); depth and quickness of mind, not just the ability to repeat information (Oxbridge selector); and those 'people who are going to be very very good at [this subject] or who are going to be very very good at, critical and engaged reading, and who are enthusiastic about it and, are going to be committed to learning' (Oxbridge selector). For several selectors, admitting the best also means rejecting an applicant if they 'cannot get a 2:1' (see degree classification in glossary, Russell Group admissions professional).

Furthermore, the then director of admissions at Oxford University, Mike Nicholson, explained how the purpose of admission at Oxford was fundamentally different from the purpose of selection at the sort of highly selective US institutions represented in the current book. In a speech he delivered at a joint US–UK event, he juxtaposed those different purposes:

> It is really important to emphasize that certainly Oxford, and many other UK universities, are primarily selecting students on their academic suitability for a particular course. There is a massive difference between a liberal arts selection [in the US] – because students will not necessarily be declaring their majors for two years into the course – and identifying who is a biochemist at the point of entry. So, I think we need to be clear that we are probably in the two education systems selecting for two very, very different initial purposes. Certainly, in Oxford there is kind of clarity of purpose we are selecting the students at the point of application who show the greatest potential to be successful at Oxford in the tutorial education system that we offer. That is a very very narrow and very focused purpose, but it is actually one that we can then form an admissions process around and target candidates appropriately. (Mike Nicholson Sutton 2013)

Both the English and the US respondents thus described that the aim of admission was to 'select the best'. For the English respondents, selecting the best academically meant selecting those with the highest academic ability and potential for a course, which was their only aim. Further discussion then emerged regarding what 'the best' means in a particular subject and social context, how to identify the best, and which evidence should and could be legitimately used for finding 'the best'. But the subsequent discussion generally did not challenge the idea of admitting the best academically.

In contrast, while admitting 'the best' academically was an integral part of US admissions discourses, it was not usually the first answer regarding the purpose of admission. Instead, admitting the best was linked to a range of other institutional objectives such as diversity and the ability to attract funding. But it was also linked to another concept that did not naturally surface in the English interviews: taking advantage of opportunities and contributing to university life. We will now look at these ideas in more detail.

Making a contribution and using opportunities

The idea that a university seeks to admit students who make use of opportunities and contribute to the institution was explained succinctly by this mid-rank selector working in the admissions offices of one of the Big Three US institutions:

> When we're out on the road, students are always asking, well, 'what are you looking for? What are you looking for?' And, the best way I've found to describe it is, 'the students who will take advantage … and students who will give.' It's like a give and take situation. And that … is the best way to describe it, because we want students to take advantage of every opportunity they have here, of all of the opportunities to do things abroad, all the opportunities they have to get to know faculty here, the opportunities to make contacts for when they leave [this institution].

As this selector explains, her institution is looking for students who appreciate the opportunities on offer, who make use of the opportunities, who have a good time, and who contribute to the university community and value their experience while they are there. Indeed, the university is looking for those who will also value their experience once they have left, as the same selector went on to explain:

> And then … give something back to the university. Make the university what it is, continue the life of the university, and … and the vibrancy that you find here, and the enthusiasm that you find here among students … I'm not a [graduate from this institution], but the [graduates] I know are so enthusiastic about being here, and about being a student here, and just love it so much. And I think that's … that says a lot about the … life of the university and what [this institution] is trying to perpetuate.

The idea of having a good time and 'giving back' to the university are linked here. Giving back can entail financial contributions to the university, but also continuing to participate in the institutional life, for example, by conducting alumni interviews as part of the admissions process.

The sentiment of participating in the university life was echoed by the selector at another Ivy League institution who described the purpose of admission as

> a part of this mission to, not necessarily promote, [this institution] because we don't really have to promote it, but to share it. ... And to find the right fits for the university. So, there's this one sense that you have to be academically qualified to be at a place like [this institution] ... but we take it a step further and we ... look at who's going to make a difference on our campus ... [by] choosing the students who are going to be happy here ... you can take research, and we've done it, who's academically successful? Who's not? What does their backgrounds look like? But in terms of who's not happy, and who are the students that may not be the right fit? It's more of a personality type than anything else. And we do pay attention to it.

This quotation reiterates some of now familiar themes about being academically qualified and making use of opportunities on campus. In addition, this respondent introduces a new angle from which to approach admission: the idea of fit and 'being happy' on campus. The institution in this quotation is a highly selective Ivy League university and the respondent states that his institution does not have to be promoted in the sense of not having applicants. However, by sharing the institution and its values and undertaking recruitment, the admissions process is intending to enrol not only sufficient numbers of academically qualified applicants but also applicants who 'will make a difference' on campus, who will be happy, and who will be a good fit in terms of their personality.

Perhaps the idea of admitting those who will contribute and participate in the university experience is most succinctly summarized by this Big Three US senior admissions professional: 'We are admitting people.' The purpose is not to admit the next highest achieving academic, but to admit a person. And a person is judged in a multidimensional way, with the academic side being only one part of the story.

Among the UK respondents, ideas relating to students' contributing to university life, making use of opportunity and being happy did not come up without direct prompting. But because using opportunities, contribution and fit were so strong a theme in the US interviews that the English selectors were asked whether such considerations came into play in their admissions process.

This Oxbridge academic considered the proposition whether fit and ability to benefit impact on admission decisions:

Presumably you don't know who's going to benefit from the tutorial system because the tutorial system is unique. And, if, in advance of having been in the tutorial system you already seem to be suited for it it's presumably because you're confident and argumentative and engaged with discussion. But presumably that's something the tutorial system is teaching, … people rather than, seeking to, to just exercise – so I think it would be difficult at interview to tell who's going to benefit most from tutorial systems … that's something that I'll have to wait and see.

Here, we can almost see the respondent working out her answer to how fit mattered while she responded to the question, perhaps showing that she might be thinking about the idea of fit for the first time. This contrasts with the responses from US selectors who volunteered information about the ability to benefit and draw on an established way of talking about this issue. Also, while the US idea of the ability to benefit and contribute considers the whole of the student experience and, in particular, extra-curricular activities, this Oxbridge tutor is straightaway interpreting the question regarding an applicant's ability to benefit from the institution as an invitation to think about the teaching and learning context and the unique features of learning in her particular Oxbridge context compared with other UK institutions.

Another academic Oxbridge selector provided a further example of thinking through the issue of fit. Again, this respondent took this idea to be about academic fit, and working through an answer on the spot, she arrived at the same answer as did the previous selector, namely that fit should not play a role:

At all stages [of the selection process] we should be looking explicitly and only at ability rather than, at … kind of social attainment or the confidence or that kind of thing. Surely, that's the last, that's precisely the thing that we shouldn't' be looking for. You're looking to … to teach people, and not just teach them a body of information but also introduce them to ways of thinking and ways of interacting, and if they already have those ways of interacting then that's great and good for them and well done, but I really don't … see the logic of saying, someone won't benefit from the tutorial system before they've been in the tutorial system.

In another Oxbridge interview, it was asked whether an applicant's ability to make use of what the university offered was important. After some thought, the respondent eventually answered that the main purpose of admissions was 'the strap-line the committee always uses, about trying to find the brightest and the best' but then went on to elaborate, 'I mean I suppose we've got something very special to offer here, and we want to have the people who make the greatest use of it.'

A respondent in a strategic admissions position at Oxbridge stated that there was, however, one area where he considered some fit with the way in which the institution operated as a legitimate aspect of selecting students:

> So what are we looking for? We're looking for potential to thrive on the course, to get the most out of a very demanding course and the focus on the exams, of course, is what I ought to add, is justifiable, we think, because our students take one-sitting-exams at the end of each year of study … our students have got end-of-year assessment, mainly in exam halls and/or by long essays. But most courses it will be, three quarters or more of the assessment, in timed exams, manuscript against the clock, answer these questions, timed exams. Therefore the focus on 'have you done well on the exams' isn't just us being macho, it is 'can you, at one sitting, take several exams, excel the first time?' Because if you need resits to excel, if you need to accumulate your grade rather than being able to nail it first time, actually your skill set doesn't map very successfully onto [what is required at this institution]. And that doesn't mean you're stupid, that doesn't mean you're a weak student, it just means that you might go somewhere else for continuous assessment of your learning and end up with a first-class degree and then you can come here to do a master's degree.

The respondent here highlighted how the particular way of learning and teaching, and especially the examination system in this institution, could be more suitable for some students than for others. Colloquially, the examinations at Oxbridge are known as 'sudden death' examinations because – as the respondent states – unlike the examination regime in some other English universities, coursework counts for little to nothing of the final grade and many subjects are only examined by a series of unseen timed examinations. At many other English universities, coursework carries a significantly higher weighting. This respondent also links undergraduate and postgraduate admissions by stating that someone might be better off going somewhere else for undergraduate study but that this institution would be welcoming to academically able graduates from other institutions who might thrive in doing postgraduate study there. There is already some formal and informal knowledge on how some universities in both the United States and England are desirable for undergraduate study, but not for postgraduate study, and thus become 'feeder universities' for postgraduate study elsewhere. But in line with the previous quotations, from English selectors fit with the university is only considered as part of academic considerations.

Overall, the idea of institutional fit, making use of opportunities, contributing to the university, and the ability to benefit were clear and uncontroversial themes in the US interviews. However, in the English interviews, this idea was not something that selectors had necessarily previously considered. When English respondents did consider this, they rejected the ability to benefit as a guiding principle for admission. This was in the context of, in particular Oxbridge, having an education system that is unlike other and previous education experiences. This observation made selectors question straightaway how they would evaluate the ability to benefit from something that the students had not previously experienced. The only fit issue that was raised among the English selectors was fit with the examination system. Here, information on how students had fared in prior single-sitting examinations was considered as a legitimate factor to take into consideration in admissions decisions.

The differences between the US and the English selectors in talking about those who will benefit from the experience thus point to some underlying differences regarding the model of learning and the purpose of a university education in the two contexts, which we explore in the next two sections.

Models of learning

We have already seen in the opening section that asking about the purpose of admissions quickly linked with other aims of the university as well as with the way in which these institutions organize their education. For example, the US respondents mentioned funding and diversity in connection with admissions whereas the English respondents, especially from Oxbridge, referred to the model of teaching and, in one instance, the model of examinations.

This indicates transatlantic differences in the underlying model of teaching and learning and the outcome of the learning process in higher education. This is how a selector at one of the US Big Three institutions explained the underlying model and philosophy of education at her institution based on the thinking of how students learn:

> By the 25th reunion they're all saying that they learned, as well as from the faculty, they learned even more from their classmates. And we have systems set up so people dine together. The features of our college are designed to reinforce … the institutional objectives. … We assign people randomly to [residential accommodation] where they're free not to live after their freshman year – everybody does live on campus except 2 per cent of the people. … We charge

them a meal plan because we give financial aid. But we have the view that dining together is a very important part of education.

This US respondent considered the primary source of learning for undergraduates the peer-group or other students. Simultaneously, it is clear that formal learning from faculty and peers is only part of what the institution aims to achieve and views as its purpose. For students, being a part of this institution is, at large, being part of an experience that centres around shared living and dining experiences and also around establishing some link with or affinity to the institution; that is, students return for 'reunions', such as the twenty-fifth-year reunion referred to by this respondent.

Interestingly, the house or college system found at some US institutions is based on the Oxbridge collegiate system that is also replicated in other English institutions. While taking meals together and having a residential student experience and infrastructures and opportunity for development outside the classroom thus clearly are also part of the student experience at Oxbridge and beyond, dining together was not at the forefront of respondents' minds when they discussed the purpose of education in England. Instead, respondents discussed the content of the curriculum and the learning experience.

As we have already seen, one thing English selectors thought was legitimate to consider was the examination system. Another Oxbridge respondent stated that at the forefront of their mind throughout selection was the sort of academic and personal experience the student would have and their role as an academic in being part of their student experience.

You're not only teaching students for three years you're, you're in charge of their pastoral care. … you don't have the kind of an anonymous relationship with them as you do in much larger groups.

While the Ivy selector emphasized the importance of the peer-group for success and a student experience, this selector emphasized the importance of the faculty–student link in learning. Overall, the academic experience and links with the faculty emerged as the key to knowing the way in which English selectors thought about the wider purpose of the university. A good outcome is one where students are supported and enabled to enjoy their studies and to be academically successful, with the academic success being the overarching aim of the university education.

Hence, rather than a fit with the larger institutional extra-curricular culture or opportunities, Oxbridge selectors look to gauge applicants' motivation for studying a particular subject as explained by this Oxbridge Science selector:

> It is so difficult to do [this subject] if you don't love it. If you hate it you will hate it more and more. You have to be fascinated by it. This doesn't mean your love has to be so deep that you want to become a professor but you have to have natural curiosity about the way the world works and be fascinated with the scientific method.

The model of learning implied here is a supported but self-motivated learner driven by curiosity and interest in the subject rather than a more general model of learning from peers and increasing a general preparedness for later studies or career choices.

This difference in discourse might be due to the differences in the undergraduate curriculum. In England, undergraduate degrees already have specialization in a particular academic subject built in. Students can study, for example, medicine or law as undergraduates. This contrasts with the more generalist and longer US undergraduate degrees, which often provide a more general liberal arts education and rounded knowledge over a longer period of time. Specialization here comes in the form of postgraduate study. In some ways, it would have therefore been interesting for example to compare the answers of those selecting for law schools (postgraduate) in the United States with those selecting for undergraduate law courses in England. It is possible that law selectors in the United States and England are looking for the same qualities in admission. This project may have missed such similarities as only admission to undergraduate courses is compared.

The same respondent as in the previous quotation elaborated further on how his own experience of undergraduate study in the United States mapped onto teaching his subject at Oxbridge:

> The tutorial system is the best way of teaching [this subject]. In eight week terms here in Oxford you can do 1 year worth of teaching of a US undergraduate course … you sit there with a student in a tutorial and you know exactly what they know and that is great and then you know what they need to learn.

While academics might have a range of views on the relative merits of teaching in the US and England, the overall sentiment and view voiced here contrasts with the views of US selectors, where an increased emphasis on the academic side of university was not desired. The following selector from a highly selective US institution noted that there had been discussions about reducing the length of time to graduation in college from four years to three years. His rebuttal to this proposition was that

> the experience of college is important. Reducing college to three years would focus way too much on the academic side. To cite Ruskin: Education is not about teaching people what they do not know, it is more about behaving differently.

This again highlights the differences between the US and the English models of learning. US institutions have a holistic view of how academic learning is one part of gaining wider learning from peers and having shared dining and other experiences and extra-curricular engagement. In England, being academically successful, enjoying academic study, and graduating with a good degree are seen as seminal. These different foci, in turn, relate to another difference between the United States and England: the idea of admitting groups or individuals.

Admitting groups, admitting individuals

In 2007, Mitchell Stevens published a book about admissions to a liberal arts college in Northeastern United States. The title of the book is *Creating a class*. The title succinctly summarizes a key aspect of the admissions process to private selective institutions: the result of the holistic admissions process is to create a holistic class. In the words of an admissions professional from a Big Three institution,

> We are putting a class together. This is about us ... we will take the ones who will contribute to campus, we build a community ... we are building a multicultural community – and we are supporting the engineering degree, the orchestra, varsity (athletics) and we are only able to take a fraction of the qualified candidates.

This means that the intake of the admitted cohort should have certain features such as having a certain number of athletes, those with special talents, a mix of racial and geographic backgrounds and representation from other 'special interest' groups for admission. Different parts of the university organization represent different interest groups, which this Big Three selector observed:

> The admissions office gets marching orders from the president, the trustees, the faculty as well as from athletic coaches and the music department ... these are the constituents you [admissions professionals] are answering to – they are setting policy.

This respondent also went on to observe that 'left to their own devices, each interest group would take a bigger piece of the pie'. He gave an example of the athletic department pushing for a higher number of athletes in a class but how the president of his institution had set a cap of athletes in the 200s for the admitted class to ensure there was balance with other interests.

The multidimensional class that is admitted, then, has a range of characteristics that are conducive to students learning from each other and contributing a variety of qualities to the group, but the class also meets organizational objectives. In fact, one US respondent went further than her colleagues by stating that the purpose of admission for her Big Three Ivy:

> It is not about fairness to the students. We are putting a class together. And we have to answer to our board. We are putting the very best class together that meets our institutional objectives

Indeed, another Ivy League elector commented how 'our selection process ... is idiosyncratic, designed to serve very specific institutional goals'.

This idea of crafting a class was met with lack of appreciation when English selectors learnt about it. I had an opportunity to hear the response of a former head of an Oxbridge college to the idea of crafting a class. During a 2009 visit to the United States, we both attended a talk on admissions. Afterwards, he remarked to me with complete bafflement that how

> they don't even pretend it is about equal opportunities over here. They just say – these are our organizational objectives, these are our stakeholders and then they admit them so it suits them! At least we are trying to be fair to the individual.

In England, the admissions processes are aimed to select the best individuals, however defined. The idea of 'creating a class' is alien to English admissions professionals or academic staff. Because of the importance of admitting a class in the US context, the English selectors were asked whether they were looking for some diversity in the admissions process. The answer was unequivocal, as illustrated by this Oxbridge selector's response:

> No. We like having diverse students but we take the best people, and if they all happen to be female in a particular year then we take them all. So ... we would never say: 'Oh we'll drop this person and take that person because that would make a better mix'. I mean we'd be very upset if they were all male ... and we'd think there was something wrong with our recruitment process if they were all male, if they were all female, if they were all something, but we would never drop someone because we would say ... that was unfair to the candidate who

had been dropped because … that would be saying, candidate A is better than candidate B but we've taken candidate B to make the numbers even.

And, just to be clear, the respondent confirmed that 'each applicant is considered individually independent of the composition of the others'.

While English respondents in this project were clear that they were not admitting groups but individuals, an influential policy paper, the Schwartz Report (2004), considered the idea of paying closer attention to the group of students learning together. It noted that 'the presence of a range of experiences in the laboratory or the seminar room enriches the learning environment for all students. A diverse student community is likely to enhance all students' skills of critical reasoning, teamwork and communication and produce graduates better able to contribute to a diverse society. The Group is aware of a recent decision by the US Supreme Court upholding a university's "compelling interest in obtaining the educational benefits that flow from a diverse student body"' (Schwartz Report 2004, 4.6). The report went on to note that institutions should make reasonable efforts to recruit from a pool of diverse applicants and be mindful of those who collectively will form the best possible group of students. While there is thus an appetite for considering crafting a class at policy level, however, there was no evidence among the English selectors as indicating this as a key aspect of admissions policy.

This section has highlighted how selective institutions in the United States aim to 'create a class' where the admitted 'class' has a range of features that meets a range of institutional objectives in different ways. In contrast, admission to highly selective institutions in England aims to find the best individuals with the highest ability and potential to succeed in a particular academic university course.

Numbers

An introduction to the aims of admission would be incomplete without the mention of the basic statistics of the highly selective institutions presented in this book. How many undergraduates do they enrol every year? What do their finances look like? What are the fees for getting a degree? What financial support is available? These numbers offer the context in which the US and the English selectors admit students.

While introducing some numbers gives helpful ballpark figures for the English–US context, the exact figures are prone to fluctuate more than perhaps the overarching aim of an institution or their model of learning. The value of endowments can raise or lose value, and in England, the structure of fees and student support has changed rapidly in a relatively short period of time.[3] With this caveat in mind, the director of admissions for Oxford provided the following comparison of numbers between Oxford and Harvard in 2013:

> Harvard are looking for around about 1600 candidates, we [Oxford] are looking for about 3200 at the end of our process. Harvard will make around about 2000 offers to get those 1600, we will make 3500 to get 3200, because the attrition rate of a candidate turning down Oxford is limited, a small number might decide for a variety of very good reasons, to go somewhere else. And, I think one of the key statistics that came out of the conversation, going back to the issue around funding and resource, Harvard have 100 million pounds a year to give in financial aid to their 1600 students, Oxford has currently about 8 million pounds financial aid for potentially 3200 students. (Nicholson 2013)

The Big Three Ivies admit fewer undergraduates per year than Oxbridge institutions and the Ivy League educates fewer students than the Russell Group. Together, Harvard, Yale and Princeton enrol around 4,300 students per year or around 1,300 to 1,650 each. Oxford and Cambridge enrol 6,500 students a year or over 3,000 each.

In terms of applications per place, it is significantly more competitive to gain an offer from one of the Big Three Ivies than from Oxbridge. The Big Three offer rates are below one in thirteen and range from as low as 5.8 per cent at Harvard to 7.4 per cent at Princeton. At Oxford and Cambridge, around one in five applicants actually enrol at the institutions. Indeed, several English Russell Group universities receive many more applications than Oxford or Cambridge and have a lower acceptance rate than Oxbridge.

Of course, at closer look, the story behind these numbers is more complicated: in England, applicants can only apply to either Oxford or Cambridge in a given year, whereas US applicants can apply to as many institutions as they wish. They could apply to all Ivy League institutions and then to a few more in any given year. In contrast, the high attainment threshold for Oxbridge means that schools will not simply support all those who wish to apply to, for example, Oxbridge in their application but will only support those with the highest grades. For an indicative comparison, in the United States this would mean that only applicants with a GPA of 4.0 would be allowed to apply to the most selective colleges.

When students are admitted to Oxford or Cambridge, there is not a 'yield' issue as indicated in the previous quotation from the previous director of admission at Oxford: a negligible number of applicants turn down their offer for a place. If students have succeeded thus far, they are unlikely not to take their place. Part of the reason that Oxbridge offers a slightly higher number of places to applicants than they intend to take is more a matter of 'meeting the offer' than of yield: some applicants gain an offer for a place, but they are unable to enrol because they failed to achieve as highly as they needed to in their final school-leaving examinations. Lower actual achievement usually makes an Oxbridge offer a void, and these applicants tend to enrol at their second-choice institutions. Converting offers into actual places is so much of a non-issue for these institutions that yield statistics are not published – if they were, they would be in the 90s for Oxbridge meaning more than 9 out of 10 admitted students will take up their place. For Russell Group institutions other than Oxbridge, conversion from offers to enrolled students is a bigger issue, and sometimes significantly more offers for places are made than there are places available to enrol the desired number of students.

Despite the fact that no restriction on the number of applications is imposed in the United States, even the highest 'yielding' university, Harvard, still loses almost 20 per cent of its admitted students to competitor institutions. Such statistics are not generally openly published in England the way they are in the United States. In the United States, yield statistics are a standard part of some university ranking systems and generally easily accessible.

The US institutions mentioned in this book are all private institutions that are built on large endowment. Harvard has the largest endowment of any US institution totalling $32.7 billion. Yale and Princeton come next with nearly $21 and $18 billion of endowment, respectively. The smallest endowment within the Ivy League is held by Brown University with $2.7 billion. This makes the institution ranked 30th in the national endowment ranking of US universities, thus showing how many non-Ivy League institutions have higher endowments than some of the smaller Ivies. The richest liberal arts colleges, Williams, Amherst and Ponoma, have endowments of around $2 billion.

The English public universities are poor in comparison. Only two institutions, Oxford and Cambridge, have endowments measured in billions. For both institutions, the combined endowment of the university and its colleges is between four and five billion, £4.9 ($8.4) billion for Cambridge and £4 ($6.9) billion for Oxford. The next wealthiest English universities are Manchester and King's College London, both Russell Group institutions, and they have £169 ($290) and £154 ($264) million, respectively.

Endowment funds can contribute a significant percentage to the operating budget of the university, which they can use for financial support for students. In the United States, the 'sticker price' for a selective university education is thus paid only by some students.

This 'sticker price' of tuition fees at the Big Three Ivies is in the low to mid-$40,000s per year. In England, the usual fee of a Russell Group education, including that of Oxbridge, is £9,000 ($15,400) per annum. However, at the most selective US institutions, fewer than half of the students tend to pay the full 'sticker price' for their education. For the students admitted in 2013, Harvard states that 60 per cent of students received at least a partial scholarship. At Princeton, 52 per cent of students were in receipt of a scholarship. For Oxford, the figure was 42 per cent.

Harvard also awards financial aid covering the estimated costs of room and board. Harvard awards needs-based scholarships for those candidates whose family incomes are up to $200,000. The 20 per cent of Harvard students with a household income of less than $65,000 do not contribute any personal or family funds to either their tuition fees or room and board at Harvard. Their education is genuinely free with no loans or strings attached.

In England, no tuition fees were payable for higher education up to and including the academic year starting in 1997. Instead, university students received government grants for their costs of living. This model reversed in 1998 when a tuition fee of £1,000 was initially introduced and grants for the cost of living were replaced by student loans. This tuition fee was increased to £3,000 in 2004 and then further increased to £9,000 in 2012. Since 2004, fees are only paid when graduates enter the labour market and are then paid as a percentage of their income once a graduate reaches a certain income threshold. International students, that is those from outside the European Union, pay higher fees than EU students.

In England, students only pay their tuition fees once they graduate and earn above a certain income threshold. Moreover, unpaid debts are written off after a period of time. This means that higher education is currently free at the point of use. Loans and limited scholarships are available for room and board. Government loans are available to cover the costs of housing and subsistence. For students starting university in 2015, loans are available up to £8,009 and up to £3,387 in grants (although these grants are to be replaced by loans from 2016 onwards).

For the year 2013, Oxford University had the most generous financial support for the lowest-income students of any university in England. Tuition fees are reduced for students with a household income of up to £25,000. Living cost support is awarded for those students whose family incomes are up to £42,601.

This is on a sliding scale of between £3,300 and £500 annual supplements. Loans are available to cover further expenses relating to living costs.

The availability of financial support means that, at Harvard, 90 per cent of US students pay the same or less for their Harvard education compared with the cost of attending a public university within their US home state. Similarly in England, students from low-income households are likely to have more financial support available to them at Russell Group institutions than at other universities.

US undergraduate degrees are stipulated to be four years, but in reality, they often take up to five or even six years to be completed. In contrast, most degrees in England take three or sometimes four years to complete. This has implications for finding support for an additional year of study in the United States, and economists would also point to the 'foregone earnings' when US students are still in higher education while English students might already have entered the labour market.

Table 1 summarizes some of these key finance and student figures about some of the institutions presented in this project.

These figures are important especially for Chapter 8 when thinking about selecting in the context of inequality.

Chapter summary

To summarize then, both English and US universities wished to admit 'the best'. The key difference between the two countries was the breadth regarding the definition of 'the best'. The US selectors considered the academic side as a necessary but insufficient admissions criterion. The selectors were interested in students who would make use of opportunities, contribute to the institution, have a good time, and go on to be successful in terms of wealth and leadership positions – and in terms of giving back to the institution. In contrast, English selectors had a narrower remit and their focus was trying to admit the best in terms of ability and potential to succeed academically. Whether admissions 'had worked' was defined by success decades after graduation in the US context but earlier in terms of degree performance and employment in the English context.

This chapter has established the different purposes that admission seeks to achieve in both England and the United States. With this in mind, the next two chapters will look at what it means to select for 'academic success' and to consider 'special interest cases' in admissions.

Table 1 Key financial and student information for selected English and US universities

	Number of applicants	Per cent offers	Offers	Matriculated	Yield	% receiving scholarship	Tuition Fees per year (2014 entry***)	Income limit up to which (partial) scholarships received	Market value of endowment assets
Harvard (US)	35,023	5.8	2,047	1,659	81%	60	$43,938	$200,000	$32.7 billion
Yale (US)	29,610	6.9	2,044	1,359	68.2	52	$44,800	$200,000	$20.7 billion
Princeton (US)	26,498	7.4	1,963	1,291	65.8	60	$41,820	$200,000**	$18.2 billion
Oxford (England)	17,216	(18.6% matriculate)		3,198		42	($15,400)	($73,000)	($6.9) £4.03 billion
Cambridge (England)	16,185	(20.8% matriculate)		3,371		Missing	£9,000	£42,601	($8.4) £4.9 billion

Source: institutional websites and National Association of College and University Business Officers and Commonfund Institute (2014).

Oxford University financial statements 2012/13, Oxbridge endowment figures include college assets. **partial scholarships might still be available for those with family incomes above this limit, usually when they have two children in college. Enrolment figures refer to enrolment in 2013. ***Tuition fees in England are for students resident in England or another country of the European Union only. Higher fees apply for international students.

3

Selecting for Academic Success

This chapter explores the similarities and differences of how universities identify the best applicants for succeeding academically at university.

United States

An admissions professional from a liberal arts college explained how in his institution admission is not entirely dependent on academic qualifications.

> Being qualified academically at a really selective place is only half the battle. That only gets you halfway there because of the 75 per cent of students that we're denying [admissions] a lot of them are academically qualified and a lot who apply at [this liberal arts college] would be able to graduate with honors. … There are thousands of kids who are academically qualified but we just don't have the room for that. At Ivies and other places it's even more extreme where you have to be really special or unique in some way to get past that point once you have already reached that level of qualification academically.

This liberal arts college denies admission to up to one in four students based on some academic consideration. The reason the other three in four do not receive an offer is not related to academic considerations. The admissions professional quoted above considered Ivy League admissions to be even further weighted towards non-academic factors. This is confirmed by a selector at one of the Big Three Ivies: a minimum standard of academic strength is necessary for a chance of being admitted; however, academic strength alone is not usually enough for getting in.

> If the student is … in the ballpark, as far as academics … the personal side is really going to be where we look, to make decisions about whether or not they're going to be admitted.

For admission to the selective US institutions, all parts of the application need to be excellent. Because there are more applicants who are academically qualified than there are places available, the personal part of the application is important and decisive. But what does it mean to be in the right 'ballpark' concerning the academics?

Standardized tests

Admissions professionals draw on a range of sources to evaluate whether an applicant's academic credentials are in the 'ballpark' or, in other words, above the minimum eligibility threshold for admissions. The primary sources of information here are performance at school, which is reflected for instance in the grade point average (GPA), performance in a nationally standardized college admissions test (SAT or ACT, see glossary), references and interviews. GPAs and SAT or ACT results are the 'currency of admissions counselling' – in other words, GPAs and SAT or ACT results are always mentioned when high schools advise students where to apply and when selectors talk about minimum standards.[1] However, even high school performance is not directly comparable across different schools because different schools can mark performance differently and have different offerings of courses available. The only part of the college application that is thus genuinely directly comparable across applicants is the performance in the nationally standardized tests. These tests are held under the same examination conditions and are marked centrally or through computer algorithms against the same criteria. This makes SAT or ACT results a 'constant' or 'common yardstick' of performance across applicants from different high schools and contexts. The tests are therefore key to unlocking the academic side of an application, as this liberal arts college selector explains:

> The first thing is the grades and test scores. If you don't have … if you're 100 points below our average, sort of like, lower average SATs, … then you could have the best essay and the best interview in the world; it's not going to make a difference if you're not performing in the tests.

This understanding of a minimum score on academic tests and high school performance was confirmed by the Big Three selector quoted below:

> There's just no way you can justify admitting this kid where [SAT] scores were in the 400s,[2] and he's a C and D student. I just can't do that. … When that kid fails his first year, that comes back to the admission office.

With regard to scores, selectors made reference to applicants 'dialling toll free'. This was admissions language for having scored 800 or several 800s on the different parts of the SAT. One of the Big Three selectors described how his university had received over 2,000 applications from high school students who had achieved the top score in at least part of the test. On its own, however, even 'dialling toll free' is insufficient for gaining admission; many students are admitted with lower SAT scores, as this observation from a Big Three selector illustrates:

> We have more applicants than we can take with perfect SAT scores. It is crucial to be in the top of attainment overall because the level of attainment among our applicants is so high. But it is not the most important aspect of admissions.

However, because SAT scores are something school advisers and applicants are looking for, US universities publish some information on the relationship between SAT scores and admissions and enrolment. For example, for the students admitted in 2013, Harvard reported average SAT scores to have been 2,237 (out of a possible 2,400). Princeton reported that 16.5 per cent of applicants with an SAT score above 2,300 received an offer for admission and that 7.5 per cent of applicants with scores between 2,100 and 2,290 received an offer. The probability of receiving an offer then decreased on a sliding scale up to the point of an SAT average of 1,500, with no admissions below this point. Yale college publishes the range of grades those who enrolled had achieved. This breakdown shows that one in four of the enrolled students had a perfect score on the SAT verbal section and one in four had a perfect score in the SAT writing section; perfect scores in the SAT maths section were a little less common. This type of breakdown of SAT scores among the admitted students is also available for each US university that uses the SAT test through the College Board, the organization that administers the SAT test.

Among the Ivy League institutions, Brown has the lowest average SAT scores at intake, yet those scores are hardly low in a general comparison: in 2013, 18 per cent of enrolled students at Brown had a perfect verbal reasoning score of 800, 17 per cent of enrolled students had a perfect score in maths and 13 per cent had a perfect score in writing. Several liberal arts colleges as well as some other private colleges have higher SAT scores at intake than some Ivies.

High school performance

High school performance is another piece of evidence admissions professionals paid close attention to. Some universities also list some high school performance statistics as part of their profiling of a newly admitted class: for students admitted in 2013, Brown University enrolled 8 per cent of students who had been valedictorians (ranked first in their high school graduating class), another 3 per cent or 58 students who were salutatorians (ranked second in terms of their academic performance in their graduating class from high school). Perhaps most surprising is the observation that over 60 per cent of this incoming class did not have a disclosed class rank on their application.

Where available, selectors consider the class rank of all applicants' high school performance. This measures how the applicant performed relative to his or her classmates. As a Big Three selector notes: '95 per cent of the students here are in the top 10 per cent of their class ... so they're number ten out of 150, or whatever it happens to be.'

High school rank in particular is viewed as a helpful way to see how much use applicants had made of opportunities presented to them in the past and to forecast how much use an applicant might make of the opportunities presented to them – relative to their peers – were they admitted to a selective college. As an Ivy selector noted:

> We don't care as much about that they're number 1, for number 1's sake. We deny a ton of students who are Valedictorians [top of their graduating class] all the time. But we want to know how they compared to their peers. ... Where a student falls, how many students were taking the exams? ... Most students who are admitted do rank in the top decile of their graduating cohorts

What selectors really seek to establish is whether the applicant is an average student in their high school context, or performs below average in a good school or academically outstanding in a context with fewer opportunities – is he or she a big fish in a small pond? But because the academic side is only part of what matters in US admissions, there might be strong non-academic reasons to admit an applicant. The class-rank information would then be given less weight as the previous respondent went on to explain:

> [But] there's no cut-off, there's no requirements, which is brilliant, in terms of giving us the flexibility to find someone who might be a great fit and incredibly strong for [this institution], but might not look strong in that one way.

Several selectors noted a trend among high schools of not ranking students or inflating high school ranks in a way that made ranks no longer useful. The dean of admissions at a private institution ranked just below the Ivy League said:

> Probably 65 per cent of the students who apply to [this institution] no longer come from schools that use the traditional class rank. And when they do, it's

very, very different, because for example, there are a couple of schools that ... have about 600 students per class and they rank. And you might have the Valedictorian [the number 1 ranked student in the graduating class] apply, but they share the rank with 55 other students.

A Big Three selector recalled an extreme example of a school where 100 students shared the rank of valedictorian; in another instance, he had seen a home-schooled student praised for being ranked number 1 (out of one). A liberal arts college selector noted other problems with taking ranks at face value:

> What happens also is sometimes the private schools, they'll tell the teachers 'you can't give the kids bad grades because no parent is going to pay $20,000 a year to send their kid to a ritzy private school for them to get bad grades'. ... They would pull them out of that school. The school knows that.

As a result of these kinds of issues, some high grades were considered with a grain of salt. At other schools, grading was known to be tough and selectors considered a GPA of 3.8 as signifying higher academic accomplishment than a perfect GPA of 4.0 at a school known to be easier. Where school records of the applicants of the previous years were available, selectors used them to decide on school-specific GPA cut-offs.

Thus, during the admissions process the usefulness of class rank is viewed very much in the context of other information about the applicant and his or her school; and SATs serve as a yardstick that allow selectors to compare applicants across schools.

Application dossiers contain information about an applicant's performance in individual courses at high school as well as some average performance score, the high school GPA. The GPA is reported on a scale from 0 to 4.0 – with 4.0 being the highest score. However, selectors often do not use the GPA score that is on an application file; instead, they create their own high school attainment measure from the information available in the application dossier. This practice is explained by a Big Three Ivy selector thus:

> So we calculated a [Ivy League name] GPA, because every school tends to do it differently ... so we have to ... standardize things in some way. So we calculated our GPA. We also looked at the ... transcript and see what kind of classes the student is taking. And you're looking for what we call solid classes, like hard academic subjects, maths, science, languages.

Because selectors found that high school GPAs were not always comparable between high schools, they found it useful to calculate their own GPA. This allowed them the flexibility to count only certain subjects. The previous respondent elaborated further on the subjects her institution would not consider in calculating their GPA.

> So, orchestra. Even though we like it … we don't count that … basically any kind of vocational classes. The only art classes we count are advanced placement classes, drafting, computer classes.

To summarize, the probability of gaining admission declines with lower test scores and lower GPAs. However, not everyone with perfect test scores, or a perfect GPA, or who is a high-school valedictorian is admitted to the most selective colleges. What is also observed is that the actual 'cut-off' point below which no one is admitted is in fact close to the national average SAT score of around 1,500. However, few applicants are admitted close to this cut-off; at Princeton, no applicant with scores below 1,500 was admitted and for those with scores between 1,500 and 1,690, 0.5 per cent were made an offer. Brown University made 39 offers to applicants with SAT reading scores below 550, and 24 offers to applicants with writing scores below this threshold. Universities also pay attention to subject choice and curriculum. Where class-rank information is available, it is used in the admissions process.

The universities in this study use SATs to establish minimum preparedness. SATs and GPAs serve as a 'deselection tool', with low scores highlighting those applicants who are likely to struggle academically. Applicants in this pool are much more likely not to gain an offer, although they could still gain admission if, for example, they are a special interest case regarding talents in sport or legacy consideration (Special interest cases in admission are discussed in more detail in Chapter 4.). The fact that low scores make gaining admission difficult does not, however, mean that the highest scores signal automatic admission. Instead, high scores confer the right to stay in the competition for a place.

Essays and recommendation letters

Academic worth can also be gauged from applicants' essays and recommendation letters. However, these pieces of the application also served other purposes such as contextualizing the application and providing support for the non-academic achievements of the applicant. A good academic reference, explained a Big Three selector, would include remarks such as the following: 'This is the best student I have seen in my career. She has changed the way I view calculus.' Such a remark could make an applicant eligible for academic-based admission.

A bad reference would say that 'the student was not the best child in the class'. Admissions professionals looked for 'whether a teacher is backing a student or not; even though they might be good, it's really clear when the teacher is really behind a student and really supportive of them, and those are really taken into consideration very much'.

Essays are usually used by applicants to highlight their non-academic background and their potential to contribute to the institution. A selector recalled only one case where an applicant wrote an essay about an academic experience to make their case for admission on academic grounds.

When applicants tried to make the case for admission on academic grounds in their essay and references, selectors looked for authenticity and a deep interest in the relevant subject. An Ivy selector had this to say:

> If the student says they're interested in physics, we look for some sort of depth … for example, the advanced labs they take in their high school, or the research they're doing outside of the school, the clubs they got involved in. We ask what books they read outside the classroom, we care about their intellectual experiences, if they know about string theory. We're looking for a hint to know: … this is someone who is going to contribute and is authentically interested in this subject … and that they're not going to switch their major to political science once they get here. That's going to make faculty members happy. It's going to add to the richness of the type of physics majors we're producing here.

Overall, it is relatively rare for students to gain admission to the most selective US institution based solely on academic grounds. The one highly selective private (non-Ivy) institution in this study that was most comfortable with allowing the academic to dominate was a specialist technical institution. A selector at the institution gave the impression that the institution was proud that 'there are nerds' and seemed happy to focus strongly on academic achievement and potential.

All other US selectors said admission based on a stellar academic record alone was the exception rather than the rule. One Big Three selector commented that an applicant would need to be 'wickedly smart – sort of category of next Fields-medallist[3] and the absolute top nationally' to be considered for admission on purely academic grounds. Such an applicant might be termed a 'mathlete' – someone with a stellar academic record and outstanding potential. In the case of such an applicant, the admissions office would ask the academic faculty at the institution to judge his or her academic performance. In general, the role of the faculty is to differentiate between the very good and the nationally outstanding ones. In the words of an admissions professional:

> The job of the faculty is to keep it real and to point out the academic stellar ones, without worrying about how they are as room-mates and the geek issue.

One Ivy League US selector recalled admitting a student solely on academic grounds, but the student was an unpleasant person and had to be 'roomed in a single', an arrangement which the institution felt defeated the purpose of a residential college experience and room-sharing. The overall conclusion drawn from the experience with this student was that granting admission based on academic grounds alone was a mistake.

Indeed, I had the opportunity to participate in a simulation exercise of admissions decisions during one of my US visits. Led by an experienced Ivy League selector, a group of twelve participants debated several 'mock applications' serving as case studies of different types of applicants. Among the application dossiers was one with a particularly stellar academic record but with thin evidence to support any non-academic accomplishments or interests. The group of role-playing selectors agreed that other applicants were higher institutional priorities than this applicant. The applicant was not admitted in our simulation exercise. The facilitator commented that the real applicant who had served as a model for this application had also failed to gain admissions to the highly selective US institution he had applied for. When I asked him whether he knew where the student had ended up, the answer was: 'I think he went to Cambridge. You know, I mean Cambridge, England.' And somehow, this answer was not a complete surprise.

England

We are geek central.

(Oxbridge admissions professional)

Indeed, while the 'geek issue' described by the US selector in the previous section was a deal-breaker for the applicant's prospect of admission, the quotation above from an Oxbridge admissions professionals shows a different weighting of academic single-mindedness. Admitting those with the highest academic ability and potential to succeed in their chosen course is the overarching, the only aim of selective admissions in England: 'I simply want to admit on academic grounds' stated an academic Oxbridge selector. Individual applicants are selected on their suitability for a particular degree course they have applied for, let it be engineering, law, mathematics or English literature. They are not selected for their suitability for a general degree programme or suitability to contribute to a particular student experience. The high-achieving, single-minded academic applicant, rejected by the selective US institution in the previous example, might in fact just be the sort of person who promises to stay focused on their chosen academic interests and to succeed academically at university. It is the sort of applicant selective universities are interested in.

This is not to say that achieving this aim of finding the best for academic success is straightforward. There is significant debate among English selectors about the most robust, and valid way to find those with the highest academic ability and potential. There is debate about the balance and weight given in admissions decisions to demonstrate ability and prior achievement and undeveloped latent potential. There is concern about detecting, finding and developing potential to thrive academically in the future that is different from demonstrated ability shown in previous examinations. There are also debates about how best to take into account the context of achievement and potential in a national education situation where educational opportunities are unequally distributed. Different academic or professional selectors, different academic fields of study and different institutions might value different ways of evaluating ability and potential. But there is no disagreement among English admissions professionals and selectors that admitting those with academic ability and potential is the aim of the admissions process.

A first example of the information selectors might take into account when evaluating academic ability and potential is provided by this Oxbridge selector: 'We look for three things: 1. Attainment to date; 2. Interview performance; 3. Test performance'.

Prior attainment and expected future attainment are considered in all selective English admissions contexts. If SATs and GPAs are the attainment currencies of US admissions, GCSE and A-levels (achieved and predicted) are the attainment currencies for university admissions in England.

A-levels

Advanced-level or A-level examinations are taken in two parts as A2 and AS examinations. A2-level examinations are taken at age eighteen, usually following an earlier AS-level examinations in the same subject at age seventeen. Unlike the high school GPA in the United States, A2 examinations are standardized and thus comparable across schools.[4]

English students usually take three A2-level subjects, but for the most selective universities, applicants often apply with four or five A2-levels. Applicants usually apply with 'predicted' A2-levels with predictions given by the teacher who instructs them in the particular subject. The pass grades, from highest to lowest, range from A* (pronounced 'A-star'), A to E. Universities then admit students based on the predicted grades. Failure to achieve the predicted A2-level grades usually means that applicants cannot enrol at their first-choice higher education institution.

For Oxford, offers for admission in 2014 ranged from A*A*A to AAA, for Cambridge, the offer range was similar with 60 per cent of successful applicants having achieved A*A*A* in their A2 examinations (2012 statistics). For 2013, Oxford noted that 'over 46,000 UCAS applicants a year achieve AAA+ … and Oxford only has around 3,200 places so even excellent grades will not guarantee you a place'.

Table 2 below shows the A-level grades of accepted Oxford and Cambridge candidates with A-levels for 2013 entry.

Table 2 Admitted students at Oxford and Cambridge by A-level results[5]

	Oxford		Cambridge	
Best 3 A-level grades achieved	**No**	**%**	**No**	**%**
A*A*A* or above	923	37.1	1,494	57.4
A*A*A	677	27.2	667	25.6
A*AA	596	24.0	347	13.3
AAA	235	9.4		
Below AAA (incl A*A*B, etc.)	57	2.3		
AAA and below			93	3.5
TOTAL	2,488	100.0	2,601	100.00

However, for the most selective institutions, the information contained in achieved AS performance and predicted A2 performance contains limited information. The reasons for this were explained by this Russell Group selector:

> For competitive admissions, you want something that differentiates between applicants. A-level performance is often not much of a variable among our applicants. Almost everyone is predicted at least three A*s or As at A-level. There is more variation now with the A* grades, and some universities look at

the percentage grade achievement in individual examinations. But the overall A-level grades do not vary very much. ... So, A-levels are not much of a selection tool really – they are more a deselection tool. If applicants are not predicted As and A*s, we look carefully why this is the case. For the majority of applicants GCSE performance and other measures of attainment are factors that actually differentiate between applicants, predicted A-level performance is often more of a constant.

Because achieved and predicted A2 and A-level attainment at age seventeen and predicted attainment at age eighteen is often so uniformly high among applicants for the most selective universities, selectors look in different places for more information about the scholastic achievement and potential of applicants. There are three general strategies for increasing information selectors consider and in many cases, all three approaches are employed: using more fine-tuned attainment at A-level, using earlier achievement information and using additional academic information (e.g. from tests and interviews) not available from school examinations.

Fine-tuning A-level results

The English selectors, especially at the most selective institutions, are looking for something that allows them to differentiate on academic grounds among applicants who are exceptionally highly qualified when compared against national achievement data. Among these high achievers, the vast majority of applicants to Oxbridge in particular are predicted the highest possible grades in the school-leaving examinations. One selective institution thus asks for the percentage breakdown of the grades achieved. Almost all their applicants achieve As and A*s – but in percentages, an A* can be achieved by someone with a score of 90 per cent or 100 per cent in their A2 units. Gaining insights into those fine grained differences is considered useful additional information for some selectors.

Obtaining the percentages in the examination rather than just the grade is thus one strategy for fine-tuning the attainment information and predicted attainment information from A-levels further.

Selectors also look in detail at the subjects studied. Generally, for A-level examinations, Russell Group universities discount any grades achieved in the subject 'General Studies' and look for achievement in applicants' core academic A-levels. Standard offers are based on achievement in three A-levels, although many applicants to the most selective courses study towards four or more full A-level subjects. In such cases, a predicted B might be discounted if the applicant is still predicted a mixture of As and A*s in at least three academic A-level subjects. This practice is similar to US selectors discounting some subjects – such as orchestra – in computing a standardized high school GPA for admission.

GCSEs

Another strategy for differentiating among high-achieving applicants is to look at earlier attainment information than A-levels. This usually takes the form of looking at performance in the nationally standardized General Certificate of Secondary Education (GCSE) examinations.

GCSEs are taken by the vast majority of students in English schools. The grades capture the academic accomplishment over two years with the final examinations usually taken at age sixteen. Students then receive an individual grade for each subject for which they took the GCSE examination. As with A2 levels, the highest pass grade is again an A*, but the lowest pass grade here is a G. Applicants for the most selective institutions usually apply with a string of A*, A and perhaps some B qualifications in their GCSEs.

Many applicants to selective higher education have taken GCSEs in more than ten subjects. Just as the selectors in the United States paid close attention to subject choices in school, English selectors paid close attention to the attainment in particular subjects in GCSEs. A short of stellar grade in GCSE art or music might not be a deal-breaker for admission to a traditional academic subject at a highly selective English university. Having a B grade or even just an A compared with an A* in the subject an applicant wishes to study may well be. This Oxbridge selector for a subject relying on writing essays explained:

> GCSEs are taken very seriously, the number of A*s – A*s signify real intellectual potential. We look for English, history, maths, languages and sciences. It is ok when they have done sciences but there could be concern regarding their essay writing skills – they need to be able to write in paragraphs, not formulae.

Another Oxbridge selector also described how selectors looked for attainment in the subject an applicant sought to study:

> And if somebody has Bs and the Bs are like maths or sciences, that's often not so bad. But if they want to study languages, and they've not done well in their languages, or languages at GCSE that's worrying.

For the selection process at Oxbridge, GCSE performance could act as a threshold applicants had to pass in order to be considered for the next stage in the selection process, the interview. The academic faculty at Oxford and Cambridge interview the majority of their applicants for undergraduate study. Only those without a chance of a place are not invited for an interview. GCSEs information can be a deciding factor when sending out interview invitations as this Oxbridge selector explained:

> A candidate on paper has to be extremely, or very measurably and seriously, short on criteria – e.g. a C in GCSE Maths, when they are applying [for this science subject] – to not get invited for interview … a grade C in GCSE English, we wouldn't disinvite them.

Again, GCSE attainment is considered in a focused way with the degree subject in mind. The selector elaborated further on the scenario of someone applying with not fantastic GCSE attainment in the subject they wished to study:

> But very few candidates apply in that situation. … The vast majority of candidates have extremely strong results to date, predicted straight As and A*s. And then when they are a little short of that they often come from schools with very poor exam results and are giving it a go and we would invite them for interview. Whereas a candidate from a school with traditionally very strong exam results who has got a couple of Bs in their GCSEs might be looked at worse than a candidate from an inner-city comprehensive. But we deselect very few each year.

Instead of having a formulaic minimum threshold for inviting applicants for interview, the attainment information is considered in the context of other information about an applicant. This other information not only entails subject choice but also the context of their schooling. We will revisit the idea of contextualized or holistic admission later in this chapter and, again, in Chapter 8.

Another Oxbridge selector for a science subject explained how the discipline had a subject coordinator who carefully considered GCSEs in the decision which applicants to invite for interview:

> Well, the problem is that almost everybody is predicted three As. So, the GCSEs loom larger than they should as you have the GCSEs. So, what he [the subject co-ordinator] did is he looked at data from the past years, to see if you had 3A*, or 4 A* or 5A*, what was your chance of getting an offer. And he found the number of stars below which you had almost no chance of getting in – in practice. … This is A vs A* – not A versus another grade. … And, so, he produced a list on the basis of how the GCSEs – using the criterion from past years – and said, these are the people we are going to desummon [not invite to interview] … we are using evidence now because we are saying, if you only have

2A*, your chances of getting in are almost non existence. So, it is being done much more evidence based'.

But again, this selector also explained which additional considerations would be taken into account before not inviting applicants for interview. The respondent emphasized how invitations and the decision not to invite someone for interview were not automatic. If in doubt, subjects erred on the side of inviting applicants for interview:

> Now, the main concern are people are desummoned on that list mainly because they didn't do all that well in their GCSEs. And, clearly, this could be because they had glandular fever, because they come from a poor school, because there was family breakup, because they are access students, and so on. So, a proportion of students were added to the summoned list because college tutors thought it not correct to desummon that person'.

A holistic evaluation of applicants' prior record and attention to the schooling context in which it was achieved could mean that some students were invited for interview despite having not stellar records. This holistic evaluation of prior attainment could also prevent invitations to interview as observed by this Oxbridge science selector:

> We even desummon people who have 'only' got an A at GCSE Maths rather than an A* if they come from a very good school.

A further challenge in using GCSEs was voiced by another Oxbridge science selector: 'some students at GCSE level don't really care, because it's too easy so they might under-perform simply because they didn't even bother to study it'. The concern here is that students who are able to attain potentially exceptionally highly at university could be missed by placing too much emphasis on early school attainment.

The challenges of selection were also experienced by another Oxbridge selector for a humanities subject. The tutor described how her subject wished to interview everyone with a realistic chance of gaining an offer but did not have the capacity of staff to interview everybody although 'Almost all of our applicants either have three A's or are predicted three As or A*s. So that doesn't help us to short list.'

This subject did not wish to go down the route of placing increasing importance and weight on GCSE performance. Instead, the subject wished to focus energy on obtaining more information directly relevant to their discipline and find comparable information for international applicants without GCSEs and A-levels at the same time. The solution this discipline came up with is to introduce an additional admissions test that all applicants sit.

Additional tests

So far, this chapter has described how English selectors can obtain more information about applicants' academic potential and achievement by fine-tuning the A-level information and by using earlier achievement information (GCSEs). The third strategy selectors can employ is to use the results of additional admissions tests or written work. Generally, Oxford University has gone more down the route of using additional tests and Cambridge University has opted to use more fine-tuned A-level attainment information although some subject at Cambridge also use additional tests. Some tests are subject specific rather than university specific and used for admission to, for example, law or medicine across a range of universities.

One Oxbridge respondent explained how 'the introduction of the test was debated at length because it is controversial' with some selectors concerned about elitism and increasing barriers to application. On the other hand, additional tests provided comparable information for international applicants and might tap into untrained potential different from the achievement measured in school examinations. She explained why, having considered the arguments for and against additional admissions tests, she supported the introduction of tests:

> I voted in favour of [the tests] ... because I think tests may be unfair but interviews are even more and at least given the fact that the students will be coming here will ultimately be assessed in terms of written examinations and not, unless you're doing modern languages or something like that, through oral examination. The interview in a sense is the anomalous thing. And I'm all for interviews, it really helps you to know a person better, but I think ... at least part of the fundamental assessment must be a written exercise. So those are the main reasons for which I think the faculty ultimately voted in favour of the test.

This account of why an admissions test was brought in also shows how the test is only one part of the process with other information, like the interview, also providing important, different information about the applicants. Once the decision to have an additional test as part of the application portfolio had been agreed, the selector also explained how a stakeholder consultation had taken place as well as an external test design process. Lead times were built in to test the test:

> The test was devised, and … then, it was all done very carefully, an independent consortium based in [other Russell Group University], was asked to collect opinions (about the test) from about two hundred colleges, schools from a variety of sectors in this country, to get their feedback. The faculty worked on it for two years to devise a test which would be thought not to be discriminatory and which would be found to be acceptable … across a wide range of schools. I think they've achieved that.

An Oxbridge science selector explained how an additional admissions test was designed to give an opportunity to shine that may not have been captured through attainment at GCSEs.

> What we do actually is compare the test results with where the candidate did their GCSEs, that school's average percentage of A* to C GCSE performance. And so, the sort of people for whom the test might make a genuine difference to whether they get a place or not are candidates well above the curve. Where the test performance is much better, it really helps a candidate but also, it would put us off candidate as well – a lot.

The motivation for the test here was specifically to provide an opportunity to show potential for a particular course at university regardless of prior schooling. The then director of admissions at Oxford explained further the role of the additional tests:

> Most of our candidates have taken some form of subject-based test. And that is a big shift in the last five years. Why do we do aptitude tests? It is partly a reflection of the fact that our candidate nature is changing, just in the seven years I have been in Oxford, we have seen our undergraduate pool go from about 23 per cent non-UK to 34 per cent. And in some of our subject discipline, Economics and Management, one of our most popular and oversubscribed courses, almost 50 per cent of candidates are applying from outside the UK and most not with A-levels. So … having aptitude tests everyone has to take for that particular subject area is a very very useful benchmarking exercise. So, regardless of a candidate's background and education, we do get some fairly useful reads on the candidates' potential and suitability for the course because what we are testing is aptitude.
>
> The tests, however, and again, this is one of the misconceptions, are very good at identifying who likely not to succeed at Oxford. What they are not is a ranking tool to identify who is definitely going to end up with a first-class degree

three years on from taking the test. And, I think again, we need to recognize that there are some students who will be admitted and who have gone through the admissions process, and things will happen to them on course that maybe mean they will not get the degree we thought they had the potential to get. There may be other students who will surprise us. But generally speaking, the admissions process is trying – at a point in time – to use all the available evidence to identify who, three or four years down the line will have made a success of their tutorial education experience. (Nicholson 2013)

Overall, some courses at selective institutions then require applicants to take an additional test as part of the application process. These tests are considered in addition to information on performance in school. But in contrast to the role of SAT or ACTs in the United States, not all applicants in England take the same tests. Instead, the tests in England are tailored to test potential and aptitude as well as demonstrated ability for specific academic disciplines. Within the same university, some subjects may choose to have additional testing and others not. Information on additional testing requirements by subject is available from university websites.

In some instances, formalized additional tests are taken prior to a potential admissions interview at university. In this case, information from the test can be used when institutions decide which applicants to shortlist for interview. In other cases, additional testing might be conducted during a selection visit to the university at the same time as admissions interviews take place.

Tests also differ with regard to whether they are used by just one university or several institutions. Examples of tests that are used across a consortium of institutions include the BioMedical Admissions Test (BMAT) for medicine and aligned disciplines and the LNAT test for law. This is bearing in mind that, in contrast to the United States, both law and medicine are available to study as a first undergraduate degree rather than being postgraduate entry only. Vocational courses like nursing and pharmacy offered in some of the selective institutions included in this project may also require additional numeracy and literacy tests in line with requirements by their accrediting professional bodies. But there are also examples of tests only used by one institution, for example, for Oxford the Classics Admissions Test (CAT) or the English Literature Admissions Test (ELAT); or the Cambridge Law Test (CLT) at Cambridge.

Interviews

Academic admissions interviews are another way how English selectors evaluated applicants. Interviews are used for all courses at Oxford and Cambridge and also in the admissions process for some courses at other selective institutions. When an interview is an integral part of the admissions process, usually all UK and EU applicants are interviewed and some applicants are interviewed overseas either by interview teams or remotely. Applicants usually participate in at least two or more interviews,[6] and selectors can refer applicants for additional interviews if they feel that an applicant would benefit from another opportunity.

Some institutions or courses also use interviews as a way to encourage students to come to their institutions. When this is the case, the interviews are more a way to recruit students than a way to make decisions about which students to admit.

Some US institutions also use interviews in the undergraduate admissions process. However, these interviews are very different from the English interviews. Instead, their main purpose is finding out more about the applicant as a person rather than being part of the systematic academic evaluation of an applicant. The US interviews are discussed elsewhere in the book (Chapter 5).

Many selectors viewed interviews as useful to 'try and find out whether you think'. One Oxbridge selector elaborated that 'interviews help finding those who can think and achieve at university as opposed to those who've simply got this far because they're good at doing exams'.

The interview then can be an opportunity to genuinely engage with the applicants and to find out more about their academic potential that was perhaps not apparent through the written records of prior and predicted achievement. This Oxbridge social science selector explained how she thought that, with the right question, it was possible to obtain information in the interview that is not already apparent in school records and other application information. She explained how it is possible to tap into potential that is distinct from ability:

> If a question can go deeper and deeper and deeper and deeper – so you start off with an explanation and you can go through certain criteria then you see whether they can apply the criteria and then you see where the weaknesses are, you can see the case – some examples that don't fit the criteria, so you deal with the concept. Then you really get a sense of how far through that process a person can go. And that becomes quite a fair way of seeing, discriminating between students …
>
> If that person just starts thinking, and starts thinking cogent, well structured, original responses, clever responses, to a difficult question – then it doesn't matter where they come from. It really doesn't. And you can be as good as that if you come from a dodgy comprehensive, special measure school and if you come from Rugby [a prestigious private secondary school] … and if you had an interview prep from a great school, you can still come and get totally stuck on a difficult question because you just can't see how to come up with an answer.

The respondent then gave an example of the way such an admission interview might work for her discipline:

> So, you give them a concept, they give you an answer and you say – 'oh, but you just said that a minute ago' or 'oh, when you say that, do you think is the case too?' … I used to do things about the second chamber [in government, i.e. the House of Lords in the UK and the Senate in the US]. Mostly it was actually about philosophy because it is very difficult to do institutional questions because they tend to be factual. So, I tend to say, well 'is that fair?' or 'Is this more democratic or less democratic' or 'is this more representative?', 'What kind of things do you think are important for democracy?' And someone might say accountability or representation or whatever. And then you'll say, 'oh, actually you just said that, so would it also be very fair then', in this country, you know, a like a notorious example where something was very representative but very undemocratic and they say 'oh, yes, sorry, no, no, oh what I meant really was that' and then I say 'Ok. So what's the differentiator, so why is that true in this case but not true in that case, what is the thing that separates these two examples, that makes this unfair and this fair?' Oh, and then they think about it and you say 'take your time' and they take their time and they say 'Oh, I think the thing that separates it is in this case there is also this criterion at work and that is not present in the other, you see.' Great! Yes, and you can see they are coming to an understanding of something, they working out the answer and they are thinking and they are coming to a new realization, and using a concept and realizing that they have made a mistake, but not being afraid of that and then saying 'oh, yes, right, but this is also the case'. And then, a really good student would say, 'yes, that is true in that example, that example is fair, but this is not really what I am talking about, I actually – this example is a better example'. So, then you say 'Right, good. What about this example.' And you try and find the grey area and you try to find an example that doesn't fit with either of these two dichotomies or something and then they go 'Aah'.. And then you both having an experience of learning. Which is exactly what you should have in a tutorial system.

The *seeing how you think* approach did not only work for social science subjects but also for natural sciences. The next quotation from an Oxbridge science selector provides a detailed example of how he structured his interview questions so that he could find about an applicant's approach to deep thinking:

> The first bit of the question is usually something like 'can you do this?' 'Do you understand the conservation of momentum? Do you understand conservation of energy? … And those are things they should have encountered at A level. … If they do get through that, then I start asking them things they haven't studied. In other words, based on what you know, I try and take it to a further

level, something that they haven't had – like spinning objects, things that are rotating, for example 'how do you think the situation would change if instead of the frictionless block we used a rolling ball-bearing? How do you think a ballbearing rolling would be different than say a hoop?' To see ... do they answer a question that they've never encountered before? Do they just guess? Or do they start talking around? Do they start asking questions about well, you know, what is the energy of a spinning thing? What would it be related to? – And that's the difference between, I think, someone who would have more potential than someone who was just really very good at memorizing a bunch of concepts.

The key purpose of the interview in both the social science and natural science example is to see applicants' thinking in action. This provides information about the applicant that is not already available from the application form. This new information is about potential and about how much further applicants may wish to push themselves and their knowledge as well as being a sort of taster of what a tutorial conversation might be like.

Many of these potential-based interview questions or exercises have no right or wrong answer; or, at least, this is contingent on the assumptions that are made. The purpose of such questions was to find those applicants that 'look good on paper' but 'really miss the point of the exercises' or 'fail spectacularly' during interviews, as well as to find those who 'really shine' perhaps despite being short of perfect school records.

But despite the conceptual difference between achievement and potential, selectors commented on the practical challenges in evaluating untapped potential through the means of an interview. This Oxbridge humanities selector commented:

Ability's not something that develops in utter independence of everything else you know. I mean what do you do? Yes, students who've come from educated backgrounds, who've been exposed more to in breadth literature or whatever have possibly a better chance of proving themselves more able for entry into a course where that's what they'll be doing. Not that that is necessarily a good indication of motivation, or indeed of ability, but certainly of a certain kind of acculturation of training, yes, for sure. And I think that's in a sense what is very difficult to assess in interviews – to see through the training.

Again, this concern was shared across academic disciplines as this Oxbridge science selector also contemplated how knowledge still played a role for the sort of questions designed to tap into potential

because, obviously, the more knowledge you have – it is not obvious – but it is likely to be easier to say something to an unexpected question

Oxbridge respondents generally agreed that one feature of the interview is that it functioned as a mini-tutorial, taster tutorial and, as such, the admissions interview had some relationship to the tutorial way of teaching. This was observed across disciplines as illustrated by these quotations: '[the interview] does relate in some sense to the way in which they are supposed to learn, the ways in which their mind is supposed to be working'. (social science selector). 'We try and make the interviews as much as possible like tutorials … giving them a bit of a dry run of the tutorial teaching style … it might even give them some taste of what being an undergraduate student … might be like' (medicine selector), 'the object of the exercise is really to see whether people will thrive in a tutorial system of teaching, where you have to be a bit interactive in order to enjoy that method of teaching'. (humanities selector)

However, there is less consensus as to whether suitability for the tutorial way of teaching at Oxbridge can be inferred from an interview or whether such potential suitability should be a selection criterion. The different viewpoints of two Oxbridge humanities selectors are illustrative. On the one hand, one selector stated that 'the people who just go to lecture and take their notes and write their essays and sit silently, I mean it's just a waste of time, frankly' (humanities selector). Other academic colleagues disagreed, stating that the point of university was teaching skills that students do not possess when they enrol. Indeed, one admissions professional in a Russell Group thought it was 'lazy' on the part of academics to look for already polished students instead of seeking to develop and teach new skills, although she was also keen to emphasise that her institutions was looking for students 'able to complete their course' and that the motivation apparent in selection interviews could be helpful in this regard.

In 2013, the then director of admissions explained the role of interviews as follows:

> We will do multiple interviews – interviewing is a helpful tool if it is done properly – … if the people conducting the interview have been properly trained, are aware that they have the potential for bias, if you have more than one interviewer in the room so that there is kind of an internal check, and you have multiple interviews, if you have all of these conditions, – and the academic interview is the focus … then, actually, there is a value to having that interview in the admissions process. Because, as a colleague of mine said recently, effectively what you have in the interview is an audition, an opportunity to see how the candidate will behave in a tutorial. And that is important. What our tutors are trained to do in the preparation is to spot

the candidate who is polished but who actually has very little substance behind the polish but also identify the candidate who is nervous and may not yet be showing their full potential. And again, the advantage of having multiple interviews is to ignore one interview and to assess how they perform elsewhere. (Nicholson 2013)

Another Oxbridge colleague from a humanities subject explained how he liked the interview process on fairness grounds as it gave selectors more of a sense of the person:

We are on the look out for this [educational disadvantage] and we feel free to make a lower offer to someone who has potential but who got a B in a subject from e.g. a [a not so good school] and we feel they have not been taught well – we would be willing to take a risk there. The interview is quite good from that point of view. In an interview one can sense potential, this person should really get a chance. Our college is really good at that. It is small, friendly and community oriented and pastorally well equipped to support students.

Not all selectors do, however, find admissions interviews useful. Some selectors view the general idea of conducting admissions interviews as flawed and some would prefer not to have any involvement in admissions decisions. Among those who generally found admissions interviews useful, several had ideas of how, in an ideal world with unlimited time and resources, aspects of the interview process could be further enhanced.

Overall, in instances where academic selection interviews were used, selectors used interview as one of many pieces of information available in the admissions process as summarized by this selector for medicine: 'In effect, interviews increase the number of measures that we have, they help with data not available or not known as well. Done well, they provide another useful way of to discriminate among applicants for admission'.

Contextualizing attainment

Selectors in both the United States and in England are interested in contextualized or holistic admissions. They do, however, understand slightly different things by this term. In the United States, holistic admission entails taking a whole range of aspects into account. Many of these considerations – such as athletic powers, race and extra-curricular involvement – are not directly related to better understanding the academic side of an application for admission. However, other aspects of holistic admission, such as thinking about how highly an applicant has achieved in the context of their opportunities are related to the search for admitting the academically 'best' applicants. When English selectors talk about holistic or contextual admission, they generally have this second, narrower definition of contextualization in mind: the idea of contextualizing the academic attainment and potential of an applicant. This section then provides an overview concerning the contextualization of academic attainment: How highly has the applicant achieved given the opportunities and barriers they faced?

US admissions committees consider applicants from the same school at the same time. This way, students can be more directly compared with each other. Selectors are looking for students who have done well within their school context and who have pushed themselves to take difficult and academically demanding courses. At the same time, selectors do not wish to penalize students for not having taken difficult courses at school when there was no opportunity to do so. If applicants have gone out of their way to seek out opportunities, for example, by attending courses at another school, college, or online, this would be a signal that the applicant actively seeks out and uses opportunities presented to them.

In England, selective universities also wish to find applicants who have had to travel a longer distance to achieve in education than others. Almost all Russell Group universities have a 'contextualized admissions' approach whereby the institution takes into account the context of achievement. Applicants who have done particularly well in a school where general achievement is low are considered to have higher potential to continue to achieve at universities than students who have done less well than other students in their school. Contextualizing applicants' performance itself has happened informally for a long time as this story about contextualizing an admissions interview from an Oxbridge selector illuminates:

> I remember … we were interviewing together, and we had this chap from a state school in the north of England, and he basically answered every question with a yes or a no … he was very very very taciturn, and hardly said anything. And we found the interview very hard going … he left the room and we both looked at each other and thought, you know, this is going to be very very hard work … but [my colleague] picked up the UCAS form, and said 'he has this fantastic record and he had had no advantages'. We took him and he turned out to be very good.

The shift to contextual admission means that institutions have a more systematic policy in place for flagging applicants who have experienced disadvantages. When universities use contextualized admission, they often look for more than one disadvantage to flag up applicants for special consideration. Multiple disadvantages could be having attended a low-performing school, being the first in the family to participate in higher education, having been in foster care or living in an area with low progression into higher education.

Selectors and universities in both the United States and England are data-hungry for as much information as possible that puts their applicants in context. In addition to using data, selective universities also undertake their own research into what predicts how well students do at university. There is research in both countries that supports the idea of finding applicants who have done well against the odds. In England, research has specifically shown that students admitted to selective universities from publicly funded schools perform better in their university examinations than students admitted with the same grades from private, fee-paying schools. The context of attainment thus matters for the purpose of finding the academically best students: it helps finding those with the greatest potential to achieve highly at university.

The selectors in both England and the United States also take into account the personal context of an applicant. One aspect of this is personal 'extenuating circumstances' such as illness or bereavement. Both, English and US selectors are interested in such extenuating circumstances as another way to contextualize attainment and to find applicants who may have the potential to succeed and achieve highly at university but have faced obstacles which mean that they have lower attainment records. For English selectors, this is generally where the consideration of personal extenuating circumstances stops. With the possible exception of having been in public care such as foster care or a care home, having faced personal adversity is not considered a bonus in admission in itself. English selectors want to see specifically how an extenuating circumstance is related to an applicant's achievement profile. If an extenuating circumstance might explain why an applicant has not done as well in an examination as their teachers thought they would do, this information would be taken into consideration. In the United States, personal extenuating circumstances and the personal context of an applicant can also be used in admission beyond explaining grades as we will see in the next chapter.

Chapter summary

Universities in both the United States and in England wish to select 'the best'. In order to select the best academically, selectors in both countries look at prior achievement in schools and, where applicable, at performance in other tests.

References and essays, personal statements, or written work are also available and considered to varying degrees. In England, Oxbridge and some other courses and universities also use academic admissions interviews as part of the academic evaluation of an applicant. Both countries also use contextual information to understand how an applicant is performing relative to other students in their school and in the national competition.

In England, evidence of academic achievement and potential unlocks the metaphorical university gate. But west of the Atlantic, academic considerations alone are not enough for being admitted to a highly selective university. Academic considerations are just one aspect of what it means to be the best applicant. Other 'special interest' considerations play a role in admission. We will now turn to what those other, non-academic considerations entail.

4

Special Interest Cases

As more people attain highly, academic accomplishment becomes less important in admissions decisions. In the second half of the 20th century, we have seen a continuous move towards a greater importance placed on applicants' personal attributes: Athletic accomplishment, alumni relations, personal circumstances or extraordinary talent. Academic accomplishment is not a powerful predictor of admission for the class of 2013.

> (retired Big Three Admissions expert reflecting on the factors that had played a role in admissions at his institution since the late 1950s)

Emphases in US undergraduate admissions have shifted away from a focus on academic ability to considerations of diversity, athletic skills, personality, personal circumstances, special talent and links with alumni. Apart from some consideration of personal circumstances, none of these factors matter for admissions in England. The explanation of why these non-academic considerations matter in the US is indicated by the admissions terminology of admitting a class. For example, admission professionals would talk about admitting the class of 2019, which is in actual fact all the students admitted in 2015 who are expected to graduate in 2019. This is a common way to talk about admissions in the United States but not in England.

Indeed, in the United States this class of admitted students would have been carefully 'crafted' to have a number of different characteristics. This group would have a certain number of athletes, students preferably from all parts of the United States and some international students, students with exceptional musical and artistic talent and some 'mathletes' or stellar academic students. Having a range of academic subject interests is also part of the diversity that selectors seek. Thus, the admitted class would have some students interested in engineering and some interested in politics. The admitted class would be ethnically diverse, some students would have track records of leading and organizing voluntary activities, and some others will have a family connection with the institution. These range of profiles would collectively describe the class of admitted students.

In contrast, the terminology 'crafting a class' is not used in admissions in England. There is no consideration for the characteristics the group of admitted students will have, with the possible exception of enrolment benchmarks by school type. The language of 'class of' – for example, the year 2019, is also not generally used. When it is used at all, it is used in a different way, to refer to students' matriculation (see glossary) year rather than their graduating year. Students who happen to be admitted at the same time to a leading English institution would each individually meet the academic requirements for studying a particular subject. They have not been jointly admitted as a group.

This chapter then is about the considerations that go into crafting a class and about the non-academic factors in admissions. Applicants who convincingly show their unique contribution to an admitted class are 'hooked' and a hook gives those applicants an edge in the competition for a place in comparison with 'unhooked' applicants who cannot make a special case for admission. This chapter discusses the following 'hooks': diversity, regional spread, athletics, legacies, extra-curricular involvement and holistic admissions. We will mainly hear voices from the United States because of the seminal role of non-academic factors in US admissions. However, we will also hear from the English selectors when considering educational contexts and music scholarships.

Athletics

In 2009, the University of Cambridge (England) celebrated its 800th anniversary. To honour the event, the then deputy vice chancellor, Professor Gordon Johnson, was invited to deliver a speech on the challenges facing the two Cambridges (Harvard University being geographically located in Cambridge, Massachusetts). In the question-and-answer session following the speech, a young American woman raised her hand:

> You have talked about university admission, teaching and research. But I haven't heard you mentioning the role of athletics. Where does Cambridge stand on athletics?

To which the then deputy vice chancellor of Cambridge University replied:

> I do believe there is a place for sport in higher education, but I am not sure that it actually needs to be at university. Loughborough does have an excellent PE (physical education) programme. I do find it hard to understand how a director of sport can be paid twice the salary of a senior professor.

There was a moment when both the American woman and the English deputy vice chancellor looked a bit puzzled – she, presumably, was puzzled because this had not been the answer she was expecting; and he because a question about athletics seemed a most unexpected one after a discussion of teaching and research.

Something was being lost in translation. The young woman making the enquiry was talking about American college athletics. The vice chancellor of Cambridge was talking about sports in English universities. The American woman was thinking of a multi-million-dollar business which was generating income from alumni and TV rights and that was an integral part of the university's identity with athletics featuring in both recruitment and admissions. The English deputy vice chancellor was talking about an academic subject that could be studied at some universities – or something that could be a recreational or competitive activity for students. Either way 'athletic' considerations are not aligned to the mission of English Russell Group universities.

In the United States, the role of athletics was explained by various participants in this project as, 'sports contribute a lot to campus life and there is lots of money involved'. 'Having athletes is one aspect of crafting a class and of crafting a community. … It is big value added for the college when crafting a class.'

What selectors want are 'blue-chip athletes'. These are already high-achieving athletes who are expected to have an immediate impact on the performance of the university team they are playing for. Part of admitting athletes was to be 'accountable to alumni, coaches and students to have a good team and to win'. Several respondents noted how the admissions office could face the blame when athletic teams were weak. One dean of admission at a highly selective private institution reported that part of his brief when he first got his post was to 'get the football team back into shape'.

Because being a Division 1 athlete is a huge commitment for students, the Ivy League has a codex on the admission of athletes. For examples, athletes can be admitted with lower GPAs and SAT scores than other applicants and can sometimes be allowed to take longer to complete their degrees. Other institutions also lowered their admissions requirements. As a liberal arts college selector explained:

> So if a kid in New Jersey needs an A average and a 1,500 [out of 1600 on two SAT sections] to get in, a recruited athlete maybe only needs 1,300. If you know they're not going to fail out that's good enough because we need them. That's the biggest advantage anyone can have in admissions, being an athlete.

While the SAT scores in this quotation might not be representative for other institutions, the idea of lowering the grade requirements for admitting athletes is. Again, the reason athletics was considered important was that

> you need your teams to win. … If the teams are winning alums will be happier and they will give more money, that might be part of it – every college wants to have good sports because that's what kids are looking for.

Other respondents echoed the observation that alumni donations increased when athletics teams were winning.

While athletic considerations could thus make a significant difference to admissions decisions, one selector at a selective private institution also explained how his institution applied what he called a 'broken shoulder test': 'Would this student contribute anything to college life if she was not an athlete?'

If the answer to this question was no, and the athletic talent was merely very good but not absolutely stellar, such an applicant would not be admitted because they had not passed the 'broken shoulder test'. This test was also used because all athletes admitted to Ivy League institutions received scholarships based on financial need rather than based on their athletic merit. This means that athletes could choose to stop doing athletics at any point during their time at college without financial repercussions. In such institutional contexts, it is even more important that the student had something to contribute in addition to their athletic talents.

This context differs from other US institutions where athletic scholarships are awarded. Such scholarships can cover tuition, accommodation, books, food and plane tickets home. Different sports and different types of universities award differently valued scholarship packages; many of these sports scholarships are endowed scholarships. An athletic scholarship exists only as long as the athlete plays the sport. An organization called the National Collegiate Athletic Association (NCAA) regulates athletes and recruitment of athletes for US and Canadian colleges and universities. NCAA monitors that academic admissions requirements do not fall below some minimum eligibility standard for college education, for example a GPA of 2.3.

The Ivy League sets its own measure and standards for recruiting athletes. This measure is called the Academic Index. It is used a bit like a credit rating; coaches use it to determine an athlete's recruitability and to ensure shared minimum standards within the Ivy League for admission on athletic grounds. Approximately two-thirds of the Athletic Index is based on standardized test scores (SAT or ACT); and one-third is based on class rank or GPA. In recent years, the Academic Index for the Ivy League had a minimum threshold of 176 out of a possible 240 (Tier one Athletic Resources 2012). This means that no athlete, however good, would be admitted below this score. In addition, the mean Athletic Index of all athletes on a university campus must be within one standard deviation of the mean scores of the whole student body. There are then four bands of academic indices with caps on how many athletes Ivy League institutions can admit with the lowest academic index. This means that only truly exceptional athletes would be admitted with minimum Academic Index Scores: 'The lower your academic index, the better you must be as an athlete.' As a rule of thumb, SAT scores of 700 or above and a GPA of 3.5 or above would be a solid academic profile for seeking athletic admission to the Ivy League.

For example, Harvard's class of 2017 (admitted in 2013) had 12.8 per cent of its members admitted as recruited athletes. These students scored, on average, 173 points lower on the SATs than their classmates who were not recruited athletes. However, perhaps contrary to a popular belief that athletes tend to come from poorer families, students from families with incomes under $80,000 were the least likely to be recruited athletes. The cost of participating in some sports explains this link between income and athlete status.

To summarize, the sort of applicant who would gain admissions everywhere in the United States would be a stellar athlete and scholar. This hypothetical amazing all-rounder person was described by this Ivy League selector in the following way.

> If you're an Olympic gold medallist, and you're brilliant all around ... and if they also have everything else in terms of academic accomplishments [then] [Big Three Ivy 1] says, yes, this is exactly what we're looking for in terms of philosophically [sic], the type of student that would utilize our resources here. Clearly, they did it already, they're going to do it again in whatever they study here. [Big Ivy 2] would say the same thing, [Big Ivy 3] would say the same thing, [another Ivy League institution] would say the same thing, so that's a student that gets admitted to everywhere they apply.

The US selectors also provided a summary of the role of athletics in English and European admissions contexts. One Big Three US selector noted that 'Europe thinks US athletic stuff is crazy', with another Ivy League selector echoing that 'in Europe, you go to college to go to college. It is not about athletics. If you want to do that, you go to your city sportsclub.'

Admissions professionals in England never mentioned athletics. Some academic selectors commented that they were aware of their students participated in certain sports, or that keeping active was a good thing to do or that too much extra-curricular involvement could adversely affect degree performance. English institutions might celebrate Olympic-level achievements of their students in promotional materials. Oxford and Cambridge celebrate success in their varsity competition between the light blue teams of Cambridge and the dark blue teams of Oxford such as the annual boat race. Oxbridge colleges celebrate wins over other colleges in a number of intercollegiate sporting events. But athletics and sporting talent are never the reason why any of the students in England were admitted to university in the first place.

Legacies

Legacies are 'special interest cases' in admissions to mostly private institutions in the United States. Legacies have a relationship with the institution that is taken into account when admissions decisions are made. There are public universities like the University of California system that do not practise legacy preferences in admission. However, some public universities like the universities of Michigan, Virginia and North Carolina use legacy preferences in admission and all the private US universities included in this book considered legacy status. As one US Ivy selector explained 'we are private, and we can do what we want, we can use our discretion and create our mission'. One of the ways this discretion is used is consideration of legacies.

Respondents mentioned three types of legacies. First, legacies are those with a familial connection with the institution because a family member had graduated from there in the past. Second, there are those with a familial connection with the institution because a parent was currently working there. And third, there are those with a connection with the institution because of the money they either had or were about to donate to the institution.

Family legacy

At Yale, 14 per cent of those matriculating in 2013 (graduating class of 2017) were children of Yale alumni. The comparable figure for Princeton was 12.3 per cent and for Harvard, the figure was just above 10 per cent. A Big Three selector explained what a family legacy was and how it was important:

> A legacy, it can vary by school how they calculate a legacy, or what they consider a legacy. Some schools will consider you legacy if you have an aunt or an uncle or

a grandparent, but at [this Ivy], you're only legacy if you had a parent who went to [this Ivy] and that can be as a graduate or an undergrad.

Another selector explained how, at his institution, only those whose parents had attended the institution as undergraduates were considered legacies; when parents had only attended as postgraduates, this was not considered a legacy. 'They're not really considered a legacy if they went to a graduate school of [this Big Three]. They're also not considered a legacy if their sibling went to [this Big Three]'. The respondent also noted though that having a parent who had been a postgraduate there 'it's something they can tell us about, and we'll see it' and the admissions professional also noted how 'in the current admissions frenzy, there are now siblings writing in' to support applications, but for legacy admissions, it was really only a parental link with undergraduate education committees considered.

A Big Three selector explained:

> If you have a legacy status … who's done everything right, but … is probably like a lot of … thousands of other students in the pool, otherwise there's no good reason to take them above any other, but if it happens to be a legacy … what happens when you're a legacy is you get a much more thoughtful consideration than if you were not a legacy.

Legacy status then increased the chances of being admitted, it provided a 'hook' in admission.

The term 'double-leg' was also used in discussions to describe applicants both of whose parents had attended the institution, although it was unclear whether this was more advantageous than having only one parent who was an alumnus or alumna. A liberal arts selector explained the reasoning behind preferential admission for alumni children:

> Legacy is you are a child or in our case we look at grandparents also but it's not as important as college alum. I guess the justification is you like seeing kids that have a family tradition with the college; I think that is one of the justifications. Also you want your alums to be happy. You don't want to go around denying all of the students who attended your college because they're going to be angry at you too. They're not going to give you another dime in money, they're never going to give you money again if you deny their kid. Legacies are still … we probably take about 50 per cent. We're still saying no to half of them but that is still double what our general admission rate is. … The only way is academic … but once they meet that level you're hooked, you're in, that's all it takes.

This was echoed by a Big Three selector who explained:

> I mean, we consider the entire application, all of the academics and everything, and really, again, it works in the same way. I mean, the student has to be admissible to [this Ivy], and then that's kind of an extra consideration.

Another selector pointed out how 'alumni status is important but it does not override a bad academic record'.

One respondent noted how her Big Three institution's policy had changed with regard to legacies. This was because while the aim of legacy admissions was partly to ensure a stable financial future for the institution, an investigation into alumni giving had found that not all alumni were useful with regard to giving to the institution: 'Just, like, parents who went to [this Big Three Ivy] and they never give any money, and they're not very useful to us'. Hence, further information about the giving behaviour of the parents might be taken into account.

Because not all applicants who were related to alumni could be admitted, one Big Three university had a chart with the competitiveness of entry which was shown to alumni when they complained that their children were not gaining offers.

Faculty legacy

Many US private institutions have some programme helping with college for the children of their academic faculty. This can mean faculty tuition fee programmes should their children wish to go to any college. But it can also entail an admission preference at the institution where a parent works which, as one respondent stated, 'helps with retention of staff'. The way this faculty legacy works is similar to the working of the alumni legacy:

> Will we give a second look to someone who's part of our community legacy? Yes – but not so that you're admitting someone who's not qualified (Ivy League selector)

One respondent even elaborated how he had enrolled at a liberal arts college for his first year at university. After one year, his father helped him to transfer to the Ivy League school where he was on the academic faculty. Transfers in the Ivy League are not that common and not all institutions have transfer programmes. Knowledge of the transfer system and the parental faculty link had been the key to allow this respondent to graduate from an Ivy League institution.

US public universities do not have faculty legacy programmes, nor do English public universities. The only part of the English education system where faculty status plays a role in admission and fees can be private secondary schools. Here, children of teachers may also be educated for free or at a discounted rate for very much the same rationale that private universities in the United States cite for their schemes – staff retention.

Development legacy

Another group of legacies were development legacies. Not all respondents delved into details in response to this question. This Big Three selector only stated that 'Certainly, those are considerations we have to make.' Another Big Three selector elaborated a little bit more, 'Of course, yes, we do have a development office, as do all institutions, and that's also a consideration, but again, there are … you know, it's not something that's automatic.' Another Ivy League selector happily explained in more detail how development legacies worked:

> We do have – which I know other schools have, too – something called a development legacy. And the development office sends up a list of students … and they don't necessarily have to be a legacy, but their parents are being cultivated and are in the position to give a, you know, a monstrous amount of money, not a couple of thousand dollars but, … your parents must be able to, like, endow a professorship, or … make a significant contribution that's really going to matter to the school in some way. And those kids, there's very few of them, but I think the standards are lowest for those students.

This selector went on to explain more about how the development list was created:

> You get on that list because there's good communication between you and the development office, and it's like, something's going to happen. Maybe a gift was already made, or maybe there's a promise of a gift, or a pledge, or something; but you don't just get on that list by just having a lot of money or actually pretending to do something for the school with that money, so … And I believe [Big Three Ivy] has something called the [reference deleted], which is students who are attracted to the development office, but they don't have the grade … they don't have the academic tops grades to be admitted right away, so they tell these kids … work for a year, and get your grades up, and then you can come next year.

In this explanation, low attaining students who are also on the development list appeared to be given an opportunity to increase their grades so that they could be admitted after a year out.

One Ivy selector explained how there was a 'Robin Hood rationale' for admitting in particular development legacies – 'you weigh up taking money from one and funding 10 others'. This was in a context where, as explained by another respondent:

> The needs of this school's, and every school's endowment has taken a big hit [in the recession], so it makes sense that they would place an even higher priority on finding more of these students if it's going to help the financial bottom line.

One Ivy selector described taking legacies as follows:

> We depend on the kindness of others. It is a balancing between principles and pragmatism. We are up front about it that, every year, we take around five students on these grounds, as 'development cases' and that allows major developments on campus such as dorms, endowed professorships, financial aid, and other building work. The kids still need to be able to make it.

A Big Three selector reflected further on legacy admissions:

> It used to make me really uncomfortable, but today, like everybody else has a place there, because it's … their parents are making this gift that really matters to the school. And in many cases, by admitting this student, you're able to pay for a lot of other students to come to [this Big Three] who wouldn't otherwise be able to. You know, so you have to look at the full system. When you isolate these little parts, it can make you really uncomfortable, but when you look at the whole thing, as if putting together a puzzle, then some of these decisions that might, in isolation, might not seem to add up, actually make sense. So you really have to take a big picture look at all of it.

Usually, legacy status was one factor taken into account but it did not grant automatic enrolment with the possible exception of being a significant development legacy.

One US respondent also asked me about legacy admission in England. Here, the case that made it to the US News – and indeed increased the enrolment of, in particular, women from the United States applying to the university – was Prince William's admission to the University of St Andrews (Scotland). Some US selectors viewed this as evidence of nepotism.[1] However, aside from perhaps any potential influence of the status of a Royal in this particular case – with Royal families being in themselves an exceptional historic anomaly in otherwise democratic countries – legacies are not routinely or openly part of the English admissions landscape. Indeed, if such practices existed, universities might face charges under consumer law and it might be construed as bribery and such practices are therefore not pursued. Many publicly funded universities in the United States similarly do not have official legacy policies the way private US universities do.

Some private fee-paying nursery, primary and secondary schools in England also continue to have legacy policies. For example, the sons or siblings of those who had themselves attended the prestigious Wetherby nursery school in London are given a definite place at the school. However, other schools are increasingly trying to eliminate birth ties in admissions decisions. For example, at Eton 'virtually all' applicants (perhaps again with the exception of Prince George or other male Royal children) are admitted through testing and interview in attempts to open up the elite schooling sector.

Race

Our society is still colour conscious, so we cannot yet afford to be colour blind.
(US Ivy League selector)

Race in admissions has strong claims to be the most controversial, most media covered, most written about and most legislated upon aspect of US university admissions.[2] Virtually all US elite colleges have a commitment to racial diversity among their students. Courts have been asked on numerous occasions to judge the legitimacy of an applicant's race affecting admissions decisions. The landmark ruling in Regents of the University of California v. Bakke (1978) found that it was unconstitutional for a public university to have quota systems by race. However, the ruling also stated that selecting a diverse student body was a permissible goal that could promote a college atmosphere of 'speculation, experimentation, and creation'. Quotas or points system for race are not permitted but considering race as part of a holistic admissions system is allowed. Since then, subsequent rulings have increasingly put greater restrictions on programs that explicitly consider race in university admissions at public universities with a ban on any consideration of race in admissions to public universities in some states.

Because all the US institutions in this project are private, not-for-profit organizations, these institutions are not subject to court decisions concerning public, tax payer-co-funded institutions and have flexibility and discretion over their admissions criteria and processes.

However, leading private institutions have put forward arguments in support of considering diversity in support letters (amici letters) of the race-conscious policies at their publicly funded peer institutions to the Courts. In the 1978 case, for example, one influential support letter by the private universities Columbia, Harvard, Stanford, and the University of Pennsylvania argued that racially neutral criteria would not allow for a sufficient number of racial minorities to be admitted. This, in turn, would impede the educational mission of institutions to educate minority leaders and to expose students from majority backgrounds to diverse views. Racial diversity was considered so that 'the leadership of the next generation – majority and minority members alike – will be the better, the wiser, and the more understanding' (Amici Curiae Brief 1978).[3]

The admissions professionals interviewed for this project explained how race was considered in admissions against the background of this national context. This liberal arts selector explained how his institution aimed to be

> the most diverse school you can, because it's something that is a selling point. It is what everybody is going to ask you, especially at a liberal arts school. How diverse are you?

He went on to explain how diversity first of all meant racial diversity: 'They mean color. When we get asked in our job "how diverse are you?" we say we have 27 per cent students of color'. However, straight away, the respondent also explained how racial diversity is only one aspect of diversity that his institution is looking for:

> But we also have students from all 50 states, we have 10 per cent international students, we have students from 50 different foreign countries. 50 per cent of [this liberal arts college]'s students are on financial aid so there is socioeconomic diversity as well. We are a very diverse place and when people say diversity that's what people want to know about it.

A colleague from an Ivy League confirmed how racial diversity statistics are a source of pride that also set his institution apart from other Ivies as they are

> the most diverse school in the Ivy League, and it has traditionally been that way. 40 per cent of our first year class are students of colour. I mean, we're without peer in the Ivy League … [all Ivies] are very committed to it [ethnic diversity]. So that's why they're so high. It drops off way from there when you're talking about the schools just below the Ivies.

Another selector also explained how his institution is looking for a 'critical mass' of students of colour. This was not a specified number but

> an educational concept that refers to enrolling enough minority students such that all students can benefit from diversity, minority and majority alike, and have meaningful interactions in the classroom, residence halls, and social and extracurricular settings.

This selector also noted with regret that even with aggressive affirmative action policies, colleges never achieved a 'critical mass' of minority students on campus. At the same time, selectors recognized that arguments made to support one policy, for example, racial diversity, could also be made for other special interest cases in admissions. One Ivy League selector noted how his institution didn't 'want just one woman in engineering'. Having a critical mass of women choosing sciences could thus also be a consideration in crafting a class.

Another Ivy League selector explained how there was a hierarchy in terms of how colour diversity was considered in admissions:

> What you want to have are black kids, after that Hispanic kids after that Asian kids and that's how it works.

This quotation ties in with scholarly work that has shown that while being black measurably increases applicants' chances of admission, the opposite is the case for Asian applicants (Espenshade 2009).

Racial diversity is clearly valued by the selectors of the private institutions that were part of this project. Even though selectors did not refer to quotas or official targets, they agreed that it was good to try and increase the intake of students of colour year on year and that 'questions would be asked' if such figures went down.

Many universities, including Ivy League institutions, publish the racial diversity of their admitted students as part of their admissions statistics. Increases in the number of enrolled minority students are celebrated as admissions success stories.

The most racially diverse university in the Ivy League is Columbia University in New York City. Incidentally, urban universities – including urban Russell Group universities – in England also have higher racial diversity than more rural universities.

Selectors in England do not have formal information on applicants' racial background when they make admissions decisions. In paper-based admissions systems, indications of ethnicity might come from names or references in personal statements. But formal information regarding applicants' ethnicity is only supplied to institutions after admissions decisions have been made.

Where there is face-to-face interaction with the applicants as part of the selection process in the case of the Oxbridge admissions interviews, the ethnicity of most applicants is apparent. In none of the selection discussions I observed as part of the project was the colour of an applicant mentioned. Indeed, only in one instance did I ever hear a reference to a student's colour and this was in a conversation many months after an admissions meeting I had observed. The selector recalled how he and his two colleagues had been particularly keen to admit one particular applicant. This student had a stellar academic record but he was also the first black applicant the selector could recall having interviewed for admissions to read this particular subject in this college. None of the selectors felt that they could mention applicants' ethnicity in their selection discussion, especially with me present as an observer. In fact, all three selectors had privately been especially keen to admit this student not only because of his stellar record but also because they thought it would be good for the college and all other students to have more diversity. But in contrast to the US selectors, these English counterparts only admitted on purely academic grounds with some personal satisfaction about how non-academic considerations might play out.

Overall, in contrast to the 'colour-conscious' approach of elite US institutions, English selectors are striving for 'colour-blind' selection. Statistical analyses in England show that applicants from minorities have a smaller chance of gaining admission to highly selective universities than their white counterparts. The reasons for this are not fully understood, but from 2017, all identifying information might be removed from university application forms to move admissions decisions even more towards being colour-blind.

Region

While one Ivy selector observed that '90 per cent of all college students go to college within 200 miles of home', the Ivies pride themselves in having regional diversity from across all US states and internationally in their intake. When looking at the websites of Ivy League and comparable institutions, there is usually some information regarding which US states students came from and how many international countries are represented. For private institutions ranked just below the Ivy, increasing regional representation is a marker of moving up in rankings as this private institution selector explained, 'We have now grown to a national and really international institution, that draws students from every state in the union, from 65 countries at the undergraduate and graduate level.'

While public institutions have different fees for students who are 'in-state' (residents of the state where the university is located) and 'out of state', Ivies do not have differential fees and no quotas or targets as such for 'in-state' enrolment.

But there is also pride among the Ivies in serving local communities. As this Ivy selector explained:

> We give a slight but real tip for locals because we see our role not only as building future leaders nationally and globally but we are also located in [place name] and want to contribute to the future of [this city] and [this state].

The pride in regional diversity was something that was perhaps best understood at the senior levels or those with a historic perspective on admissions. One selector from a highly selective private institution explained how historically, the value of regional diversity could be traced back to the Civil War era. This was a time when a Big Three Ivy made efforts to offer admission to students from 'every state and territory', hoping to remove prejudices by bringing them into friendly relations. This was based on the underlying idea that 'people gain greater understanding and learning when brought into contact with people dissimilar to themselves'.

However, a liberal arts college selector with just a couple of years' experience in admissions was less clear on the purpose of a regional spread in admissions. He also explained how which US states an applicant applied from could make a difference to their chances of being admitted:

> I've never understood it and it's something in admissions I don't care about at all. What do we care if there is some yahoo from North Dakota at the college? At [this institution] especially we have students from all 50 states and that is something we like to be able to say that we're such a diverse place that we have students from all 50 states. So you do not get in from Manhattan unless you are a student of color or a legacy because there are so many students of color in Manhattan and so many legacies and so many athletes live there that they take up all the spots ... but ... what that means is that we have to make a really strong effort to get those kids from like the Midwest. In that part of the United States where it's 40 per cent of the land area but it's 5 per cent of the population and nobody lives there. Kids that are going to college from there, they are not even going out of the city or ... they're not going to some liberal arts school in [state name] that they have never even heard of. What that means when you have three kids apply from Wyoming and if they're decent you've got to take them, you need to accept them and, we're getting 500 kids applying from New Jersey you have to be fantastic to get in from New Jersey because there are so many other kids applying. In Wyoming you don't have to be as good because you are one of five kids that are going to apply

Another aspect of regional diversity was the admission of international students. One Ivy League selector explained, 'we highly value our international students, because of course, they bring such diversity and interest to the campus'. Harvard had led the way to include international students in their 'needs-blind' admissions policy and institutions took pride in their international intake statistics which are published alongside the US home states of their incoming students. An example of how regional diversity is advertised is provided in Table 3.

Table 3 Harvard admitted students 2015 (class of 2019)

Geographical breakdown			
New England	18.1%	Mountain	3.2%
Middle Atlantic	20.7%	Pacific	17.4%
South	16.7%	Territories	0.4%
Midwest	8.9%	International	12.2%
Central	2.5%		

Source: Harvard College 2015: A Brief Profile of the Admitted Class of 2019.

Admissions professional from a selective private institution just outside the Ivy League also explained with pride how his institution had internationalized:

> If you looked at [this institution] in the 70s, it was very much [place name]'s college and it's now grown to a national and really international institution

Geographic location and the impact this would have on the geographic diversity of the student body could thus play a role in either boosting or decreasing an applicant's chances of gaining admission. Applicants from under-represented regions might be looked upon more favourably than applicants from regions that sent a lot of strong applicants. Being a local applicant or an international applicant would also be considered in the admissions process.

A final consideration regarding geography was that admissions professionals were less interested in applicants who seemed driven to apply to an institution because of its geographic location rather than the academic and student experience on offer as this Ivy selector observed:

> We get a lot of students who apply ... but they're not really wanting to be at [this institution], they just want to be in [the city where the institution is]. And we look for students who really want to be at [this institution].

Selectors in England did not mention geographic targets for admitting their English students. However, some institutions have aims to increase their international student intake. In contrast to the elite US institutions who appear to do so to celebrate diversity and who will offer needs-blind scholarship, a key aim of such international institutional strategies at undergraduate and postgraduate level in England is generating higher fee income.

Through local outreach schemes, English universities can seek to increase the number of local students who enrol in their institutions. Neighbourhood and postcode data can also be used to contextualize applicants and to increase the representation of students from, for example, neighbourhoods with a low transition rate into higher education. However, overall, geographic considerations appeared to be of lesser importance in the discussions with English selectors – in particular with academic selectors – than with the US selectors.

Special talents

If the music department says 'we need a brass player to be able to play Marlow'
then it matters.

(Big Three selector)

US selectors are not only in touch with the athletic department but also with the music, drama and art departments. Orchestra, art and drama are 'things that need to keep ... going, at the university, for it to be what it is, and so those are considerations that we have to bring in to the committee room' (Big Three selector). Again, as with legacies and athletes, the academic part of the application needs to be in the right ballpark and then, on a 'case by case basis ... there are considerations made for that kind of thing' (Big Three selector).

Part of crafting a diverse class is having diverse talents present among the students. Such talents could relate to contributing to campus life in terms of music and art. In addition, those with stellar academic potential can put a case forward for being a 'mathlete', or in other ways academically outstanding. Applicants claiming a special talent can often send in additional material to support their case. Such additional material could be checked by the academic faculty.

> Students can send in supplementary materials, and they can send in a portfolio
> of their artwork, or they can send us a CD, or tape of music ... they can send
> us research, abstracts or science papers, and that kind of thing. And what we'll
> do is send some of those things to faculty, who evaluate those and then send
> their evaluations back to us, and then we include that in their file. ... So, even if

they're not applying, necessarily, to study music here, if they are an exceptional musician and they get a very high evaluation from a member of the faculty, that … will be taken into consideration quite seriously (Big Three selector)

Members of the relevant academic field would comment on the special talent of the applicant and 'point out the academic stellar ones' but they would not make the ultimate admissions decisions.

The faculty's academic judgement on the special talent of the applicant would be added to the application file. It would be an additional piece of information to consider. However, it was still for the admissions office to decide how the special talent would play out in crafting a class. In making this decision, admissions committees would not only consider the special talent and the academic record, but think about what sort of person the applicant would be on campus, if they would be a good roommate and a 'good citizen' who participated in campus life. The committee 'want to be assured that the person will make a difference in the world in the future and put their education to good use'. (Ivy League selector)

Overall, selectors found that special talents other than athletics were 'less visible' (Ivy League). Athletes could generate income for the institution through winning and alumni contributions going up. There was therefore a direct link between admitting an athlete and other goals of the institution. Other talents may not have an as straightforwardly quantifiable impact on the institution. As such, US selectors described how special non-athletic talents carried less weight than other talents in crafting a class.

Special talents are not generally considered in English admissions. There is one exception to this observation: The organ and choral scholarships awarded at Oxbridge and some other universities.

Oxbridge organ scholars provide music in College chapels, and participate or lead general music activities, some might even act as the director of music. In return, organ scholars receive free or subsidized rooms and meals, a piano to practise in their room and a small (nominal) honorarium. Many organ scholars go on to full-time organist posts.

For those applying to Oxbridge in 2014 for admissions in 2015, there were thirty-one organ scholarships available with at least five awards requiring the award holder to study music.

The standard for these scholarships is that applicants already play the organ to level 8 (the highest standard accredited level of playing an instrument in England) or already have a diploma in organ studies. There are rigorous trials with auditions and harmony tests with the Oxbridge trials taking place in September, about twelve months prior to enrolment. If an organ scholar wishes to study music as their academic subject at university, successfully completing the organ trials and a sufficient academic record meet the admissions requirements for music. If applicants wish to study another subject while being an organ scholar, they have to meet those additional academic admissions requirements as well, including the academic performance in their school-leaving examination and performance in any additional admissions tests.

Not all subjects can be studied while having an organ scholarship, typical exclusions are medicine and aligned subjects or laboratory-based subjects – this is because laboratory timings often conflict with rehearsal timings and Evensong.

Organ and choral scholarships then are potentially an exception to the English admissions system that is otherwise based solely on academic attainment and potential. A music scholar could potentially be admitted with slightly lower test scores than another applicant who was not a music scholar. This is similar to the concessions made for special talents in the US admissions process. One Oxbridge respondent explained that while the admissions process would normally try to select those with the highest academic potential to succeed, that is, those most likely to attain a First-class degree, the approach to organ scholars was different. If someone was designated an organ scholar, selectors would look for evidence that the applicant was academically capable of doing the course and of achieving at least an Upper Second class degree. Because of this shift in focus, some colleges consider the organ scholar place as a 'floating place' that is awarded to a subject in addition to their standard admissions quota. This additional place is given to whichever subject an organ scholar wishes to study and means that no non-organ scholar applicant would lose out on a place for admission to an organ scholar.

While special talents are not routinely considered in higher education in England, they are considered by some private schools, notably private boarding schools, in awarding scholarships. These schools might have music and art scholarships, or general 'talent scholarships'. For example, the elite private secondary school Harrow awards outstanding talent scholarships for athletes and for exceptional musicians.

Extracurricular

You need to be committed to extra-curricular activities and willing to make a contribution

(Big Three selector)

Academic accomplishments alone were not usually sufficient for gaining admissions to an Ivy League institution. Selectors looked for people who were

> the right fits for the university ... we look at who's going to make a difference on our campus. So, we look at their impact in their extra-curricular activities and everything they do outside of school – religion, culture, family, things that are important, and then hobbies, and then their perspectives that they'd be bringing to small, seminar-style tutorials. (Ivy selector)

What institutions were looking for in extra-curricular engagement was commitment and contribution. One Big Three selector explained how points on a scale from one (highest) to five (lowest) were awarded for different extra-curricular activities where, for example, 'a non-academic one, it's somebody who's achieved something at the national level. A non-academic two would be somebody who's achieved something at the state level, and then three is leadership in your school'.

Another Big Three selector explained how taking into account extra-curricular activities was designed to create a 'well-rounded' student body as well as having some students with focused talents. However, a liberal arts college selector was a bit more sceptical about the extent to which extra-curricular involvement and leadership could make a difference in selective admissions:

> Extra curriculars are something people talk a lot about in college and people think that is something that will really make the difference and in a few cases it can. Unless someone has done something incredibly interesting that can really make the difference but otherwise ... every student is doing some community service, every student is doing clubs or some sort of thing. ... So extra curriculars for students ... parents will say is that what makes the difference and it can but only in a very small percentage.

This respondent went on to give one example where an applicant with 'amazing qualifications academically, high grades that were off the chart' had further distinguished himself in his application by having undertaken work with a doctor on metabolic diseases among a certain population group and this work had been published. This counted as 'exceptional extra-curricular involvement'. Overall, mere participation rather than leadership seemed insufficient for admission.

This desire to admit well-rounded students and leaders at US institutions was not mirrored in discourses in England. As noted by the then director of admissions at Oxford University:

> There is a presumption that if applying to Oxford, you have to be incredibly well-rounded ... you don't. (Nicholson 2011)

Some English selectors explained how they were aware, and sometimes pleased, with the extra-curricular involvement of their students while at university. One Oxbridge selector elaborated:

> One of my students plays netball, one is in the Harry Potter society, one was in a play in the [theatre in town]. ... I got one person who judges debates at the ... Union and goes round the country judging debates and debates herself.

But, crucially, this selector explained how he was 'pleased with that' extra-curricular contribution of his students, but he didn't 'think that should be a selection criteria' and indeed, reaffirmed that.

> I don't select on that basis ... I am really pleased with that but I don't think that should be a selection criteria. Very strongly think that ... I think we would select people we like. We would be more likely to select pretty people than ugly people and so on. People of similar accent to you. These are horrible faux pars. We should not be selecting people we like.

Not all selectors were altogether pleased with the actual extra-curricular activities of their students while at university. Another Oxbridge selector observed how

> from the point of view of the community, there are all sorts of ways in which people contribute and ... have done terrific things in their time at [this college] and contributed. But at the end of the day ... they might well have cost us points[4] because they achieved a 2:1.

But this selector agreed with the colleague in the previous quotation that, regardless of how one viewed extra-curricular involvement, it should not play a role in admissions. He explained how an outstanding extra-curricular contribution was not something one could or should take into account.

> Our criteria are approached in terms of academic potential and I think it's, and quite frankly it's people who are the most promising at the start.

Another selector confirmed, saying:

> I haven't considered at all a person's wider contribution to [the institution] ... I haven't looked at a person from a wider perspective. Even when I look at the other things that they do – it is only really how it is related to their academic performance.

Indeed, in one admissions Oxbridge meeting observed during this project, selectors arrived at the following assessment about an applicant: 'socialite, great member of the JCR'. The Junior Common Room (JCR) is the umbrella network for students' social activities in colleges. Being singled out as exceeding on this front but not academically meant that this student was not admitted.

And just to eliminate any doubt about the role of extra-curriculars in a comparative US–English perspective, this selector explained:

> I don't care if they [applicants] are a good person. I care whether they do the course well. You look at American references and they are all about 'being good'. I simply want to admit on academic grounds ... anything else would take us back to the bad old days when your dad paid money for you to get in ... and I think it is corrupt to take into account the character of a person or whether they play netball for the university.

In contrast to US selectors who considered signs of being a civically engaged person as desirable for admission, the idea of selecting students based on their extra-curricular and other aspects the institution considered helpful were strongly rejected by English selectors. Indeed, they thought that for them such considerations would create more problems than they solved.

Socio-economic

> We had a new president who came in ... and said 'I want to make [this institution] more socioeconomically diverse. I want you to go out and find these poor kids and bring them to [this institution]'. (Liberal Arts school selector)

In the past decade, there has been growing awareness that diversity in terms of race and special interests can hide a lack of diversity in terms of wealth on the campuses of elite US institutions. As the admissions professional in the previous quotation laid out, this is something institutions are aware of and seeking to change. An Ivy League respondent stated how his institution was proud to be 'the most socio-economically diverse' when measured against the number of Pell Grant recipients among their students. The Federal Pell Grant Program, to give the scheme its official name, provides need-based grants to low-income students in post-secondary education.

At the most selective and prestigious institutions, the lack of socio-economic diversity is not for want of financial support awarded by the institutions for those applicants needing it as this Big Three selector explained: 'Money is not a barrier for admission'. Her colleague at another Big Three institution explained further how financial support worked:

> [we offer] need-based financial aid. So the cost of [this institution], minus the estimated family contribution, which includes the student portion, leaves them with a financial need ... and we meet that financial need 100 per cent for all four years. So there's actually very few institutions that do that, but I think all of the Ivies do it. (Big Three selector)

The details of financial aid packages are different across the Ivies, however, the very poorest students (usually with family incomes below $65,000) generally do not pay anything towards the cost of college with increasing contributions on a sliding scale depending on income. Ability to pay does not play part in the decision to admit an applicant as this selector explained:

> We are needs blind ... we know if they've applied [for financial aid], but we don't know what their income is, or anything. The fact that they've applied doesn't play any factor in the admissions process or in the committee.

In recent years, many leading Ivy League institutions, technical universities and liberal arts colleges have extended needs-blind admissions to international applicants. Following Harvard and MIT's lead, international needs-blind admissions was introduced at Yale in 2000, Williams in 2006, and Amherst and Dartmouth in 2008.

US respondents stated that needs-blind admissions with fully meeting the costs of college for poorer applicants was a strong commitment that had not waivered during the recession as this Big Three selector explained:

> This academic year ... the college will pay $145 million in scholarship aid and the scholarship is the money you give someone and you don't get it back. And you hope someday they'll remember that you gave it to them and you certainly hope they'll give it back then. But you don't require them ... you don't lend it to them. It's the opposite. It's not like a loan. So that's a huge expense especially at a time when we're all feeling quite battered. But it's the highest priority and we hope for better times.

Often related to socio-economic background but distinct is whether or not an applicant has a family history of higher education or is the first in their family to go to university. Some institutions publish those statistics. For example, for the 2013 admissions cycle the following percentages of admitted students were the first in their family to go to university: Williams College 16 per cent, Columbia 15 per cent, the University of Pennsylvania 14 per cent and Dartmouth 11 per cent.

England

This Oxbridge selector explains how there is also concern in the English admissions system to be aware of socio-economic differences:

> At each stage there are flags for the less privileged candidates and so we look at them carefully.

Other selectors explained how they had participated in awareness training for selection interviews to highlight that for applicants from 'certain socio-economic backgrounds the thought of talking to an adult about literature is just not the thing … therefore the experience of being sat down in a room with two strange adults and asked to expose yourself on those grounds is not necessarily, going to be easier for some people than a lot of people.'

Just as US admissions, admissions to all public universities in England is needs-blind in the sense that the academic decision to admit an applicant does not take into account ability to pay. The national policies with regard to university fees have been changing rapidly in the past decades though. Starting in 1998, England has witnessed a shift from free tuition and student grants to tuition fees. Since 2012, all the universities in this study have started charging £9,000 per year in fees for UK students. Tuition fees only have to be paid back once students graduate and are then paid back on a sliding scale relating to income. Full grants or bursaries to meet the full cost of living are relatively rare although, again, the poorest students at the wealthiest universities have the best chance of getting grants they do not have to pay back. Student loans are, however, available to all students but these loans have to be repaid with interest later on.

In contrast to the policy of leading US universities to meet the financial need of international students, those whose normal residence is outside the European Union pay higher fees than applicants from England or other European Union countries. While the decision to admit them as such is not based on financial consideration, there are very limited institutional scholarships at undergraduate level to help with the cost of study.

English universities do not tend to publish information about the percentage of students who are the first in their family to go to university although some universities use this information internally. However, English universities monitor the postcode data of their UK-based applicants so that they can highlight when applicants come from geographic areas with low participation rates in higher education. As part of a contextualized admissions approach, this information can mean that applicants are looked at more closely in the admissions process.

Schooling

In England, intake by school type is closely monitored by individual institutions and against performance indicators set independently by the Higher Education Statistical Agency. Performance indicators are set by the percentage of undergraduate students coming from state schools, different socio-economic classes and areas in which few students continue into higher education. This in a national context where fewer than 1 in 10 adolescents attend a private school, but at leading universities, as many as half the students have attended private schools. Increasing the intake of students from state as opposed to private schools is thus an aim across selective admission. We will revisit the topic of schooling and external benchmarks in more detail in Chapters 7 and 8.

The main way schooling is used in admissions is then to contextualize the academic achievement and potential of an applicant. The academic performance of an applicant was mapped against the performance of the school and selectors looked for 'outliers' who had performed well compared with their peers.

This could mean that an applicant who had done very well in a not-so-good school would be looked upon kindly. One selector noted how his academic colleagues 'would be prepared to lower down the criteria to allow people with disadvantaged background to come in as long as they don't need to be drastic'. Some institutions operate more formalized policies of having a minimum academic standard all applicants need to meet. Once students make this cut-off, there can be discretion whether students need to meet the top of the entry requirements (e.g. A*A*A) or would be admitted with slightly lower attainment (A*AA).

Schooling is closely related to socio-economic status because of the ability to pay for private school and because academically poor performing schools tend to be in poorer areas. Viewing schooling as a special interest case for admissions is thus some, albeit imperfect, proxy for trying to increase the representation of those from less privileged backgrounds in selective higher education.

In contrast, none of the US selectors discussed school type as a 'special interest case' in admissions. There was no discussion of targets by school type, although the schooling profile of incoming classes was monitored in some published statistics. The lack of emphasis on schooling in the United States could be because there is a more overt discourse of socio-economic diversity rather than a 'proxy' discourse of schooling as a special interest case in admissions.

Extenuating circumstances

The holistic admissions processes in both the US and England allow for applicants to draw attention to special personal circumstances. In England, the bodies that award A-levels and AS-levels also already take extenuating circumstances into account in their gradings. Extenuating circumstances can relate to illness that has affected examination performance, accidents, bereavement, divorce, caring responsibilities or other individual circumstances. Information about extenuating circumstances can come from the recommendation letters or through the personal statement or essay. Some institutions in England also have additional forms available for applicants wishing to make a case for special circumstances.

A liberal arts college selector recalled two examples of how he had observed the working of extenuating circumstances in his admissions context:

> I had a student once whose father died in 9/11 and she wrote an essay about that and how in high school she works as a children's grief counsellor with kids who have gone through trauma and that helped her overcome her own trauma. It was this really moving essay and really well written but also such an amazing story there I said 'I want this kid to be at [this institution]' so I didn't pull her even though she was a white girl from New Jersey.

In this first example, the applicant had faced bereavement but had overcome this adversity and turned it into something positive. This made the admissions office interested in her and saved her from being taken out of the pool of admitted students when her place came under scrutiny. Given the earlier observation how selective institutions strive for a regional mix, the applicant had been considered for being taken out of the pool partly because she was a 'white girl from New Jersey' and was therefore competing against a lot of many otherwise similar white applicants from this part of the United States.

In the second example, an applicant's academic accomplishment was particularly noteworthy because it had been achieved against the context of adversity as the liberal arts college selector went on to recall:

> I had another student once and the essay read like it was June and her mother throws out her abusive alcoholic father and then in July she almost dies from

some heart condition and then, … she was in the hospital all summer then she still came back to school in September even though they told her she should probably not go back to school. She still went back to school and she took the hard courses and did really well despite all of the crap that happened to her.

There is usually not a formulaic way to take such extenuating circumstances into account – for example, there is no tariff for an adjustment in academic requirements for certain types of events. However, after some lobbying from a charity, the UCAS application form in the UK asks applicants whether they have been 'in care', meaning that they have been in public care – often a children's home or foster family. This information is aimed to help increase the admission of those from care backgrounds in higher education as this group is vastly under-represented. This information is then generally systematically flagged up to selectors to signal that any applicant with this flag has already succeeded against the odds – although not all selective universities do this. One university also flagged up when an applicant had been a refugee.

Chapter summary

Your background can make the difference between being admitted or not. Because diversity is important in the role of educating others.

(US Big Three selector)

There are special interest cases in admissions. In the United States, this means generally a hook with regard to athletic powers, race, extra-curricular involvement, a special talent (including academic excellence), region of application or personal context. For example, Dartmouth proudly celebrated the diversity of the new incoming class enrolling in 2013 as follows:

The accepted students have a variety of talents and accomplishments. Two have been named winners in the Intel Science Talent Search. Several have performed on the popular National Public Radio musical program, From the Top. One is a winner of the VEX Robotics World Championship, and another is an accomplished short-track speed skater who is training for the 2014 Winter Olympics. (Chapman 2013)

In England, considerations about school type and socio-economic context could be taken into account in admission to evaluate students' academic potential.

However, when celebrating diversity in admissions, one also has to be mindful that not all possible types of diversity may be included or celebrated in crafting a diverse class or individual admission. For example, I observed in an admissions meeting in England how selectors were very lukewarm about an academically excellent home-schooled applicants. Selectors thought the applicant was a 'risky choice' as he had no social experience of schooling. When I asked a US Ivy League selector whether this applicant would have fared better in the US holistic admissions system, the answer was that while home-schooled applicants were certainly among the admitted students, they were also considered as risky choices that needed to be 'carefully considered'.

Mental health was another type of diversity that seemed to concern selectors. In one instance, a US selector retold an application case study where the application files contained indicators that the applicant was 'prone to feel low' and this raised concerns not only for the applicant but also regarding the effect this would have on their roommate and the sports team this applicant wished to participate in. The student was not admitted.

Diversity with regard to religion, sexuality or disability status were also not part of institutions official diversity drive although English universities would maintain to select 'regardless' of those characteristics and free from inadvert discrimination.

To conclude then, considerations other than academic talent play a key part in making offers for admission in US universities. This contrasts with England where – other than organ scholars – none of the 'special interest' categories of US selection come into play. In England, considerations are only given to contextualize the academic ability and potential of applicants with different personal and schooling circumstances.

With these considerations about the purpose of the admissions processes in England and the United States in mind, the discussion now turns to the actual application and selection process.

5

Applying

So far, this book has described who the selectors are and what institutions are looking for in admissions decisions. But how does the process of recruitment and admissions actually work? What are the nuts and bolts of the process? How do applicants apply? How do selectors select? How are decisions made? How do they craft a class? The present and the next chapter provide some answers to these questions.

For some, the process of preparing for university might have already started when they were a twinkle in their parents' eyes. However, the actual process of gaining admissions usually begins in the last year of secondary school. At this point, many students will have already been on university campuses and open day visits; some young people may have participated in some outreach scheme, and potential athletes will have already been in touch with coaches and perhaps received an early letter that they are likely to be admitted. Now it is time for applicants to decide where to submit their applications. Applicants in England also need to decide which degree subject they wish to study. Universities make offers for places, and applicants decide where they wish to enrol.

The last year of school is the time to sit any additional tests that are required for admissions. This is usually the SAT or ACT tests in the United States. In England, there are national tests for some subjects such as medicine and law and specific tests for some universities, in particular, Oxford. The Oxbridge admissions process requires applicants to submit their application by mid-October – or by September for potential organ scholars. The deadline for most other English universities and courses is January. US applicants can often also work towards two deadlines. But in contrast to England, the different US deadlines relate to different admissions pools. Many institutions operate an early and a regular application deadline. The 1st of November is a frequently used deadline for the early pool; decisions are then available in December. For the regular admissions route, deadlines tend to be at the end of December or early January with decisions available in March or April.

Table 4 Activities and deadlines in the final year of school for students wishing to apply for higher education

Final year of high school/secondary school	Ivy League example	Oxbridge	Other universities in the UK
September and earlier	Listen to talks by universities about what they offer, attend university fairs, attend open days or visit potential institutions in person or through a virtual campus tour, use internet to research universities. Possibly sit ACT or SAT; research institutions (open days, internet)	Register for subject-specific additional tests; Application systems through UCAS opens; Organ scholarship deadline	
September October	Last month for sitting ACT for early choice applicants	15th October application deadline through UCAS	Deadline for equal consideration for only medicine, dentistry and veterinary sciences
November	1st of November – binding early choice deadline for application and financial aid; Last month for sitting SAT for early choice	5th of November is the test date for many subject tests for admission to Oxford; Receive invitation for interview or information that not invited for interview	Interview invitations might start arriving for subjects requiring it
December	Binding early decision decisions available; Regular admission deadline 31st of December through Common Application	Interviews for UK/EU students (potentially over telephone or internet)	
January	Mid-year grades sent to colleges; Last month for sitting SAT for standard applicants; Admissions meetings start	Receipt of admissions decisions, usually an 'unsuccessful' or a 'conditional offer'	15th of January is the standard application deadline for equal consideration for the majority of remaining courses and universities
February	Last month for sitting ACT for standard applicants		
March	Full committee meetings, finalize class; 1st of March deadline for financial aid for regular decision applicants	Standard decision deadline for applicants to accept up to two admissions offers: 31st of March	
Late March/April	Admissions decisions mailed		
May	Applicants decide which offer to take by 1st of May; Deposit deadline; Waitlisted students might be contacted with admissions offers		
May/June		Study very hard for the final examinations at school as the results in these examinations determine university destination	
August	Housing Assignment, course choices	Sit A-level (or equivalent) examinations; A-level results day; Either confirm offer with the first-choice university or, if the grades are no quite as high as hoped, confirm with the 'safety school' or, if unsuccessful, consider 'clearing' process through UCAS	
September October	Academic work starts (unless deferred entry)	Academic work starts (unless deferred entry)	

Table 4 gives an indicative timeline of what the last year of secondary school involves for US and English applicants to higher education.

All applications for undergraduate full-time study at UK universities, including Oxbridge, Scottish, Welsh and Northern Irish institutions, are managed through a central clearinghouse called UCAS. The UCAS application allows applicants to make up to five application choices. For example, an applicant could apply to study the same degree course at five different universities. Or an applicant could apply to only two universities but ask for admission to three and two degree courses respectively.

UCAS charges £12 for applying to one university course and £23 for applying to between two and five university courses. A restriction on choice is that applicants cannot apply to both Oxford and Cambridge in the same year. One US participant in this project described this practice as 'anti-competitive', whereas an English selector argued that it prevents Oxford and Cambridge competing for 'the same student' and costing public money in the process.

In the United States, there are no limits to the number of institutions that applicants can apply to. There are generally two admissions portals applicants can use: the Common Application used by over 500 US institutions and the Universal College Application used by just over forty institutions. By using a standard form, students can submit the core of their application to several institutions. The selective institutions in this project then usually require applicants to submit an additional 'supplementary' application that is specific to the particular institution.

There is no formal restriction on the number of different institutions a US applicant can apply to. Application fees per institution tend to be in the range of $70–$90, and fee waivers on economic grounds are also available. Just over 1 in 4 students apply to more than seven colleges for admissions.

Timing of application

In the United States, three types of early admissions programmes are available: early decision, early action and restrictive early admission. In early decision programmes, a student has to accept the admissions decision and enrol at the institution they applied to through early decision. The admitted applicant is not allowed to enrol at any other university and the application is signed by parents, the school counsellor and the student. In contrast, early action admissions decisions are not binding and students can still apply to other institutions for early or standard admission. Restrictive early admission means that an early action application is sent to just one institution.

A Big Three selector explained how the historic routes of early admissions programmes are found in the 'special relationships' that selective institutions had with private schools in the 1970s, when selectors

> went to the schools and interviewed the candidate and the counselor. We then gave them an A, B, or C rating and decided straight away whether they would get in. If you had [this institution] lineage, you were given an A-rating. This was unfair because this early admissions process was only offered to some privileged kids, we then felt it should be broadened out to public [state] schools.

Formal early admissions policies were developed to make the early admissions system fairer and were made available to all applicants. In 2014, the Big Three Ivies operate functionally very similar early admissions programmes although under somewhat different names. Harvard operates a restrictive early action programme, and Yale and Princeton operate a 'Single Choice Early Action programme'.

The idea is that early admissions programmes benefit institutions and students: the institution benefits because the early programmes create greater and earlier certainty concerning who will enrol and thus help manage student numbers. For the students, early admission means greater certainty about their university destination earlier on.

An increasing proportion of new students are admitted through early programmes, giving rise to the claim that 'early is the new normal' (Ivy League selector).

Up to half of the incoming class at selective institutions might be admitted through early schemes, and the admission rates can be almost four times higher than in the regular pool. Institutions maintain that standards are the same in early and regular decision and that the higher admit rate for the early pool reflects the greater strengths of the early pool compared with the regular pool. Table 5 summarizes the overall acceptance rate and the early acceptance rate in the Ivy League for the class entering in 2013.

However, there remains some controversy surrounding the early admissions schemes. Some admissions professionals view early admissions policies as primarily benefitting the institution and not serving the applicants. For example, binding early admissions programmes do not allow students to compare financial aid packages from different institutions. This can be particularly disadvantageous for poorer applicants.

Table 5 Acceptance and early acceptance rates in the Ivy League for 2013

School	Overall acceptance rate (%)	Early action or decision	Early acceptance rate (%)
Brown	9	Decision	19
Columbia	6.9	Decision	20
Cornell	16.2	Decision	29.5
Dartmouth	9.8	Decision	25
Harvard	6.3	Action	18
Penn	12.4	Decision	25.3
Princeton	7.9	Action	18.3
Yale	7.1	Action	14

Source: Admissions Consultants 2013.

There is also some concern about the representativeness of the profile of those who applied through early programmes. One Big Three Ivy selector who would like to see early programmes discontinued argued thus:

> People who apply through early programmes will usually be whiter, richer, and more domestic … no matter how you cut it, there is almost always some difference between the early and the regular programme.

Another Ivy League selector indicated that they gave a bonus for legacy applicants in early decision 'to give them the edge' but did not apply this bonus in their regular decision round. The aim of this policy was to incentivize alumni children to commit early to the institution.

A proponent of early programmes from another highly selective institution, however, argued that the research from his institution had investigated

> whether these progammes advantaged the better off. Initially they did, the early pool had more privileged applicants. But our outreach programmes had the effect of diversifying the early pool and now it is a very diverse pool.

There have been attempts to discontinue early admissions programmes. This would require joint action by leading institutions. However, because of antitrust legislation, institutions cannot have such an agreement in place as they cannot exchange information that might affect student choice, for example, information on future fees and general future policies. The early admissions game in the United States thus seems to be here to stay.

Some US selectors straight away considered the earlier admissions deadline for Oxford and Cambridge in England as anti-competitive. To them, it was surprising that there was not more sector-wide protest against this specific early deadline for Oxbridge. This early deadline is not one of the key topics in English admission. There are, however, voices arguing similar to some discussions in the United States, that applicants need to be better supported, organized, networked and informed to apply early and that not all schools and parents support applicants equally in this endeavour. Because the applications to Oxford and Cambridge occur through the same central application service, UCAS, as all other undergraduate applications, the early deadline also means that the other institutions where any Oxbridge applicant has applied to receive these applications early. Although universities do not see which other universities an applicant has applied to, the perhaps unintended effect of the early deadline system is also that a large proportion of the highest attaining students in England apply earlier to university than some of their peers with slightly less stellar prior attainment.

The elements of an application

> We are working with a lot of information … and we are looking for information throughout the admissions process. We have the information that comes to us through UCAS, so we have a reference from the students' school, we have got a personal statement that the candidates themselves have written, we have their prior academic record and we have some predictions about their future success. And all universities will use this to a greater or lesser extent. The advantage that Oxford has, we can ask for more, indeed, we do ask for more. … This year, 90 per cent plus have taken some kind of subject-based additional aptitude test. (Nicholson 2013)

A full university application in both the United States and England shares the following core elements: some personal background, achievement in school to date, trajectory of current school performance, information about the school, a recommendation letter and a section written by the applicant. Where applicable, the application will also contain the results of additional tests and information on any additional considerations.

Beyond these shared features, there are some differences in the details of the two application systems. For example, the English form asks applicants whether they have a disability. The reasoning is that this will allow universities to put support in place early on, although this may not always be how applicants view this question. Indeed, because declarations of disability increase after firm admissions offers have been made and accepted, several universities now ask for this information again at a later stage in the admissions cycle.

The US application forms ask for the occupation and education of both parents and siblings, the English forms ask only about the occupation and education of the highest earning parent. UCAS collects only this particular information from applicants who reside in the UK and not from European or other international applicants. US application forms ask all applicants to self-identify with an ethnicity, but in England, this question is asked only of UK applicants for admission. While information on race and parental occupation is available as part of the holistic admission to US universities, these two pieces of information are not disclosed to selectors in England until after admissions decisions have been made.

US selectors also have access to information on marital and family status, religion, armed forces affiliation and languages spoken at home as part of an applicants' personal background section. Such information is not systematically available on the UCAS application form. However, in contrast to the US selectors, English selectors have information on whether an applicant has been in care (i.e. with a foster family or foster home) or was a refugee.

The US application elicits information on extra-curricular activities, leadership, hours spent doing an activity and whether the applicant intends to participate in these activities in college. Universities can also purchase an array of additional information from the testing companies that administer the SAT and/or ACT. This is not part of the standard application dossier in England. These differences in what information is required align with the different status of extra-curricular involvement in the English and the US selection processes.

To summarize the similarities and differences, Table 6 offers a comparison of a typical English and US application files for admission to a selective university.

In both countries, not all information necessary for a complete application is available at the point of initial application. For example, US applicants might not have taken the SAT or ACT test yet. Once applicants have completed the test, they can ask the organization administering the test to send the test results directly to the universities that an applicant has applied to. Applicants for admission to English universities might also still sit a subject-specific admissions test such as the BMAT for medicine or the LNAT for law, and again, such test results will be released to the institutions that an applicant has applied to once the test has been completed. For several courses at Oxford, there are additional subject tests

Table 6 What is in a typical application file to a highly selective university in the United States and England?

Ivy League example Common Application form	Application file	Oxbridge
Yes (but with supplements and not all institutions accept the Common Application form)	Standard application form across institutions	Yes (and additional test or written information if required)
Yes	Previous grades at school/transcript	Yes
Yes	Predicted grades/mid-year report	Yes
Yes	Information about the school	Yes
Yes two letters are required	Reference/Recommendation letter	Yes, one letter is required
Yes	Essay/Personal statement	Yes
Yes	Test results	Yes, where applicable
Yes	English as a foreign language if applicable	Yes
Yes	Extra-curricular information	No
Yes	Additional information/extenuating circumstances	Yes
Yes	Personal circumstances	Yes, but not all information is available to selectors at point of selection
Yes	Parental education	Yes (less detailed than United States)
Yes	Parental occupation	Yes (less detailed than United States)
Yes	Sibling information	No
Yes	Criminal records disclosure	Yes
Yes	Help with application form/ Outreach participation	Yes
No	Disability	Yes
Yes	Future plans	No
Yes	Armed forces affiliation	No
Yes	Race	Yes, but not available to selectors at point of selection
No	Refugee; in care	Yes
No (Yes for universal application)	Early decision agreement as part of application	No
Individual fees $75 (e.g. Harvard) or fee waiver request	Cost of applying	UCAS charges £23 for up to five application choices and £12 for only one application

Figures correct as of June 2014.

usually taken on or around 5 November. All Oxbridge applicants residing in the UK and elsewhere in the EU have to participate in the mandatory interview process. For both Oxbridge institutions, this process takes place in December and can require one overnight stay at the institution. There can be additional tests when applicants are at the universities for their admissions interview.

Applicants to selective US universities will often be contacted by a previous graduate from that institution to arrange a non-academic interview. Such interviews can take place anywhere in the world where there are alumni. The alumni then provide the admissions office with written comments concerning their impression of the applicant.

Both, US and English selectors seek to base their decisions on the most up-to-date attainment and performance information. US applicants thus tend to send in 'mid-year transcripts' in January that show their high school grades. The offer a US university makes at this point then is unconditional with no further requirements attached. Applicants applying for early admission will have their offers confirmed before the mid-year transcripts are available. In England, admissions offers for applicants are normally conditional offers. This means that the offer is conditional on the applicant achieving certain grades in their school-leaving examination. If these offer conditions are not met, then the offer becomes void although there is some discretion to allow for individual circumstances such as extenuating circumstances.

Key elements of the application form are school achievement and test performance, references, essays or personal statements, interviews and a social background section.

Achievement information

The reasons for looking for school performance and test results were discussed in Chapters 2 and 3. This section now briefly summarizes the nuts and bolts regarding how school and test information enters the application file.

Both, US and English application forms request prior academic attainment information. In England, the majority of applicants have an attainment transcript of the grades achieved in their GCSEs and in the United States, applicants have their end-of-year results from the previous academic year and their calculated GPA. English applicants also put down the grades they have achieved in their penultimate year of schooling (where available) and the referee, their class teacher enters the predicted achievement for their final school-leaving examinations. References and recommendation letters can provide further information regarding particular grades or aspects of school attainment.

In the United States, SAT or ACT test results are used across selective institutions and some courses or universities in England ask for additional tests.

References/recommendations

In addition to achievement information, application files contain a reference or recommendation letter from someone in the applicants' secondary school.[1] US university applications tend to have two to three references supporting them as a Big Three selector explained: 'There's two teacher recommendations, and then also the guidance counsellor recommendation'. There is generally only one reference through the UK UCAS application system. In both countries, there are different views regarding the status and importance of this support letter: some selectors consider references as useful and important whereas others find references useful only in exceptional circumstances or not at all. Several US respondents considered references to be more important at the most highly selective universities than at slightly less selective institutions.

The purpose of the US references was to 'bring life into the student'. This is considered important in terms of the residential college experience at highly selective US institutions where selectors are interested in finding out answers to the following questions: 'What kind of room-mate would this person be?' 'Would you like to have breakfast with this person?' 'Would you like to work on a research team with this person?' In short, selectors are trying to find out 'what sort of person' the applicant is.

Advice to high school students is thus to choose a referee 'who likes you', 'knows you well' and 'can set you up for success'. Selectors do not want a 'laundry list' of accomplishments or a 'sleek and pseudo-charismatic' reference but genuine deep insight into the applicant and their circumstances that may not be available from other parts of the application. Badly written recommendation can negatively affect chances of being admitted and reflect badly on the high school. However, a Big Three selector maintained 'We admit kids, not schools' and that admissions staff were able to consider references in context.

A respondent from a liberal arts college voiced some overall scepticism whether a reference could make a genuine difference:

> There are letters of recommendation that honestly aren't that important because we know they are going to positive. We know they are going to be positive because no kid is going to get a teacher to write a bad recommendation …

Unless it's 'This is the best kid I have ever seen in my time as a teacher' – that is going to make a difference.

Just as their US counterparts, English selectors also had mixed views regarding the usefulness of references. As one Oxbridge selector remarked 'school references are probably becoming more and more positive and undifferentiated' and a colleague remarked how, as a result, the references are of 'no use at all'. Other selectors noted how the references were useful when they contained information not available from other parts of the application; however, this respondent also noted that references 'are often very uniform and it is only occasionally that you get something else'. Therefore, another Russell Group selector remarked how 'if there is any caveat at all in the reference this does make you wonder'. One Oxbridge selector gave an example where there 'were signs in the reference that maybe he [the applicant] wasn't as hard working as he could be' and as a result there was doubt as to whether the student would achieve the required grades for admission. This information was taken into account alongside all other pieces of information.

Furthermore, admissions professionals also apply contextual knowledge about the school when reading references. For example, selectors are aware of the differential counsellor to student ratios in different schools with the most prestigious private schools having fewer students per counsellor than large state-funded schools. As this Big Three Ivy selector explains:

> Public secondary counsellors are very taxed ... college counselling is only a fraction of what they do, because they're doing scheduling, they're involved in crisis management, they're involved in so many other day to day development pieces of a student's life. Whereas at a lot of private day schools and boarding schools, they have offices that are dedicated solely to college counselling ... public [state funded] schools don't necessarily have the time or the resources dedicated to really focus on the college process.

Just as in the United States, there were also differences in how informative and useful references from different schools were viewed in England. One selector remarked that 'the teachers won't always realize what we want to know' and that some schools are clearly more experienced than others in writing references as one Oxbridge selector observes:

> You can see very different sort of levels of Oxbridge experience in the references, that schools write ... to characterize crudely: You get some terrific write ups from public [private, fee-paying] schools that send a lot of candidates and you have to get extremely artful in reading between the lines in realizing that this is ... not a first rank candidate but someone who is being sold quite strongly. ... Sometimes state schools seem to be terribly frank ... and if you put simple

reliance on references this might disadvantage them [applicants]. But I think
people are reading those references with that sort of contextual intelligence.

This point again highlights how references are one aspect of the admissions
process that is read in the context of the application and their school. References
were also 'an opportunity for the student or the guidance counsellor to tell us
about things that may have affected them during school' (Big Three selector).
This aspect is also considered useful in the English context.

One English selector commented on how references had the potential to
provide additional information about an applicant and how this potential was
often not realized. As she explained:

> A teacher who's taught someone for two or three years, may well have a lot more
> information about the about the person than [A-level examination grades], but
> of course you can't get that information truthfully and reveal it.

References in England are 'open' and can be read by parents and the students'
and several selectors commented how this had resulted in more uniform, less
genuinely informative references over time.

There was also some acknowledgement that there were different national
cultures of writing references. An Oxbridge science selector remarked that
North American references are generally glowing and 'unless the person can
walk on water it is a bad reference!' Another Oxbridge arts selector contrasted
this with continental European references where there was 'little exaggeration'.
She therefore thought that such references should be interpreted as 'good if they
do not say something negative about a student'.

Because most references are glowing, selectors in both the UK and the US
commented on unsupportive references that had stood out in their memory
over time. One Big Three selector recalled reading a reference that stated the
applicant 'appears to be personable and alert. But he isn't'. An English selector
remembered a reference that had a disclaimer on it stating that 'this reference
is written based on direction from the parents. The school has not advised the
applicant to submit an application for admission nor does the school support
this application.' But even in such instances, selectors argued that it was unlikely
for an applicant to be denied admission solely on the grounds of one reference.
However, other parts of the application would have to be exceptional to
counterbalance such lack of support.

To summarize the role of references, selectors commented on a general shift
towards references becoming less useful over time because references were open
and private schools in particular were under parental scrutiny to write strong

references. Where references were not glowing, this had to be interpreted in the light of the school experience of writing references and potentially national context of the reference culture. References were useful when they highlighted unusual circumstances that had affected an applicants' academic journey. Indeed, UCAS provides specific advice on how to write helpful references, although take-up among teachers seemed variable.

Essays/personal statement

The application essay in the United States is between 250 and 650 words long, and some institutions require or allow for an optional second essay in the supplement part of the application form. In the UK, applicants complete one 'personal statement'. This is similar in length to the US admissions essay, although length is counted in characters (1–4,000) rather than words.[2] Table 7

Table 7 What are US and UK universities looking for in personal statements/essays?

US essay (Common application essay prompts)	UK personal statement (UCAS guidance)
Some students have a background or story that is so central to their identity that they believe their application would be incomplete without it. If this sounds like you, then please share your story.	**1. Why are you applying?** For example why you want to study at higher education level; why that subject interests you; what your ambitions are when you finish your course.
Recount an incident or time when you experienced failure. How did it affect you, and what lessons did you learn? Reflect on a time when you challenged a belief or idea. What prompted you to act? Would you make the same decision again?	**2. What makes you suitable?** Skills, knowledge, achievements and experience you have that will help you do well. These could be from education, employment or work experience, or from hobbies, interests and social activities.
Describe a place or environment where you are perfectly content. What do you do or experience there, and why is it meaningful to you? Discuss an accomplishment or event, formal or informal, that marked your transition from childhood to adulthood within your culture, community, or family.	**3. Which of your skills and experiences are most relevant?** Check course listings to see what level of understanding you need to have and what qualifications or skills they're looking for. This way you can link your experiences to the skills and qualities they mention, and you can put them into a structure that's most relevant to the course providers.

gives an overview of the essay/personal statement prompts given to applicants when they complete their application form.

In addition to these standard prompts, the supplementary part of US applications can contain further prompts for the second essay. For example, the Harvard supplement gives applicants examples on what to write about in their second essay, such as 'Unusual circumstances in your life; travel or living experiences in other countries; a list of books you have read during the past twelve months; how you hope to use your college education; an intellectual experience that has meant the most to you, what you would want your future college roommate to know about you'.

The importance attached to personal statements and the information that selectors are looking for vary between institutions and selectors. As a broad generalization, US selectors are interested to see whether applicants can write and tell their personal story and explain how they might contribute to their campus community if admitted. As another broad generalization, some institutions in England use the personal statement in a formulaic way to map the skills cited in the personal statement against the skills required for a particular university course, whereas other courses and universities do not systematically consider the personal statement.

A Big Three Ivy selector explained what her institution was looking for in the essay:

> First of all, is writing skills. The student needs to be able to write well. If it's an Ivy League school ... they are going to be doing a lot of writing. And [at this institution], you have to write a dissertation. So you need to write well. And then also, ... we're looking for more qualities that don't necessarily show up in other parts of the application, like, maybe, imagination, creativity, telling a story ... something interesting about their background, or something they did. We're asking them to be really self-reflective in their essays.

Another Ivy selector explained that he took the writing skills almost as a given, but that his institution 'loved great essays' because they gave an opportunity to hear the students' voices. Another Ivy selector asked himself when reading an essay: 'What's the student's story? How do they think? What do they choose to tell us in their essays? What do they think that they would bring to the table at a place like [this institution]?' An admissions colleague from a liberal arts college selector elaborated on how the essay could bring an applicant to life and tell the human story behind the numbers and accomplishments:

> The essay will make a difference if they have an amazing story. If they have had hardship in their family that is something that can really help. Mostly that's

sort of the human element of admissions … we're not computers we're actually people, so if you're the guy reading that kid's essay and it really like moves you or speaks to you then in a lot of situations you're going to try to take that kid. If, despite all of the crap that has happened to them they still had good grades and good SATs and that sort of thing. You're going to say that kid is actually so powerful and this is such an interesting student, this is somebody we want to have at the college so you'll go out of your way to take that kid, and that can definitely make a difference.

An essay that captured selectors' attention or imagination then had the potential to make a difference in admission. However, when asked how much of a difference a great essay would make, one selector clarified that the essay might only make the difference between being admitted rather than put on the wait list and not between admitted and rejected.

The liberal arts selector from the previous quotation gave examples of essays he remembered and how these essays had played out in the admissions process. He recalled essays of hardship, illness and grief but where applicants had turned the negative experience into something positive, for example, through helping others. These applicants had maintained their high grades against this background of adversity. The admissions committee then looked particularly favourably upon these applications when it came to deciding between these applicants and others with a similar record but without a strong essay contextualizing their accomplishments. However, just standing out was not enough for applicants to obtain this contextual consideration as he also explained:

> The kid wrote an essay that in third grade she wanted to be different so she wore mismatched socks every day. Every day from then she wore mismatched socks and it seemed hilarious to me and I wanted to keep that kid in the class but in the end I had to pull her and put her on the waiting list.

Another Ivy selector explained how he was looking for fit with his institution and academic and other values and some indication that the applicant genuinely wished to study at this particular Ivy:

> We're more intellectual than some of our peers. We're very diverse. Do you want to be a part of that diversity and [our curriculum]? You can go to a place like [another Ivy], where there's no curriculum. You just pick whatever you want, and that's very attractive. Why not go there? So, we play, like, devil's advocate there, in terms of that perspective.

Fit with the particular context of the institution, rather than a general fit with higher education, was regarded as important by this selector.

So, essays that really made a difference in making a case for extenuating circumstances told a strong story, and they contextualized how the achievement of the applicant was particularly noteworthy because of the adversity they had faced in achieving it. They also made the case for why this applicant was a particularly good fit for the institution they had applied to.

While US selectors and some English selectors valued hearing the students' voice, there were also concerns about this element of the application on both sides of the Atlantic because of concerns that coaching can affect authenticity in this part of the application.

One Big Three selector acknowledged that it 'is perhaps worrying how important the essays are because you can buy them from the internet'. Indeed, any visitor to the book store of an Ivy League institution cannot fail to notice book titles like 'essays that got into [Ivy name]', 'essays for medical school' and 'essays for law school'. Schools were another explanation for difference in quality in college application essays as noted by this Big Three selector:

> At some schools they definitely get coached … if you're at a private school, you're going to have counsellors go over your essay with you, or maybe your English teacher, or … it depends on the school, what kind of help they're getting with that.

Some schools and their teachers are known to give extensive feedback on the essays and to offer significant help in editing and outlining. In addition, selectors knew of stories where 'parents write their kids' college essays all the time … some U.S. parents are nuts' – a concern that was shared in England.

Applicants for higher education in England write only one personal statement, and this statement is the same for all institutions they apply to. For some subjects at some universities, selectors ask for additional written work, but this written work can be previously submitted school coursework and is not comparable to writing a second reflective essay as is the case with some US admissions. The English personal statements are intended to give more information about the motivation for applying to a particular subject and about relevant skills and achievements that applicants brings to the subject. A fraud detection service run by UCAS aims to safeguard the authenticity of the submitted statements (UCAS 2015).

One Oxbridge selector recalled how he explained the importance of the personal statement during a visit to a school: 'We are looking for people keen to study the subject they have applied to and evidence that they really like it.' He gave the example of how in modern languages students have to do a lot of reading, and they have to 'enjoy sitting down with a book and reading it. Otherwise they won't enjoy the course.' If an applicant shows that they enjoy Camus or Kafka, this is good, but 'basically we are looking for evidence that they like reading, it doesn't matter very much what. In last year's admission round, three applicants said in their personal statement that they had read Dorstojewski. That is good. But Stephen King is better than nothing'. Another selector explained how she was looking for 'commitment to the subject and, interest in it, and energy, you hope a lively, mind'.

Whether the personal statement matters at all in selection is subject to some debate, and the answer varies across institutions and individual selectors. In one Russell Group, personal statements are centrally read and scored and then the results are entered into a weighted formula for admission. In other universities, statements are not part of the selection process, although only one selector who had been part of admissions for the first time actually stated that he had not read the personal statements because he had run out of time. He then realized in the committee meetings that everyone else had read the statements, if only to aid recalling the applicants for the purpose of making final selection decisions. Many of the academic selectors do not consider the personal statement, or they prefer the information obtained in an interview where it is available.

One Oxbridge selector for a humanities subject recalled how her initiative to have the personal statement systematically assessed was unsuccessful:

> I did ask people to give a numerical mark to the personal statement and a lot of colleagues in other colleges objected to this. I thought you could do it, because, my sense was that I was looking for you know – outstandingly good, outstandingly bad and somewhere in the middle – … I do think you can, rank these, but that was very controversial and in fact dropped from the [systematic admissions considerations].

Objections to having the personal statement systematically assessed included 'what they say in the personal statement never seems 100 per cent coherent or convincing', 'most of it is irrelevant', 'very rarely that you find something in there' as well as concerns about whether applicants had actually written the statements themselves. Even the selector who had argued for systematically assessing personal statements concluded that she thought the personal statements was 'less persuasive' than the other factors evaluated in admissions.

Some academic selectors considered the personal statement to offer information about writing and thinking ability, ability to express themselves, and ability to structure a piece that was relevant to the academic content of the course that applicants were seeking to study. As one selector pointed out: 'You get a sense of the candidate's personality, and their intellectual style, how well they can order their thoughts'.

'The personal statement is interesting because it gives you an idea of you know, how the student thinks – if he or she has written it them self that is.' Such information on writing ability might not be as relevant for a natural science subject as 'in mathematics, to be honest, they [the personal statements] do not count for much. But this is something where subjects are really very different.'

Some Oxbridge selectors for arts or social science subjects found the personal statement useful for starting the interview: 'Obviously one of the things you do with the personal statement is to sort of make a note of anything that you'd like to ask the candidate about in the interview'. Another selector provided an example:

> If Ms Jones said she liked going to Stratford to see Shakespeare plays or she says she is interested in the discussion of pain in St John's gospel then this triggers interview questions. And, if they had said something – say, they said something interesting, like 'I really think this about the world economy' or 'I really think this' – well, then ok, let's see whether we can push them on that!

Some academic selectors then used the personal statement as a starting point for conversation and indeed encouraged students in writing the personal statement 'to flag up what they want to talk about in their interview'. Some selectors did not pursue this line of enquiry further if students could not elaborate on what they had written in the personal statement, whereas one selector noted it was 'disappointing' when students had flagged something for discussion in the interview and then could not talk about it.

Because there is no one-fits-all formula for writing personal statements and what selectors are looking for in them, the effect on selectors when reading a personal statement could also be different. One Oxbridge selector recalled:

> I think there may be, differences in the way a different selector reacts to personal statements. There was a candidate for a joint school [a degree programme in more than one department] who had written a very fanciful personal statement. Wherein, once upon a time, there was a little girl called, whatever her name, whose dearest wish was to study at [Oxbridge]. And so on in this vein. To me, such a fanciful style is off-putting. I'm afraid this made a very bad application with us [in our department] – the candidate didn't convince us that she was, in the top flight. The tutors in the other subject must have liked it, because this girl got in, for the other subject she obviously did carry conviction. I can't say whether that was because of her fanciful personal statement or despite it.

As with the reference letters, many selectors are concerned about how much genuine information personal statements contain. There was concern about whether applicants had written themselves, how much help they had had and how much effort applicants had put into the activities they recounted.

> We do not take personal statements into account. Now, a) they are written by the school b) they tell you they are doing fantastic things, the play the flute to Grade 8 and they paint old ladies' houses. And it is all very impressive. Many times it is the school that has arranged those things because they knew it looks good. And public [elite fee-paying private] schools can do that better than state schools.

Indeed, academic research on personal statements shows that the grammatical mistakes as well as the type of experiences discussed in personal statement differ by school type. Those in private schools make fewer grammatical mistakes and they also refer to more high-brown work experiences, holidays and volunteering experiences compared with their state-school-educated counterparts (Jones 2013). Currently ongoing work also suggests systematic differences by applicants from different ethnic groups in writing personal statements.

Another selector commented how applicants have a personal statement that 'has gone through the 10 zillionth draft and is about how great they are and why you would be stupid not to take them.' There is specific concern about how much their parents and friends help with the writing. One selector recalled how his daughter had wanted help for her boyfriend's youngest sister's personal statement. As a result, 'the personal statements have become much more undifferentiated, because people have been trained to write things'. Therefore, the personal statement has lost some weight.

Alumni interviews

> When I talk to students, I basically tell them there has to be strength in every area of the application. Obviously, the academic level is very high ... essays really need to be excellent ... the two teacher recommendations, and then also the guidance counsellor recommendation ... and then, of course, there is the optional interview. (Big Three admissions professional)

All the US institutions in this project made some use of alumni (see glossary) interviews as part of the admissions process. This was usually a strongly recommended part of the process for applicants. Interviews are conducted by an alumnus or alumna (see glossary) of the university who lives near the applicant and who is matched with a prospective student for having a conversation as this admissions professional explained:

> With alumni interviews, which our alumni, for free, as volunteers, interview all of our candidates all over the world. So we have alumni meetings when we go to Shanghai or when I was in Anchorage. And then those students become applicants, we give very basic legal information we can give, so that they can contact these applicants and meet them for an interview and then send us their feedback.

These alumni conversation notes are put into the application file as an additional piece of information.

The purpose of the interview is more social and it is to get to know the person rather than just an academic evaluation of their scholastic achievements as this Ivy admissions professional explains:

> It's a chatty interview, where it's not like being with the faculty member. They want to have an intellectual and a serious conversation, but they're not talking about their testing or their grades ... It's more, how does this student think? How ... what are they thinking about [this university]? ... generally, it might be something like the student would say, 'I'm really interested in film studies' and, ... the alumn would say, 'I love films as well, let's talk. Tell me some of the films you've seen recently'. And it's like, how they react to those kind of questions, to us, gives us the gauge, or another form of their curiosity, how they communicate, and being part of an experience that, again, is heavily based on the perspective you bring to the table. And if you're not able to communicate, or you're not able to offer or contribute to the conversation, then, what perspective are you bringing? ... in a philosophical way, we use the interview as another barometer to check everything else we're doing. Because sometimes students are fantastic on paper, they've spent a lot of time on their paper application, but they don't necessarily shine in the interview.

A liberal arts selector explained how at his institution, interviews were more of questions like: 'What questions do you have? Let me tell you about [this institution]'. Another selector said that they encouraged their alumni to think about 'what kind of room-mate would this person be?'

The matching of alumni and prospective students occurs by geographic location – this can sometimes mean that not all applicants can be matched with a previous graduate and be interviewed. In such cases, applicants were not disadvantaged in the admissions process as this admissions professional explains:

> We don't guarantee an interview, so a student isn't penalized if they don't have an interview. The only time I'd say a student is penalized – and we're pretty honest with this –, is … if they're offered an interview and they say, 'no'. I mean, what kind of interest level could there be?

Furthermore, when the admissions office had less information available about the school, for example, because they had never visited the school, alumni interviews could play a key role in providing information.

Finally, one respondent also commented on how the alumni interviews functioned as a way to keep alumni invested in their alma mater and up to date with developments. This in turn, could translate into continued attachment to the institution and could lead to donations. This observation again highlights how admissions at selective US institutions is part of a holistic approach towards various aspects of the university beyond the core admissions function.

A – perhaps unintended – effect of alumni interviews was recalled by one US admissions professional who had an alumni interview with a Big Three alumnus.

> One thing he said to me was here at [this Big Three Ivy], … 'we will make a class of 2,000 but we can take all the ones who didn't get in and make another class of 2,000 and it would be indistinguishable with the first one' … so I thought – why am I wasting my time with this place? And I ended up applying to [other selective institution] instead.

The quotation highlights the often small differences between some of those who are and those who are not admitted. Furthermore, alumni may have particular views about admission that may not always be completely reflective of the actual admissions practices and perhaps intended admissions message of their alma mater.

Academic interviews

In England, there is some occasional and limited use of non-academic interviews as part of the selection process. At Oxbridge, such interviews can happen around the same time as the subject-specific academic interviews for admission. Such general interviews never replace the academic interviews and many colleges do not have them.

Where general interviews happen, they tend to be conducted by a senior member of a college with an aim to assess aspects like 'general intellectual ability', 'personal organizational skills' – 'it is more about their personal, circumstances, and their ambitions, and their interests' (Oxbridge selector). Such general interviews did not seem to carry the same weight as academic interviews in the subject students sought to study.

Academic admissions interviews are discussed in more detail in Chapter 3 and throughout other discussions in this book.

Personal information

The application forms in both the United States and England ask for various pieces of personal information. This includes information like gender, date of birth, home address parental history of higher education and also ethnicity. Most of this is self-certified, for example, information on ethnicity. In England, universities have been alerted to the fact that applicants might not wish to disclose some information at the application stage; for example, regarding a disability and social class. One Russell Group university found that the number of applicants disclosing a disability increased if students were asked whether there was anything the university could do to support them after applicants had received a firm offer for a place. Other Russell Group universities now also ask for any additional disability disclosures after offers have been made.

Chapter summary

We're very open what we are looking for.

(Ivy League selector)

The application systems in the two countries ask for some similar information but there are also aspects of the two application systems that are specific to the national contexts. For example, questions about extra-curricular involvement addressed in US admissions essays have no equivalent in England. Furthermore, while self-declared information about ethnic origin is an important admissions consideration in the United States, such information is removed from application files in England. While the United States has non-academic alumni interviews, the focus in England is on academic interviews. A caveat to the description of the application details and files in this chapter is that the information here could be subject to change more rapidly than other aspects of the book.

As the different pieces that make up the application file come together, the process of selection begins. The next chapter describes how selectors decide which applicants will be given an opportunity to become newly enrolled undergraduates and which applications are unsuccessful.

6

Selecting

This chapter is about the nuts and bolts of how the selection process works for selective institutions in England and the United States. The descriptions offered here give a general overview of selection in action. However, there are differences between institutions in selection practices. The particular descriptions in this chapter are thus more indicative of the general processes rather than a comprehensive overview of all the nuances of different contexts.

Reading

We look first at the transcript, then we review the counselor's letter [school recommendation], the essay, the teacher recommendation, the extracurricular activities, the test scores and interview report and any supporting material. Applications are read by two readers and the files with the most promise go to committee for a discussion and a vote. We have a waitlist so we can enrol exactly the right size freshman class, some years we admit students off the waitlist, some years we don't. (Ivy selector)

In US institutions, completed application files are allocated to readers. The first 'reader' to receive a file is usually the one who is responsible for the geographic region from which an applicant applies. The file is then passed to a second reader. The reading process is explained by this Big Three selector:

Each of the admissions officers is responsible for a different geographic area … and I read all of the applications that come from those areas first. Then I will send off some of the applications to other readers … so there's two readers on a lot of the applications, and then those evaluations are sent back to me, and I will then decide on who I feel should be presented for a committee.

During peak reading time, around January and February for regular decision applicants, additional part-time readers might be hired by admissions offices to share the reading load:

> We have 20 admissions officers actually reading applications, and then we do have outside readers … six, maybe eight additional readers who help us with second reads. (Big Three selector)

The reason for having a specialist first reader is that this person knows the school and regional or national context of the applicant, and he or she has travelled to this area and liaised with high school counsellors. This first reader should also be familiar with the examination systems used by individual schools and, in the case of international applicants, the examination system in that country. This specialist regional reader is therefore in a position to put the applicant in context. As this Ivy selector elaborated:

> It's very important to put the students in the context of their environment. You can't expect the student to be going to [unknown state] High School to come out looking like someone who went to Exeter [elite private boarding school]. They just haven't had the same opportunities. So they still have to be really strong in their environment, and they still have to show us that they can do the work at [this Ivy], but you really can't compare.

When first readers do not already know the school context of an applicant very well, they do research on the school, which can include checking the location of the school on the internet as well as finding out more about the school curriculum and the number of students who continue into higher education. This process is described as 'very time intensive' and laborious.

Contextual knowledge is also important when reading the files of special interest applicants. Athletes or other special interest applicants might therefore be allocated to special readers or their applications are read by the area specialist and the specialist for a particular talent in order to, as one selector observed, 'create a level of integrity in our process, which is very important'. For athletes and other talents, the application file might also be read by the athletics department or music department or another relevant department that might have an interest in the file.

One Ivy League respondent stated that she reads between 1,000 and 1,300 applications as a first reader for the area she is responsible for and around an additional 1,600 as a second reader. She observed: 'It's a huge amount of work, yes. It's seven days a week, reading applications.'

The majority of applications are read by more than one reader. One Big Three selector described how there are very few instances where an application file might only be read by one person. This is when

> it's clear that they're not going to be able to handle the [this Ivy's] curriculum: The school reports are not backing up the students. It's very clear that those are not going to be the kind of students that we would accept [here].

In such clear-cut cases, there was no second read or committee decision and discussion prior to making the rejection decision. The opposite scenario, where an applicant was so stellar that this made the person a definite admit, also meant that their file did not need to go before a committee but would still need to be read by two readers:

> If it's going to be a sure admit with no discussion, it has to be read by two people, and it has to be given a certain evaluation … if both people feel that this is a sure admit, there's no discussion at committee; it just goes through as an admit. But two people have to agree on that, and it rarely, rarely happens.

This institution captured valuations on a numerical scale, and for an applicant to be a sure admit, both readers had to give the highest possible grade on this scale which was an exception.

Another Ivy selector commented on the sort of person who was admitted to every institution they applied to:

> If you're an Olympic gold medallist, and you're brilliant all around at everything. … I mean, why would you look at an Olympic gold medallist in our society and not value them?

Another Big Three selector reported how her institution had a report card on every applicant file where the reader marked key aspects of the application. These included the GPA as calculated by the university, whether the applicant had any alumni relation and also whether they came from a racial minority. In addition, 'readers comment on intellectual curiosity, love of learning, originality'. Another selector explained in an information session that

> when reading applications, we ask: 'Can you survive academically on campus? Can you survive in the classroom? Are you going to thrive here on campus? Are you going to have fun here?'

Therefore the vast majority of application files are read by two readers, and the files are then sent to a committee where applicants are further discussed and decisions are made.

In England, the online application through UCAS means that data arrives centrally in the admissions office. Universities increasingly have electronic systems for processing applications, although some prefer print-based processes. Furthermore the processing of the application form upon arrival can vary depending on whether the university operates a devolved, centralized, or mixed system. In a centralized system, applications are read and graded by full-time admissions professionals. As in the United States, there are some institutions that hire additional readers at this stage. Their role can be as straightforward as applying attainment cut-off points to the application files and making an offer to every applicant with higher achieved or predicted attainment than the cut-off. One Russell Group respondent reported that her university also graded personal statements and took those grades into account in an admissions formula. In another centralized system, the 'cut-off' point approach to admission is supplemented with a committee meeting approach for applicants who are flagged as coming from disadvantaged backgrounds. This means that those applicants cannot be 'automatically' rejected because they do not meet cut-off criteria. Instead, a small committee might look at whether there is potential in other parts of the application that might support a positive admissions decision. Sometimes, such borderline applicants might be called for an additional admissions interview.

There is also variation in practice in the decentralized, academic-led systems. One approach is to send applications to individual academic departments who have a designated person for admissions. This person might simply apply cut-off points of attainment the way some central admissions systems do. In such cases, the selector might even be a relatively junior academic who is given this role as part of his or her administrative or service duties.

In collegiate universities like Oxford and Cambridge, admissions is also led by departments and subject tutors, although college tutors also review the pool of admitted students for their college. This focus on the academic subject an applicant has applied to rather than the residential college is a change from how admissions used to be undertaken (e.g. Hughes 2013). Today, part of the aim of the admissions process is to admit applicants regardless of which college they applied to; in other words, each applicant should be admitted on the basis of his or her strength when compared with other applicants for the same subject, and not just compared to the ones who have applied to the same college.

Therefore, Oxbridge tends to have subject tutors with a university-wide remit for admission in their subject. These subject tutors, potentially in some joint procedure with individual college tutors, initially review all applicants for admission to their subject. This initial review establishes the interview shortlist.

At this point, selectors look primarily at the applicant's attainment record. In the event of exceptional circumstances or being flagged as disadvantage, invitation for interview will be sent to applicants who might not have otherwise been invited.

Where information from additional subject tests is already available, it can also be used to decide the shortlist for interview.

Committee

The US admissions committee is the place where individual applicants are discussed and votes are cast to admit or reject an applicant. It is also the place where classes are crafted.

The composition of the admissions committee is described here:

> The committee is made up of admissions officers, usually the dean or the director of admissions ... probably two associate directors – the next level down from dean or director. And then, sometimes faculty, deans of residential colleges. Usually a committee is made up of about five people, and there has to be a majority vote for someone to be admitted to [this Big Three Ivy]. (Selector, Big Three)

Committees have several admissions professionals in them and tend to operate on a 'one person, one vote' system. When academic faculty members are in committees, they also vote on the admissions decisions. Voting in committees tends to be done by region and by individual schools within regions. As this Big Three selector explains:

> So we look at all the cases at the same school at the same time. And we have this computerized docket, which has entered in, the GPAs, the test scores, and you can see if they're a legacy student. And then the kids with the highest GPAs appear at the top of the screen. So then we discuss, and then we vote.

By looking at the applicants from the same school simultaneously, committees are able to consider how applicants perform relative to others within the same context and therefore avoid rejecting an academically higher ranked applicant but admitting a lower ranked applicant from the same school.

Another Big Three selector explained the committee process in her institution:

> we have what's called a 'slate', and on the slate we have put down grades and scores, and we have certain evaluation systems that we use for the personal

aspects of the application. It's just a number system, basically, one through nine, and so they see all of that, and then we kind of go through the slate for each application, and then I will present some short summary on many of the applicants, and ... decisions are made based on those.

The committee stage is also the point at which discussion and debate as well as advocacy for individual students can occur. Readers might disagree on the merits of an applicant and make their case. One Big Three selector observed how the committee would 'actually go into the application and pull up different parts, the essays, all the teacher recommendations, or they'll want to look at the transcripts. ... And so we'll go into things in much more detail.'

While bespoke advocacy for an individual did not appear to be an overly frequent occurrence, individual selectors reported to occasionally push for applicants whose story had moved them. As one Ivy selector remarked 'I mean ... we're people. Like, we cry when we read certain essays.' He then went on to elaborate this point:

> What is easy to advocate for are the stories. The stories that are so compelling that you know everyone's going to feel that way about the student who's homeless, who has no parents around them, and yet they managed to score a 1,500 out of 1,600 on their SAT and they had straight A averages; and no one in their school even knows that they're homeless, except for their counsellor and the administrator. It's unbelievable stories like that. They're not the norm ... but you read a story like that and how can you not advocate? ... And sometimes they're not as clear-cut as that, because sometimes they had SATs that were below ours, and we do admit students who are way below our range; and we do that because we know they can be successful here, and we find this evidence in other ways.

Admission in such cases was not a simple reward for having overcome adversity and having achieved against the odds, but the admission of such unusual students was linked to their ability to act as a 'teaching tool' and to contribute to the student experience at the institution.

For highly selective admission in the United States, being described in committee as 'solid' equals a decision not to admit. Similarly, in admissions meetings observed in highly selective UK admissions, an applicant described in the deliberation as 'competent and nice' met a similar fate. Being nice, competent and solid is not enough in this competition for these highly competitive places at the most selective universities.

After deliberations, votes, and debates, the class of admitted students will take shape.

Deliberation

In the academic-led interview-based Oxbridge admissions systems, key admissions deliberations take place before and after the interviews. The deliberations before the interview create the shortlist of those who should be invited for interview. As a general tendency, even if one selector feels that an applicant should be interviewed, the applicant will be invited for the interview.

> We tend to have a view that if one of us feels strongly that someone should be interviewed, the others will go along with that because we respect each others' views. And that, that's actually a nice aspect of the whole process … we tend to respect each other's judgement, particularly in areas where it's closer to, the other person's expertise.

After the admissions interviews and the completion of interview report forms, the tutors who have interviewed the applicants for a particular subject in a college discuss their admissions choices among themselves. There is then also a discussion among the tutors for the same subject from different colleges.

Typically, academic selectors often agree on their clear-cut 'top choices' and those they definitely do not wish to admit. The largest amount of time is taken with the marginal decisions of those who could be admitted but there are not enough spaces to admit all of them. Those are the most difficult decisions to call. In one Oxbridge college admissions meeting observed for this book, the decision came down to filling the final two places from four of the remaining potential applicants. The three academic selectors agreed that 'we are in impossible territory, really' and that filling those final spots was 'an inexact science' where 'you cannot put a sheet of bread paper between' the remaining serious contestants.

Fortunately, in this particular case, selectors were reasonably confident that they would be able to place the two applicants they did not take for their college elsewhere in the collegiate university. The decision to reject a student for a place at the particular college would thus not necessarily mean that the student would not gain a place at the university. This is where the 'intercollegiate meeting' of subject tutors from different colleges comes in.

The intercollegiate meeting is an opportunity for tutors to compare notes on all applicants and to send strong applicants they could not offer a place to in their own college for consideration at other colleges. Conversely, college tutors also came to the meeting with a view of finding applicants they could offer an additional interview to from other colleges and who might then be admitted to any of their remaining places. This process is informally known as 'exporting' (sending applicants to other colleges) and 'importing' (receiving applicants from other colleges).

There has been a general move towards removing any college information from application forms, and to rank all applicants for a particular subject consistently before college decisions are confirmed. This is called 'college-blind' selection. As one Oxbridge selector remarked: 'It's a big improvement to what happened before … when people were inclined to take their own weaker first choice candidates, rather than go out looking for better ones (because) doing so was so laborious and so uncertain. I think it has done … quite a lot, to reduce the element of lottery in the admissions process.'

Still, there can be importing and exporting of applicants from other colleges. This negotiation process can consist of sometimes passionate 'pitches' as this example from a meeting shows. One college tutor remarked on an applicant that she had been the 'best candidate on paper' and that all was perfect except that one of the three college tutors 'didn't want her', so it would be a 'crime if she didn't get a place – I'd have had her.' Other pitches could be less enthusiastic, for example, stating that the candidate had a solid academic record and hence deserved another chance to be interviewed but that none of the tutors had been impressed with the interview performances. Yet in another case, a tutor wished to have the opinion from a colleague in a different college as the candidate had been so nervous during interview that they didn't get much out of the applicant. This was recommended by the chair as a good use of the opportunity to have additional interviews.

Some deliberations can enter difficult territories and several respondents remarked privately that they thought there was still room for further improvement to the current system. For example, students wishing to study at joint schools, that is, in two departments, need to be admitted by both departments. Examples include students wishing to study philosophy and physics or modern languages and law. This contrasts with 'single honours' applicants who only need to be admitted by one department. This can lead to tensions when one department is keen on an applicant and the other department is not. In one intercollegiate meeting, a college was asked to admit a single honours applicant based on their overall ranking among all applicants and wished to challenge this decision as they were much keener on an applicant who had applied for joint honours but who had not been admitted by the other joint school. Indeed, one college tutor suggested calling the applicant who had applied for joint honours to ask whether he would accept a place for a single honours programme. However, the intercollegiate meeting vetoed this suggestion as it was not within their standard admissions procedures to ask applicants whether they would change the degree subject they had applied for, indeed, such changes may need to come formally through UCAS. As a twist in this story, this applicant had actually applied for single honours in the previous admissions round but had not been successful, and then had reapplied in the current year for a joint honours programme. In the end, this applicant was rejected and the college had to take the – in their opinion lower-ranking – single-honours applicant. The incident highlights some element of fluctuation in candidate quality over time as well as an element of luck in the selection process.

Incidents like this may explain why one selector reflected on the admissions process thus:

> You walk away really feeling quite sad for some of them. Because you know, you are making decisions which affect their lives. (Oxbridge selector)

Shaping the class

> You look at athletes, you look at legacies, you look at minorities, you look at building projects. You may have to put people back in as well as taking them out. (Ivy selector)

At the end of the initial committee stage, US universities have a pool of admitted students. But 'what always happens is, we admit too many students. So there's a round of what they call pull-backs, and they get pulled out' (Big Three selector). At this stage, universities might have too many admitted students, but they might not have all the students in the pool who they wish to have in this new class. Thus, some students might still be fished out from the pool of 'not admitted' students and are offered to join the newly crafted class after all.

As the admitted class is beginning to take shape, institutions keep a close eye to 'run any statistics you can think of' (Ivy selector) such as the GPA, SAT scores, the number of legacies and athletes, and also the number of admitted students from different racial groups. The process of selectively 'pulling and adding' students fine-tunes the overall profile of the class. It is at this stage that 'group characteristics' like belonging to a certain ethnic or geographic group or having a certain talent are considered more important than individual GPAs and test scores.

An example of adding students to the pool of admitted students is described by this Big Three selector: 'What always happens is, we never have enough black

or Hispanic students, so then we have to go back into the pool, like try bring
more of those kids in.'

Several selectors described the process of pulling students as the 'least
favourite' aspect of the admissions role. This process involved going through
the list of admitted students and taking some out who were currently among the
newly admitted class.

One liberal arts selector described how shaping the class worked at his
institution when they have to remove applicants from the admitted pool. He
first explained how there were a range of applicants he could not remove:

> If you're a legacy, if you're a recruited athlete or if you're a student of color that
> has the biggest advantage at least where I work –you are 'hooked'. Or if you're
> from Wyoming State where we don't get kids from.

This sentiment was echoed by a Big Three selector, although this respondent
also added 'art students' alongside the athletes, students of colour and legacies as
being protected from being pulled from the admitted class.

The liberal arts college selector from the previous quotation went on to
explain how he thought his institution had a particularly limited number of
places for 'unhooked' applicants compared with some of the bigger universities
and colleges:

> The thing with the liberal arts schools is that we are so much smaller than the
> big universities, the number of spots that get taken up by the students of color
> you need, the athletes you want … (you need the same amount of kids for the
> basketball team at a school with 1,000 students versus a school that has 10,000
> students) …, legacies – then there are only this many spots for unhooked kids.

The only applicants this liberal arts selector could remove at this stage were
the 'unhooked' applicants who were not legacies, white, and not athletes, and
not from an unusual geographic location. In his experience, these 'unhooked'
applicants 'are the white kids from New Jersey' who were perfectly admissible,
but there were too many of them and therefore, some were pulled from the
admitted class – 'that's always the hardest thing when you work in admissions
and have to do that'.

At this liberal arts college, selectors also had perhaps more individual
discretion than selectors at the Ivy League institution to 'protect kids'. This
selector could exercise discretion to not pull a kid he really liked 'even if it means
I have to pull a kid who is better than them academically, but it is because they
are stellar for some reason … and I say I've got to have this kid, I don't want to

pull them, I want them to be at [this liberal arts college] so I'll pull somebody else instead of him'.

None of the other respondents in this study reported being able to individually pull applicants from the pool. Such decisions were generally reached through further committee meetings, which this Ivy selector reflects: 'Looking at different applications again … we might come back to a file two or three times with different committees'. The principle of protecting 'hooked' and pulling 'unhooked' applicants still applied.

Overall, a Big Three respondent remarked: 'The process is more art than science, it is not formulaic, all we can promise is to give full attention to each application' and another Ivy League selector observed how 'decisions are more scientific than just dropping a pile but so many factors go into decisions that individual results can seem somewhat unpredictable to parents, families, and kids'. Because so many factors play a role in the crafting of a US selective university incoming class, it can be difficult to predict the admission fortunes of many applicants who are competitive but perhaps not absolutely outstanding or hooked in a particular way.

In England, there is no comparable process of 'shaping the class' in terms of the overall class characteristics, although the idea is periodically considered in some public debates such as the 2004 Schwartz report (Admissions to Higher Education Steering Group 2004). In academic-led system, the closest that happens is admissions professionals or academics with strategic remit for admission questioning colleagues on particular admissions statistics. A typical example here would be a team of selectors having to justify why they have only selected five men or five private school applicants for a subject rather than a mixed male–female or private–state school-educated cohort. There are also various limitations to the number of students who can enrol for a subject and these numbers will be monitored centrally. Where admissions tests are used, there is also monitoring and reviewing as to whether there are systematic differences in performance for male and female applicants and applicants educated in different schools. But there is no overall shaping of a class the way it is observed in the United States.

Offers

English admissions offers are either 'conditional' or 'unconditional' offers. Generally all applicants whose final secondary school performance is not known receive conditional offers. This means that the applicants' offers of a place are under the condition that they attain certain grades in their school-leaving examinations. For Russell Group universities, such offers typically range from A*AA to AAB. An increasing number of universities have some contextualization of offers. This means that some offers could be slightly lower than the standard offer if applicants apply from particular disadvantaged schools or neighbourhood contexts. Every year, there are also some applicants who apply to universities when they already know their grades, for example, because they have taken a year out since finishing secondary school. For such cases, the school-leaving grades of the applicants are already known, these applicants apply with confirmed rather than predicted grades and are thus 'post-qualification applicants'. There is some evidence that selectors like the certainty of knowing the grades of applicants and that this increases the chance of gaining admission. Furthermore, these students receive 'unconditional offers' if they are offered a place, meaning that the offer is not contingent on further attainment.

The final school-leaving results in England are announced in mid-August. This is the time during which offers for university places are confirmed. If applicants achieve or exceed the grades of their conditional offer, they can accept the offer for their place for study, with degree courses starting usually within six to eight weeks after school results are known. But every year, there are also students who do not perform as highly as they were predicted to; that is, they are applicants who 'miss' their grades as specified in their conditional offer. For the vast majority of applicants, this means they cannot take up their first-choice offer place, but the UCAS system allows applicants to hold a second offer place as an 'insurance offer'. Often, students can enrol at their 'insurance' university choice if they do not make their first choice, or if unsuccessful they can enter the UCAS Clearing process which matches applicants with any remaining unfilled university places.

Contextualization can also come into play when students 'miss their offer grades'. Here, there is sometimes discretion to still admit students who have done less well than their predicted grades if their performance is still stellar in the context of their school. Individual extenuating circumstances such as illness can also be taken into account. Different universities can have different approaches and tend to consider 'dropping' offer grades and admitting students who had not achieved their conditional offer grades on a case-by-case basis. For students who 'exceed' their offer conditions and expected grades, there is a small time-window when they can 'adjust'; this means they can try to gain admission to a course that requires higher entry grades than the course or university for which the applicant holds an offer.

An Oxbridge respondent remembered some incidents where students had dropped their grades:

> The student seemed to have very good interview grades and actually did brilliantly – actually she got one of the second highest scores nationally in the [national admissions test for this subject] – but she didn't get her 3As – in fact, she ended up getting an ABC! … that was very surprising. But she wrote a letter asking us to think again, and she had also done the US SATs and she had done very well. But, no, we didn't take her. Nor for the other two who were English applicants who also didn't make their AAA offer.

While the United States also operates a pre-qualification system, offers for places are definite and not impacted by the actual grades students achieve in their final year of school. This is bearing in mind that SAT and other test results are already known at the point at which universities make admissions decisions.

Yield

Chapter 2 introduced the idea of 'yield', that is, how many applicants to a particular university take up their offer for a place. At Oxbridge, yield is higher than 9 in 10, almost everyone who is offered a place will take it up. Indeed, the reason even Oxbridge make marginally more offers than they can enrol is that a certain percentage of students will not make their conditional offer. However, other English universities and US institutions systematically admit more students than they have places available. This is because some admitted students prefer taking up a place at a different institution. Indeed, US students are encouraged to apply for a 'competitive', a 'reach' and a 'safety' university based on how challenging it is likely to be for them to gain admission. The idea is that applicants will tend to accept the offer at the highest ranking institution that admits them. Some applicants will be admitted to all universities they apply to, some will not be admitted to the 'competitive' ones but might be admitted to their 'reach' university and should be admitted to their 'safety' university. Many applicants thus have a choice of where they wish to go to university. The sorts of US universities included in this book have some of the highest yields in the United States, but even Harvard, which has the highest yield, loses around 1 in 5 applicants to other universities.

In the United States and English Russell Group universities, there is a history and experience of managing student numbers. Financial aid offers as well as taster weekends and online connections with existing students can be used to entice admitted students to accept their places. Institutions are keenly aware of who their 'crossover' or 'peer competitor' institutions are. These are institutions that are often similar in prestige and rank and that compete for the same applicants. If the institution is slightly higher ranked, there might be crossover between their marginal admitted students and the strongest students admitted by a slightly lower-ranking institution. A respondent from a university ranked just below the Ivy League explained how:

> A student who is a top academic student, that is getting into all these [crossover] institutions, we're still losing the majority of those students that are probably in the top half or top 1 per cent of our pool to our cross-over schools. I think maybe because of academic reputation.

This private university had developed a special Presidents Scholars Program for around fifteen newly enrolled students per year aimed at trying to matriculate exceptional students. Unlike their large-scale financial aid scheme based on need, this scheme was a way to try and entice students away from – usually slightly higher ranked – crossover institutions. However, this respondent also noted that his institutions still needed to make around thirty of those scholarship offers to yield fifteen fully funded students because for half of the offer holders, even a full scholarship did not swing their enrolment decision in favour of this university.

Another selector from an Ivy League Institution also elaborated on how universities might lure applicants away from competitor institutions.

> See, with the American system of higher education, what's so brilliant about it is, [liberal arts college] can woo someone, who might go to [Ivy League], but [liberal arts college] gives them a full scholarship, based on merit, not based on financial need. Whereas [Ivy League] would only give financial need. So, [Liberal Arts College] can enrol someone who is a powerhouse, and then that brings up the quality of their education.

The respondent thought it was a virtue of the US system that schools could compete for students and 'become hot', whereas the less competitive English system meant that institutions were stuck in 'a caste system of quality'. This observation might be less true in 2014 than it was even two years ago, and the same respondent also acknowledged later in the conversation that universities in the UK could 'get hot': 'St Andrew's, I'm sure, got hot after Prince William went there.'

Another Ivy respondent explained how an example of the sort of applicant who would likely benefit from enhanced offers for a place could be a Hispanic, Latino, African American or Native American student who had done well in standardized tests and at school. Because students from those ethnic groups tended to score lower on the test than whites or Asians, the high scorers were particularly sought after by universities wishing to enrol an ethnically diverse student body.

Until relatively recently, English universities have not openly competed for students by offering different scholarships or other incentives for going to a particular university. Since the introduction of increased tuition fees, this scenario is now slowly changing. In 2013, the University of Birmingham offered 'unconditional offers' to applicants to a selected number of courses if they made Birmingham their first choice. Other English institutions are offering accommodation discounts and bursaries for students from poorer families. The impact of scholarships and bursaries on student choice in England is not yet fully understood. Moreover, in contrast to the United States where financial aid packages are sent alongside admissions offers, often, students in England do not find out whether they are eligible for even a small needs-based bursary until they have enrolled. It is thus fair to note that universities' competition for students through financial aid packages in England is in its infancy as compared to the competition for some select students in the United States.

At the end of the selection and admissions process, the final statistics of the enrolled class in the United States are taking shape. Selectors will look at the average GPA of the incoming students and the number of those who had perfect GPAs, as well as their test scores, the range of high schools, US states and international countries represented and the sporting racial and legacy diversity of the class. Information regarding the last three categories is not always published in institutional reports. Institutions might also report some more unusual statistics like how many of the incoming students had started their own business, had volunteered in particular areas, had previously held student government offices in their schools and had learnt to play a musical instrument.

In England, universities publish information about their newly enrolled students with regard to what type of school they attended, what percentage came from neighbourhoods with a low participation in higher education as well as some information on the gender and ethnic profile of new students. Sometimes, such statistics can be found on universities' websites, such information is also centrally collated by the Higher Education Statistical Agency. There is no systematic information available concerning the extra-curricular activities, volunteering or musical talents of new higher education students akin to the way universities showcase such information in the United States.

Chapter summary

The evaluation process for admission at highly selective universities in the United States considers a broad range of criteria as part of the individualized review of every application. In England, there are some key differences between academic- and professional-led evaluation systems, especially when academic systems involve interviews. Some professional-led admissions systems might base their decision whether or not to offer a place to an applicant relatively straightforwardly on prior and predicted attainment, where available, results from subject-specific admissions tests and some contextual consideration of such attainment. Academic interview-led systems have the added element of considering interview performance and having often extended deliberations among academics regarding the admissions decisions.

Table 8 summarizes the similarities and differences in the selection process among the competitive American and English universities described in this book. The comparison shows that some dimensions are comparable between the two countries. Both countries evaluate academic accomplishments, the school context, extenuating circumstances, recommendation letters, geographic considerations (either for geographic diversity or as a proxy for disadvantage) and other considerations. In addition, US selectors also value students' characteristics and attributes and extra-curricular involvement and leadership.

With those features of the selection process in mind, the next chapter investigates which challenges selectors face in the selection process and to what extent these are shared among the United States and the English selectors.

Table 8 Similarities and differences in what US and English universities are looking for in admission

US	England
Academic achievement, quality and potential	
Cumulative GPA	GCSE attainment
Pattern of grade improvement during high school	Achieved/predicted A-level or equivalent attainment
Quality of curriculum	Quality of curriculum
Solid college-prep curriculum (four years in each subject)	
Strength of senior year courses	
Core (required) curriculum/courses beyond core curriculum	
Advanced Placement, IB and honours/college courses while in High School	
Test scores (SAT I and II, ACT, AP, etc.)	Performance on subject-specific admissions tests
Internships in area of academic interest	
Participation in enrichment or outreach programmes	Part of outreach programme or partnership school
Class rank	Performance above the school average
	Interview
Educational environment//Contextual data relating to school	
Strength of curriculum (inc. availability of AP, IB, honours)	
Average SAT I and/or ACT scores	GCSE score profile and/or AS score profile
Percentage attending four-year colleges	Higher education transition rates
Competitive grading system in high school	
Competitiveness of class	Performance of school mapped against national performance
Academically disadvantaged school	
Extenuating circumstances	
Overcoming personal adversity/unusual hardships	'In care'
Language spoken at home/ESL	Disability (for support purposes and to avoid discrimination)
Frequent moves/many different schools	Refugee status (one example)

(Continued)

Table 8 Continued

US	England
Recommendation letters	
Counsellor & teacher recommendations	Usually only considered as deselection tool if highlight something negative
Character	
Civic and cultural awareness/Diverse perspective/Tolerance	
Commitment	
Intellectual independence/Enthusiasm for learning/Risk taking	
Creativity/Artistic talent	
Concern for others/Community	
Motivation/Determination/Grit/Effort/Initiative/Persistence/Tenacity	
Leadership potential/Maturity/Responsibility	Consideration of specific characteristics may be given for particular courses or universities when highlighted in the personal statement or reference
Geographic considerations	**Geographic proxies for disadvantage**
In-State resident	Postcode
Economically disadvantaged region	POLAR or ACORN for UK applicants
From school with few or no previous applicants	HE transition rates of area
Other considerations	
Demonstrated interest in college/good match	In a handful of exceptions annually: Organ scholarships at Oxford and Cambridge
Strong personal statement	Personal statement usually only considered as deselection tool if exceptionally grammatically incorrect
Evaluative measures	
Academic recognition and awards	
Artistic talent	

Table 8 Continued

US	England
Depth in one or more academic areas related to student interests	
Evidence of academic passion	Interest in/passion for academic subject
Grasp of world events	
Independent academic research	
Intellectual curiosity	
Writing quality – content, style, originality, risk taking	
Characteristics and attributes	
Personal background	
Alumni connection	
Cultural awareness/experiences	
First generation to go to college from family	First generation to go to university
Low-economic family background	Low-economic family background
Under represented minority	
Personal disadvantage	
Professional diversity	
Faculty/staff connection	
Military veteran/Peace Corps, America Corps, etc.	
Extra-curricular activities, service and leadership	
Awards and honours (athletic, artistic, musical, civic)	
Quality and depth of involvement	
Leadership	
Community service	
Impact student's involvement had on school and/ or community	
Scholarship athlete	
Work experience	

Source: US list based on Spencer 2011.

7

Challenges in Decision-Making

Selectors on both sides of the Atlantic face some shared challenges in decision-making. These challenges occur, regardless of whether it is professional full-time staff doing the selecting or academics or whether the aim is to find the best academic students or those with the highest potential to achieve a thick fifty-year reunion contribution. This chapter discusses the challenges of not being selective enough, drawing lines where there are none, the art of deselection, the challenge of incommensurability and prediction in the context of uncertainty and achieving procedural fairness while complying with legal and governance requirements.

Not selective enough

The first challenge in selection is perhaps a somewhat counter-intuitive one: even the most sought-after universities are admitting more students than all selectors think are their first and preferred choice of new undergraduates.

In both the English and the US systems, every year there are some students who will be admitted wherever they apply. For the United States, such a student could be an academically solid Olympic gold medallists from a US state that does not send many students out of state, a student of colour with good grades who is also a recruited blue-chip athlete or a concert-level oboe player who has already performed in Carnegie Hall and also dialled toll-free (see page 53) on their SATs: 'If you are a student of colour and you are from Wyoming you will get into every college you apply to' (liberal arts selector).

In England, the 'sure admits' may have up to five offers to choose from. They are those who have achieved a string of ten to fifteen A*s in their GCSEs, they are predicted four A*s in their academically rigorous and relevant A-level subjects, and their performance is well above average within their school context. If applicable, these students have also scored in the top percentile of any additional subject-specific tests and have given thoughtful and mature responses to interview questions showing depth of knowledge and genuine passion for their subject that puts them head and shoulders above other interviewed applicants.

In these rare cases, the decision to admit is clear-cut. But selection does not stop at this point, although there was one academic Oxbridge selector who contemplated the idea: 'one should maybe think about reducing the number of places. Otherwise one risks a kind of dilution, with the ... [Oxbridge] brand of education really' whereas other selectors realistically evaluated that 'money follows the students' and that admitting more students than the exceptionally few was necessary for universities to survive. But despite the high rejection rates of selective institutions, a perhaps counter-intuitive observation is that selection is arguably not selective enough because the admissions process continues to admit more students after the stellar exceptional students have been offered places. This then leads to the next challenge: selecting between very similar applicants.

Drawing lines where there are none

An Oxbridge selector explained the challenge of not being selective enough and then, in his words, drawing lines where there are none as follows:

> We are trying, basically, to draw a distinction where no distinction exists. (starts drawing normal distribution on piece of paper). We got a normal distribution ... of the people we interview. Now, clearly, everybody agrees that these people they are terrific (points to the outliers on his sheet of paper), ... and we are trying to draw a line there (shows on piece of paper line between the outliers – where he said one should stop – and the peak of a normal curve) ... and, you can't do it. In admitting the marginal applicants we are basically trying to differentiate between people on the normal curve and you can't do it.

The admissions challenge here is to find those applicants who will make up the group of admitted students who are not the sure admits. These students need to be found from a large pool of applicants who have a chance of being admitted. They are the applicants who are left in the pool of eligible contestants for a place after some applicants have been clearly admitted because they are so stellar and after other applicants have been rejected because they are without a realistic chance of getting an offer – usually because their academic grades are too low.

This challenge was shared with selectors across the Atlantic where an Ivy League selector observed how, with marginal applicants, decisions 'are not clear cut, there is no right or wrong answer'.

A more optimistic take on this challenge – and perhaps contrary to the Oxbridge observation above – was voiced by an Ivy League selector who explained how his institution needed other students to create a class out of stellar individuals. More specifically, he was looking for 'glue kids, the students who are holding it all together'. These glue kids could have a range of possible characteristics; they might be all-rounders who created campus life through their participation, engagement, volunteering and academic accomplishments. Other admitted students might be a little lopsided with a single hook – for example, their legacy status or athletic powers.

The applicants in the middle of the distribution, those who may or may not be admitted, take up the majority of the discussion time in committees on both sides of the Atlantic. They are the ones that committees might come back to again and again and are the ones who might get an additional interview at Oxbridge to help the decision-making process. These marginal applicants may have been deemed worthy of a place at some stage in the process. Or – more seldom – they may have been in the pool for rejection letters and been reinstated at a later stage in the admissions process following some holistic review of how the class of admitted students is shaping up in the United States. This could be the case to fine-tune, for example, regional, racial, athletic or other attributes sought after in the collective profile of the admitted class.

The art of deselection

Another way to think about the challenge of drawing lines where there are none could be called the 'de-selection' challenge. Admission then is about applicants staying in the competition for a place through the various iterations of an admissions process and having passed through hurdles where others fail. A Big Three selector reflected that for someone not to be admitted '99 per cent of the time it isn't that there is anything wrong with that person, but simply that there are better ones in the competition'. This was echoed by the dean of admission at another highly selective US institution who noted that 'low scores are more keeping you out than high scores are getting you in'. Admission then is as much the art of deselection as of selection; it is the process of seeing which applicants an institution can justify not to admit.

Selection and deselection happen throughout the admissions process. For example, in the Oxbridge admissions processes that require an interview, some 'de-summoning' occurs prior to this interview stage. At this stage, some applicants are not invited for an interview. This then excludes those applicants from further consideration for a place. An Oxbridge selector explained how this would happen if 'we really just don't think that person has got a chance, it is not fair to bring them up [for interview]'. Being invited to interview means staying in the competition. While the outcome is still uncertain, the applicant has 'survived' one deselection hurdle and has a continued chance to secure a place.

Deselection continues right to the final stages of the admissions process. In US committee meetings, when the class of admitted students is taking shape, final adjustments of balancing athletic, regional, academic and other special interests are made to decide on the last spots in the class, this process is described as 'pulling kids' from the pool. In Oxbridge subject meetings, the final number of places is allocated. In those final allocation meetings, there can be applicants who are right at the borderline. In one iteration, they are in the pool of admitted students. In the next iteration, they might be out.

To remind ourselves, the English admissions process is all about academic attainment and potential, so the strategies employed by decision-makers try to find some academic tiebreaker. One Oxbridge selector described how, faced with a situation where there was only one spot left for her subject but several applicants, she and her colleagues put all the remaining application forms in front of them. This was the stage at which someone with a B in GCSE art might be deselected from the pool, not because of concern that the student would not thrive in the course, but because there were other applicants who only had As and A* grades. At this stage, a student with an A rather than A* grade in mathematics might also have to go. In other words, the person with the best GCSEs, everything else being equal, might secure the last place.

Alternatively, selectors might pay particularly close attention to the school context of an applicant. Everything else being equal, the same A* grade – or potentially even an A grade compared with an A* grade – achieved in a less good school can be given more weight and judged as a greater accomplishment than the same or perhaps even slightly higher grade achieved in a high-performing school.

Incommensurability, relational standards and luck

Another challenge is 'incommensurability'. This challenge, encountered in both the United States and England, entails that different parts of an application do not all point in the same direction. One applicant might have a great attainment record but a less strong personal statement, another applicant has a strong personal statement and strong references but has not done well on a test. Selectors are then comparing applicants who have scored highly on some parts of the application or institutional priorities but less highly on other aspects. So, how can applicants be compared when they have shown different strengths and weaknesses in different parts of the application?

Since none of the most highly selective English or US processes use a formula for admission, professional judgement has to come into deciding the relative emphasis of different elements of the application. Such academic freedom and judgement is enshrined in English law in the Higher Education Act 2004. Moreover, discussions concerning the incommensurability of different information can also be apparent when selectors try to understand just one piece of the application file. This was explained by an Oxbridge selector who had faced challenges when interpreting the results of an additional entrance test:

> So the marks [of an admissions test] were really bizarre. You get a brilliant student who had done a fantastic answer to one question in the exam but hadn't finished the third (question) so had a very low mark. And, so we were sitting there thinking, well that is ridiculous because this student is obviously very good. And then you get into a stupid conversation is what is really important the fact that they can finish or is what is really important the fact that they can shine in the work that they do.

The challenge in this example was to not to simply consider results at 'face value' but also to think about how this test result had been achieved and what one great answer but an incomplete test meant in relation to the admissions criteria. The considerations here also highlight how procedural fairness (everyone is marked against the same matrix) and discussions of substantive fairness can sometimes diverge. Indeed, we shall return to the discussion of procedural fairness later in this chapter.

An example of incommensurability across different attainment measures was observed in an Oxbridge admissions meeting. Here, the variations in performance of one applicant with a perfect score on her school-leaving examination was discussed. The applicant had undertaken the International

Baccalaureate, a well-respected school-leaving qualification, and her perfect score was understood as a significant and stellar accomplishment by selectors. However, this applicant had scored rather low on an additional admissions test. The incommensurability challenge is the difficulty in making sense of two competing pieces of information, a high and a low score. The selectors sought to solve this challenge by considering the following question: 'Are the final year examinations at [this institution] more like the International Baccalaureate or more like the admissions test?' In other words, is the high score on her school examinations or the low score on her admissions test going to be closely related to how this student will perform at university? Is this applicant likely to be a high achiever (predicted by her IB score) or someone who scrapes by at university (suggested by her test score)?[1]

In the United States, one Ivy League selector recalled how the final fine-tuning of the class led to detailed considerations of two applicants with a similar academic profile, where one applicant was from an under-represented state within the United States and another one playing an instrument in demand for the orchestra. The question was whether potential for the orchestra or potential to meet enrolment aims by geography should carry greater weight in deciding which of the two should be offered one of the final places in their admitted class.

The last example also illustrates how admissions standards and decisions are relational, in other words, the decision to admit or not to admit a particular applicant is often linked directly to the strength of claim another applicant makes for a place for undergraduate study. Selectors in both England and the United States were aware of this as exemplified by these two quotations:

> Admission to Ivies can be a bit like the lottery and fluctuate from year to year. (Ivy selector)

> Last year was a very strong year. Lots of very good people were disappointed. And this is where myths arise about [Oxbridge]. Because one year … a school sends a brilliant candidate to [this institution] and they get rejected. And another year they would have been accepted … but what can you do … it is very sad … when people don't get in and they have got every chance of being good enough. But there are just people who had been better. (Oxbridge selector)

How good an applicant is in a particular year is then partly related to how good other applicants are. This means that, in the margins of admissions processes, there is an element of luck as well as judgement in getting into a selective university. Some of this luck relates to who else has applied to the institution, or in the English case, to a particular subject at an institution in that particular year. One Oxbridge selector recalled how he and his colleague had reflected on the first admissions interview of the season and 'had thought that first applicant had not been very good' when they had tried to compare this person with the applicants from the previous year. However 'when we saw the other candidates, the first person actually looked good in comparison to them'. The opposite instance was recalled by another Oxbridge selector who remembered writing a letter to an applicant who had just missed out on a place which stated 'we would have loved to have taken you but we couldn't this year because of our other applicants.' For marginal applicants, being admitted or not can simply depend on the strength of the competition in a particular year.

Another Oxbridge selector explained how the fluctuation of quality in applicants year on year made it 'very difficult to give someone an absolute score' for the interview. He went on to explain how he therefore ranked applicants not on a numerical score but in relation to each other, even though at the end of the process he had to then return some numerical scores for book-keeping:

> The easy thing is, you can usually put people in a rank order, you compare them relative to each other. So what I'll do is, … I'll take the first person and I'll lay the sheet down and then when the second person comes up beside well I'll ask: 'is this person better or worse than the other one?' and I'll put them on top or underneath, and I just keep doing that. And by the time the interview process is done, I have a stack of papers with a rough rank order of who I thought was top and who I thought was the worst.

Selectors on both sides of the Atlantic were aware of the consequences of not admitting a student who was outstanding in their local context but not in the national competition. An Ivy selector explained this as the 'small pond big frog phenomenon' whereas the English colleagues preferred using the metaphor of big fish in the proverbial small pond. In either case, teachers, parents, and where applicable, counsellors see a student who is the best in the local context of their school but when they apply to a leading national university, these applicants are no longer the best. Moreover, these students are also increasingly competing against international applicants and their claims for admission. Institutions went to some length to try and admit those big frogs and fishes but not all of these stellar local students were admitted.

Incommensurability could also occur with regard to selectors not agreeing on their reading of an application file or the interview performance of an applicant. In an Oxbridge selection scenario, two academic selectors had a robust disagreement about an applicant and decided to send the person for a third interview as they could not agree on a decision regarding the applicant's interview performance. One of the people involved in this incident recalled: 'I thought the student was excellent … but she [my co-interviewer] really didn't like him. And we had some quite heated exchanges.' The committee process in the United States is designed to allow for collective decisions in cases where there are different readings of the same application file.

Another challenge in decision-making is luck with regard to who happens to do the selecting. While most decisions discussed in this book were arrived by committee and deliberations, certainly in the Ivy League and Oxbridge institutions, some other selective institutions have perhaps less resources at their disposal and some decisions might face less scrutiny from committees. One liberal arts college selector who was relatively new to his role reflected:

> It's one of those things, it amazes me sometimes that people spend so much time on their applications but what makes such a difference is what person you get that is reading their file. That 23-year-old who is going to be reading your essay what do they think of that? If they really connect with what you are saying that can make all the difference for you … It's the same thing also doing interviews because I remember when I was a student doing interviews I had a kid that I really liked but I knew one of my fellow senior interns … if they had interviewed this student they wouldn't have liked them … I'm now writing an evaluation that can make all the difference to whether they get in or not but it's all about who I was and whether I conducted their interview or the next person did. That is something that sort of boggles the mind and how much of a difference that can really make.

While perhaps other selectors would highlight the safeguards in place to mitigate against an interview making all the difference, and English selectors would highlight safeguards against selecting people one likes in general, the observation that there is a remaining element of luck in the selection process seems real.

Uncertainty and evidence

> *We are in the future business. We want to predict how this kid is doing in 4 years, in 10 years, life.*
>
> (Big Three selector)

> *I mean, it is a very difficult – it is crystal ball glazing – you are really looking into a crystal balls whether these people are the best people.*
>
> (Oxbridge selector)

Selectors in both the United States and England face the challenge of predicting the future based on information about past accomplishments and potential. In order to decrease risk and increase good decisions that correctly predict those who will do well, institutions on both sides of the Atlantic are 'data-hungry organizations' (Russell Group selector), 'obsessed with information' (Ivy League selector) and study the factors that are associated with success in degrees (England and the United States) and in the United States, also the factors that are associated with 'success in life', however defined.

Institutions and national bodies invest into significant research to find out how students do in higher education and in their particular institutions and what factors are predictive of success. A non-exhaustive list of examples of institutional research projects included an investigation of the added value of interview scores for admission (Oxbridge), the impact of 'flagging' disadvantaged applicants for special consideration (Russell Group), monitoring of intake from applicants from the poorest neighbourhoods in the country (Russell Group); investigations of the relationship between ethnicity and degree performance (Russell Group and England-wide research); a project looking at the added value of counsellor recommendation (Big Three Ivy League); an investigation of who was 'successful and happy' at university (Ivy League) a project that modelled who would benefit from changes to financial aid allocation (Ivy League); the relationship between financial aid and dropout (Big Three Ivy and a cross-institution project in England commissioned by the Office for Fair Access); a project looking at the profile of students using the careers service (Russell Group) and projects looking at type of employment or further study after university (both US and UK).

When selectors had a choice between admitting an applicant for whom they had little predictors of university success compared with one where they could predict success, selectors preferred the known to the unknown. For example, during an Oxbridge admissions meeting, an applicant who had been home-schooled all his life was discussed. The question was how this applicant would fit into the structure of institutional and residential life of a college and university environment. The student was ultimately not admitted as this seemed like a 'risky choice' and there was little to go on that would predict his behaviour at university. When I asked an Ivy League selector how this student would have fared in his admissions process he said, 'we admit some home-schooled applicants every year. But we are also cautious.' The Ivy selector could relate to the concerns his English counterparts had voiced about this being a risky choice and the desire to have some evidence to help making decisions especially for the majority of applicants who are neither outstanding nor poor and where small differences mattered.

Potential risk-averse behaviour was also noted in relation to the accountability an admissions office owes to the institution when students fail. Here, an Ivy League selector explained how:

> When someone fails, or when someone gets into academic trouble, internal admissions files are taken out, and looked at. … They're basically looking for any red flags. The dean [of admission] is very afraid of finding a red flag and having one of the academic deans say …: 'this was in the file; why did you admit this kid? … like, this kid has a criminal record and was admitted.'

This concern then can also contribute to erring on the side of caution. Selectors on both sides of the Atlantic acknowledged that further mistakes could be made, sometimes with the best intentions as noted here: 'We constructed a three-dimensional person out of a two-dimensional person and when she came here, she did not live up to it' (Ivy League selector). The sentiment was echoed by an academic selector from Oxbridge stating, 'Lots of the people we didn't take would have done perfectly well and some of the ones we take are not doing so well.' This again highlights how there can be little to differentiate between some applicants in the admissions stage and occasionally a candidate who was not picked might have turned out to be a stronger choice than someone who was selected.

Overall, selectors acknowledge that they were working with an array of imperfect measures and proxies in the admissions process to help them admit the students with the most potential and ability to achieve. By combining a range of factors and knowledge of aggregate patterns of what predicted progression and success among potential students, each in itself somewhat imperfect, holistically, selectors thought to maximize their chance of reaching the best and fairest decision. Moreover, the fundamental counterfactual question of what would have happened if different decisions had been made, is difficult to address as this Oxbridge academic observed: 'We never know about the ones we don't take. It's the problem with all admissions research everywhere, isn't it?'

Procedural fairness

The admissions system is now many order of magnitude better. The desire for change came mainly from within, a desire to 'try and ensure that we do our best to select the best candidates' a desire to be fair. If you teach them in tutorials, you like to make sure that you teach the best you can get ... but the government also helped. Government rules about fairness (legislation, threat of litigation) was an important trigger otherwise the system has a great deal of inertia – let's do it this way because this is how we have done it last year – there is a great deal of resistance to change in any system. The press and the government forced us to think: You cannot say it is a fair system if it takes a candidate with 2 As and a B but not one who achieves 3 As because that person has applied to a different college. It has forced us to think about how to demonstrate fairness. (Oxbridge selector)

Implicit in a lot of challenges in admission on both sides of the Atlantic is the notion of fairness. As a generalization, selectors in England were aiming to be fair to the applicants for admission. Selectors in the United States aimed to be fair to the institution and the applicants. Furthermore, US selectors had their eyes firmly on the aim of admitting a class through the admissions process that had certain collective strengths and characteristics. In contrast, English selectors were making individualized decisions about each applicant's fit with the academic requirements of their course.

English selectors voiced the value of fairness in selection in various ways. This might be as straightforward as stating 'I want to be fair' or by discussions about procedural fairness. Procedural fairness includes wishing to have one gathered field of applicants (Oxbridge), and can include considerations regarding who to invite for interview, testing interview questions to avoid ambivalence, interviewing in pairs, offering multiple interviews, having the same time for each interview, changing the order in which applicants would be interviewed over two days to avoid recall bias, taking into account personal extenuating circumstances and paying attention to life-experiences for applicants who had taken time out since school. Selectors also attended interview training which encouraged them to reflect on the potential for their own prejudices, and views to influence admissions decisions and raised awareness of the different backgrounds of applicants and the impact of first impressions.

Increasingly, Russell Group institutions have some checks in place to prevent applicants flagged as disadvantaged or having participated in an institutional outreach scheme from being rejected without senior managerial sign-off or a senior committee decision.

There were some examples of how concerns about fairness played out in the admissions process. In one instance in an academic-led admissions process a selectors lodged a complaint during an admissions meeting about unfair treatment of an applicant to allow for an applicant's case to be reconsidered.

In detail, an example of how procedural fairness played out was in an Oxbridge context concerning the decision which, if any, applicants from a remaining group of three marginal applicants to invite for interview. This decision followed clear-cut decisions of which applicants would certainly come for interview and which ones would certainly not come. In a group meeting of three academics, no selector wanted to make a strong case for the three marginal cases. There was some consideration of schooling and context, but ultimately, the selectors decided that there was no way to objectively differentiate between those remaining three marginal candidates and no one among the three was invited for interview so that all criteria would be equally applied to the three.

In an example of disagreement over what fairness meant, a first-time selector considered it 'bullshit' to take into account that an applicant for admission had overslept due to medication on the day of their admissions test. This met with robust disagreement from the chair of the selection committee who argued that discounting the test performance was the way it had to be in order to be fair – 'in case of litigation and because it is a genuine factor to take into account.'

Several selectors then particularly mentioned how 'college-blind' admission had been introduced to give Oxbridge applicants for the same subject the same opportunity for getting a place. Intercollegiate meetings between tutors for the same subject from different colleges then provided a ranking of a pool of all applicants with the top ones being offered a place. Another selector remarked how considering the process to be fairer than it used to be meant that 'I am much happier these days, I don't lose sleep over it as I used to.'

US selectors reported making admissions decisions by region and by school to be fair and to avoid admitting a student with a lower rank in their school than a higher ranked classmate who might not be admitted. A Big Three selector also noted how she was aware of the risk of supporting particular applicants simply because they are known to the selector:

> Sometimes you will meet a student at a high school who seems like the best kid you have ever met and you want to go out of the way and do whatever you can but that's not fair to all the other kids that never got the chance to meet you who are as qualified.

Both the US and the academic-led English system thus have some checks and balances in place to arrive at decisions that reflect the views of a range of people and whereby the positive or negative view of a single evaluator is not usually decisive on its own. Often, professional-led institutions in England admit solely based on predicted academic grades and here, selectors might simply make an offer to everyone who applies with the predicted grades. Some institutions here allow leeway for special consideration in individual cases.

A critique of academic-led systems is that they can be perceived to have less transparency and consistency although there are safeguards mitigating against these possibilities. While complete consistency meets the requirement for procedural fairness in treating everyone predictably the same, consistency may not always meet the desire for substantive fairness. There was at least one example during this project of a centralized Russell Group admissions office having a consistent but not evidence-based way of grading all personal statements of applicants. This is against recommendations from research of how personal statements need to be contextualized to account for the differential opportunities of applicants to have certain experiences. Fairness thus does not then always follow from consistency of a process if the process itself is not designed fairly.

Legal compliance

Considerations of fairness in admission can be linked with consideration of the legal context and the threat of litigation as this Ivy League selector observed: 'with so much litigation in this world one had to be careful'. Or, as an Oxbridge selector remarked when asked whether he interviewed alone or in pairs or a team: 'Always in a team. I don't interview alone any more. It's legally too dangerous.'

There have been numerous high-profile legal challenges to admissions decisions in the United States. These court decisions have focused on public institutions with the private institutions that feature in this book not subject to judicial review. Through amicus curiae letters, however, private US institutions have made clear their support for, for example, considering race as a factor in admission.

English institutions have not been subject to the same high-profile legal challenges to test principles for admission. This is partly because universities prefer settling challenges to their admissions decisions out of court and partly because courts can review the process or way a decision has been made but not the actual academic judgement contained within an admissions decision. Having said this, legal challenges of those unsuccessful for admission to Oxbridge have led to the a firm focus on comparing those who have applied for the same subject together rather than focusing on applicants on a college basis. In addition, English universities have clear equal treatment mandate including treating those from different racial groups equally (Equalities Act 2010). Positive action, that is, encouraging applications from under-represented groups, is allowed and encouraged, however, positive discrimination, treating individuals differently at the point of admission because of, for example, their race, is not allowed in England. Admissions also has to be compliant with consumer law (CMA 2015). Staff training is in place to provide academic selectors and professional selectors with an understanding of the legal context in which they make admissions decisions.

Governance

There are also some organizations in both England and the United States that influence how admissions work is undertaken. We have already been introduced to UCAS as the UK-wide service for university applications to full-time undergraduate courses. In this application process, some governance rules and conventions are followed. For example, applicants for undergraduate study can only apply to either Oxford or Cambridge, applicants can only apply to a maximum of five different courses, and the way offers for places are accepted and confirmed is also governed.

Another key player in the governance of higher education institutions is the Office for Fair Access (OFFA). OFFA was set up in 2004 as part of the increases in tuition fees described in detail in Chapter 2. All English universities and colleges that want to charge more than £6,000 in tuition fees must have an 'access agreement' with OFFA. OFFA then monitors the progress institutions make towards their agreed access targets.

All English universities in this project charged £9,000 in fees and were thus subject to OFFA access agreements. In these agreements, institutions have to lay out how they work towards making their institution more accessible for groups that are currently under-represented in higher education such as students from low-income families and from areas where there is little history of participating in higher education. Universities frequently agree a target of, for example, increasing the number of students from the lowest socio-economic groups or from state schools. Some of the funds generated through the higher fees have to be invested in outreach and supporting low-income students at university.

There are two further bodies that support admissions professionals and aim to safeguard fairness in university admissions in England. The organization Supporting Professionalism in Admissions (SPA) was also set up in 2006 to provide a central source of expertise and advice on admissions issues. SPA provides a good practice framework for an integrated strategic approach to admissions. SPA also offers resources, and advice and expertise on conducting professional admissions processes that lead to fair access to higher education and support social mobility. Finally, the Quality Assurance Agency (QAA) for Higher Education advises and monitors standards and quality in UK higher education, including student recruitment, admission and enrolment. The QAA publishes the UK Quality Code for Higher Education which entails requirements that all higher education providers need to meet in order to maintain their accreditation. Chapter B2 of this quality code is particularly concerned with admissions to universities and lays out requirements regarding admission and recruitment. Specifically, the code expects the following from all UK universities:

> Recruitment, selection and admission policies and procedures adhere to the principles of fair admission. They are transparent, reliable, valid, inclusive and underpinned by appropriate organizational structures and processes. They support higher education providers in the selection of students who are able to complete their programme.

In the United States, accreditation is a voluntary peer-review process although institutions need to participate in the process in order to access federal financial aid. While all of the UK has only one accreditation agency, there are six regional accrediting organizations in the United States. For example, the New England Association of Schools and Colleges' (NEASC) Commission on Institutions of Higher Education accredits Harvard, Yale, Brown, Dartmouth and MIT. Princeton is accredited by the Middle States Commission on Higher Education, and Berkeley and Stanford are accredited by the Western Association of Schools and Colleges (WASC).

Another cross-institutional player in the United States is the National Association for College Admission Counseling (NACAC), founded in 1937. NACAC caters for guidance counsellors in high schools as well as for admissions professionals at universities and colleges. NACAC has a statement of principles of good practice which includes mandatory good practice in admission that all members have to comply with.

The eight Ivy League universities also have a joint 'Ivy League Athletics Admission Statement'. This statement includes the joint Ivy League policy to provide financial aid to students, including athletes, only on the basis of financial need as determined by each institution's Financial Aid Office. There are no academic or athletic scholarships in the Ivy League. Ivies also subscribe to the Academic Index used to determine the academic eligibility for admission of Athletes and to prevent athletes with little chance of completing the academic side of college from being admitted (see Chapter 4 for more details). Athletes hoping to enrol at the Ivy League and other Division 1 or 2 athletic institutions[2] also have to undergo some initial certification through the National Collegiate Athletic Association (NCAA). This organization furthermore provides a range of resources for aspiring college athletes through its eligibility centre including advice on academic requirements.

The governance structure around admissions in both England and the United States means that institutions, as a minimum, have to ensure that their admissions procedures are compliant with mandatory regulations and laws, for example, as they relate to competition, consumer protection, equality and others as applicable. Institutions also have opportunities to lead the development of innovative good or best practices that go beyond governance requirements.

Cooperation and competition

For higher education institutions, it is important to comply with any additional governance concerning admission that is separate from actual legislation. Often, the existence of governance also allows some collaboration where applicants' best interest would not be served by different universities each pursuing their own institutional self-interest. For example, an institution might be tempted to offer a full scholarship to an athlete who has little chance of completing the academic requirements of higher education. This could serve the institution in the short term as they are winning games and generating income, however, this action also has the potential to be a disservice to the student as they might not graduate, it might lead to discontent on campus about differential admissions standards and other institutions might be tempted to join a race for lower standards for athletes in the pursuit of winning games. The Athletic Index then is a way for institutions to cooperate in ensuring some minimum academic standards.

In England, an example of navigating competition and cooperation among higher education providers is the case of outreach. Here, universities generally agree that enhancing opportunities for previously under-represented groups in higher education is a good thing. However, individual institutions also have targets, normally set by themselves and approved by OFFA, of how they will increase the participation of students from under-represented groups. Universities are thus happy to cooperate with each other in outreach involving relatively young adolescents. However, in the final year of schooling, universities can be more competitively minded and might target activities at recruiting students to their institutions as opposed to providing general information about higher education.

Engaging with the media

Another admissions challenge can be dealing with the media. The media in England, the United States, and indeed, beyond, is interested in admission to the Ivies and other selective US institutions and also in admission to Oxbridge and the Russell Group. As one Ivy selector remarked: 'the media is fascinated because it is a high stake game, because it is a mystery, and it is a ritual that is great to watch'. Another US selector remarked how admissions was 'a great spectator game in a society that is obsessed with success and status'. Indeed, in 2005 the United States even had its own admissions reality television show *The Scholar* which offered college scholarships as prizes.

Some Oxbridge selectors also observed that they felt Oxbridge was receiving more 'unwarranted' media criticism than any other English universities but that they had to up their game rather than complain about it.

There was a feeling among US selectors that the media could 'make or break' a campus and that admissions officials had to 'Be nice to the media. You need them, they need you. But they are not your friend. If you want a friend, buy a dog.' (Ivy League selector).

There was some concern on both sides of the Atlantic that nuances of how admissions worked in practice could be missed in media coverage where 'anecdotes are reported as facts' (Russell Group admissions professional). At the same time, there was recognition that journalists, the media, social media and online information had 'democratized' access to information and that institutions could use this to increase their visibility and also their accessibility for a wider range of potential applicants than previously possible. University press offices are thus part of the media landscape in both the United States and England and proactively embrace and engage with a range of social media including Facebook, Twitter and YouTube.

English universities are also subject to freedom of information requests which means that the media or any other member of the public can ask, within reason, to see records of, for example, meetings or admissions statistics.[3] Many universities have responded to the number of freedom of information requests by proactively putting a lot more information in the public domain than they had previously done. In addition, trusted journalists have obtained access to observe admissions process and to report in their newspapers. An example is the *Guardian* coverage of Cambridge admissions in January 2012 (Vasagar 2012).

Chapter summary

This chapter described the challenges selectors face in the admissions process. While individual contexts vary between and within the two countries, there are shared challenges regarding not being selective enough, drawing lines where there are none, the art of deselection, the challenge of incommensurability and prediction in the context of uncertainty and achieving procedural fairness while complying with legal and governance requirements. Against this context, selectors feel that they manage to navigate around the challenges on aggregate but that sometimes an individual admissions decision taken in isolation might not make sense to everyone affected by the decision. There was then some consensus among US and English selectors that 'we have a great track record on aggregate but don't get it right on every single count' (Big Three selector).

However, perhaps the greatest substantive challenge in admission is investigated in the following chapter: How can fair admissions be achieved in a context of inequality?

Fair Admission in the Context of Inequality

Colleges and universities depend on a pipeline that promotes opportunity and academic preparation for all students.

(William R. Fitzsimmons, in Phillips Exeter Academy (2007))

I remember years ago – in the early 70s, the [subject] tutor … used to say: Oh, yes, but for somebody from that, comprehensive, … or whatever it was then – this is a very good performance!

(Oxbridge academic selector)

Approximately 1 in 3 students at the 146 most selective US colleges come from the top quarter of the socio-economic status (SES) scale as measured by parents' income, education and occupation. Just 3 per cent come from the bottom quarter of the SES distribution (Espenshade 2009). Those from the bottom 20 per cent of income are 25 times less likely than the wealthy to enrol at a top college.

In England, young people who are from poorer families as identified by their eligibility to have free school meals are half as likely to continue into higher education than those not eligible for free school meals. While 37 per cent of the general public are identified as working class, they represent only between 11 and 14 per cent of the most selective Russell Group institutions. Why are there those differences in who attends selective universities?

The single greatest challenge and public media controversies in university admissions concern how admissions should take into account the wider social context of differences in education and beyond that students experience long before they file their applications for study at a university. Selectors are acutely aware of how different previous educational experiences influence and shape the range and strengths of applications: 'Education in America is very unequal. We can't close the door of our institution as long as the pipeline is not sorted' (Ivy League selector).

Studies in both England and the United States repeatedly find that students from different socio-economic backgrounds and different ethnic backgrounds perform differently in achievement measures in education, be it SATs and GPAs in the United States or GCSEs and A-levels in England. Of course, there are always high-profile individual exceptions of poor students doing exceptionally well in education against the odds – but these students are not the norm.

Selectors were also keenly aware of the relationship between test performance and socio-economic background and schooling as this Big Three selector noted:

> Some start their SAT test prep in the 7th grade – there is a whole industry for test prep. Some spent as much time preparing for the test as they do in school … and then some private college consultants charge $1000 an hour or so for test prep.

In SAT tests and the like in the United States, Asian students top achievement tables ahead of whites, with fewer high-achieving Hispanic and black students. In England, Chinese and Indian students sometimes outperform white and mixed-race students, whereas black and Bangladeshi and Pakistani students tend to perform lower in GCSEs and A-levels.

US admissions controversies and discourses have historically focused mainly on race and have only recently moved to overtly talking about how racial diversity on campuses can hide a lack of socio-economic diversity. The opposite is the case for England. Here, inequality in access to higher education by 'social class' has been the dominant theme for some time, with only more recent attention to the modest racial diversity at some of England's most selective universities.

The present chapter then explores how inequality poses challenges with regard to prior opportunities in schooling and at home before describing ways in which universities in the two countries are responding to these challenges.

The challenge of differences in families and schooling

For some education-minded parents in both the United States and England, thinking about a child's education may begin before conception or birth and may involve moving to an area with good early years education opportunities, calling prospective schools when the first baby scan arrives and, where such an option exists, to put children's names down for elite private schools at birth. For example, the single-sex pre-preparatory school in London attended by the two Royal princes, William and Harry, advises that 'Registrations are accepted from birth (we do not register babies before they are born) … parents are advised to contact the school office as soon as possible after the birth of their son'

(Wetherby 2015). In the United States, early year application dates tend to be on annual cycles – for example, New York families mark the 'Labor day' prior to enrolment as the key time when application forms to private kindergarten become available – many applications are then submitted the very same day. American books like Schoenstein's book *Toilet Trained for Yale* (2002), *The Ivy Chronicles* (2005) by Karen Quinn about kindergarten admission and Chua's *Tiger Mum* (2011) about bringing up children in the competitive Yale university town of Newhaven have highlighted not only how early some parents start thinking about their children's future but also to what lengths they might go to achieve their aspirations for their children.

The early years are also particularly expensive years in private education. The fees of, for example, over £18,000 per annum for an early years place at Wetherby's, London or of $42,000 per annum for an early year place at Trinity, New York, easily dwarf or equal the tuition fees of even the most expensive universities. They also put the private consultant fees some US families pay to place their children into kindergarten into perspective. The competition for desirable education is particularly heightened in urban centres like London and New York.

Participating in expensive and prestigious early year and middle school education is only enjoyed by an often privileged minority of children in both countries, and can set children up for a trajectory of educational success that enhances the chances of culminating in admission to higher education generally and in addition to highly selective higher education in particular: some private nursery schools have a preferential admissions policy for the children of alumni and they may provide a well-established pipeline to other private schools in the next stages of education. For example, the elite private school Harrow in England enrols 85 per cent of its students from private preparatory schools.

Private schools in both countries and at any stage of schooling are aware of the importance families place on where students continue their education after leaving a school and often showcase such information on their websites. Depending on the stage of schooling, this information may capture progression into private primary or secondary schools or higher education. In the latter case, 'Oxbridge admission' for England or 'Ivy/MIT/Stanford' admission in the United States are noted separately – especially if such rates are good for the school. Both countries also have research and league tables that look at which schools have the highest transition rates into those selective universities.

According to *Forbes*, Trinity School New York had a 41 per cent transition rate into these selected US universities (Laneri 2010). A table of the top feeder high schools for the Ivy/MIT/Stanford has a strong presence of New York City private schools and New England prep schools – although publicly funded schools focusing on maths and science and other magnet schools also show high transition into selective colleges (The Wall Street Journal 2007). In England, the two private London schools Westminster and St Paul's Girl's school have half of their UK university-bound graduates going to Oxford or Cambridge with a further 35 per cent attending a select group of eleven other leading universities (Westminster School 2013; St Paul's Girls' School 2014).

Fewer than one in ten English children attend private schools. Yet, at the most selective universities, privately educated students can make up half of the student body. An analysis by the charity the Sutton Trust found that just forty secondary schools and colleges out of a total of 2,750 schools provided about a quarter of all Oxbridge entrants in 2011/12 (Sutton Trust 2008). Again, many of these forty schools are private schools with some notable exceptions of usually academically selective state-funded schools. US statistics on private schools suggest a similar trend.

While the majority of students at private school are from very wealthy families, notable financial aid and bursaries initiative by some of the most prestigious schools like Eton College in England and Phillips Exeter Academy in the United States are opening private schools to high ability students without the means to pay for their education. With $1 billion endowment and a strong vision for the academic future of the school, Exeter Academy has 45 per cent of its students on scholarships, dwarfing Eton's £250 million endowment supported aspiration for 5 per cent of their 1,300 students to be on full scholarships. Similar to higher education where scholarships are more readily available at the absolute top institutions, the second tier of private schools with smaller endowments are usually less able to offer scholarships. While scholarships based on ability and ability to pay become somewhat more common in secondary or high schools, scholarships or bursaries for the very early stages of private primary school education remain scarce.

The state-funded school sector in both the United States and England also educates some of the highest achieving young people. Entrance examination performance and/or living in the geographic catchment area of the school are key ways for getting into those schools. Examples include Boston Latin School, Stuyvesant High School New York or Thomas Jefferson High School for Science and Technology in the United States and the publicly funded academically selective 'grammar schools' in England which educate around 4 per cent of all English secondary school students.[1]

While in theory open to everyone with the ability to succeed, in practice, some parental or school support is required for potentially eligible students to know that these schools exist, to prepare for the required entrance examinations, and to submit applications on time. Research in England has shown that children from more affluent families are more likely to attempt the entrance examinations for grammar schools, that a disproportionate number of students in state-funded selective grammar schools have previously attended private, fee-paying primary schools, and that grammar schools have fewer children on free school meals in them than there are in the population of high achieving children. However, Asian students are well represented in grammar schools in England, a finding that is repeated for magnet schools in the United States where, for example, Chinese Americans have developed a successful system of disseminating information about the existence of these schools and the requirements for securing a place within their community (Waters et al. 2013).

However, the strong link between geography and catchment area for many state-funded schools that do not have entrance exams means that the state and private schools with the highest attaining students in them in both the United States and England can have rather similar socio-economic profiles. The premium in prices for properties located in desirable catchment areas can exceed the costs of several years of tuition fees for private school. In England as well as the United States, there are league tables and comparisons estimating the effect of a good school on property prices.

Furthermore, well-informed English parents are aware of the pressures universities are under to recruit more students from state schools (see Chapter 7 on governance). Some parents therefore 'play the education game' to their advantage by sending their children to private schools for the early part of their schooling and moving them to excellent state schools for the final years of their education.

The children who generally do least well in the system are those with interrupted schooling due to frequent moves and unstable home contexts. In England, the charity ButtleUK has raised awareness concerning the low attainment and particularly low transition rates into higher education and the even lower transition into selective higher education for children who have been in foster care families or care homes. A minority of 7 per cent of these children – compared with 47 per cent of children who have not been in care – participate in higher education and few apply to selective higher education. Children who had to flee their home countries also experience poor education outcomes although it can be more difficult to capture statistical information on their progression.

In the United States, undocumented migrants graduating from US high schools have significantly lower transition rates into college than equally qualified legal migrants or non-migrants, a finding that is at least partly due to their smaller chance of accessing funding or in-state tuition rates for college.

These findings on different attainment and schooling for different groups are partly driven by different access to the 'hidden curriculum' of how the education system works and which educational opportunities and support might be available. The English scholar Basil Bernstein (1974) and the French scholar Pierre Bourdieu (1986) have written about the effects of differences in ability to understand the 'assumed code' of educational systems. Generally, the educated middle classes are better placed to support their children through the way systems work. Indeed, one Ivy League selector noted how he had found navigating the process of helping his child go to college 'very difficult – and I am an expert in the field! So, how difficult would it be for low income kids without all this knowledge to navigate the process?'

An example from higher education of how detailed knowledge of a system can work in practice is the following observation: 'children of college professors very frequently will end up in liberal arts schools … because the professors know that the teaching is best at liberal arts schools because professors actually have to teach … you get to work with the professor' (liberal arts selector). Also, some knowledge is required to appreciate how a liberal arts education can be complemented by pursuing graduate study at a bigger, more recognizably branded research university later. Similarly, middle-class families in England know that a good route into a prestigious legal career is studying a non-law degree at a Russell Group university and then studying law in a short conversion course afterwards. This is the sort of knowledge that will be less obvious to first-generation university students or those who have no links to professionals.

The US scholar Annette Laureau (2011) also show how, from early childhood, different families have different parenting philosophies with middle-class families consciously structuring their children's environment and activity through concerted cultivation whereas working-class families use a more natural growth model. For an admissions system that rewards evidence of engagement and rounded portfolios or stellar performances, opportunities given through concerted cultivation might arguably advantage middle-class applicants. The exceptional achievement of self-starters who create rather than use opportunities given to them, however, also has to be acknowledged.

Networks or social capital and information, advice, and guidance – or the lack thereof – also explain differences in attainment and educational choices and progression in a line of work attributed originally to the US scholar James Coleman. For parents who do not know the higher education system very well, the extent to which they can support their children is then not so much an issue of a lack of aspiration for their children, but some parents are not well positioned to advise their children on their educational journeys. Schools also differ in terms of course opportunities and subjects they provide, for example, US 'schools with higher percentages of students eligible for free and reduced price lunch programs ... were less likely to offer AP, IB, and enriched curricula' (NACAC 2011). In other words, the poorer the students in a school, the less likely is the school to offer the robust academic curriculum highly selective universities are looking for. Ratios of counsellors to students vary significantly between publicly funded and private schools with more one-on-one support available in private schools. Similar patterns are true for England.

Another US selectors noted how university admission is an 'emotional, not just a rational and logical process' and thus emotional support was crucial for successfully navigating the process. Some children, like those in foster care and refugees, might not have any family member supporting them. In England, there has been a long tradition of research – for example, by Diane Reay and colleagues (2005) – thinking about how some young people perceive higher education to have a certain culture or to be for a certain sort of person. For students with little history or knowledge of universities in their families, there can be concerns about 'fitting in' and having to adjust and learn a new way of being in the world. Such concerns can prevent students from applying to higher education and can affect experiences at universities.

Overall, the existence of differences in attainment and progression in education is well established and linked not only to issues around educational opportunities. Such differences reflect other, often multiple, differences in wealth, health, family structures and housing that persist in wider societies. So, how can universities and their selectors attempt fair admission in this context of differences in earlier opportunities and other inequalities?

Tackling admission in the context of inequality

The challenge for elite colleges today is to get more students from the bottom half and bottom quarter of the income distribution.

(Big Three selector)

There was a time when universities in neither the United States or England would have perceived the attainment gaps and the diversity of opportunities in earlier schooling and family context as a problem for university admissions. Until the middle of the twentieth century, the idea of universities as a finishing school of the well-off and direct or indirect exclusions based on wealth, religion, gender, disability and race was common in both England and the United States. Indeed, Jerome Karabel (2005) has documented how Harvard, Yale and Princeton have gone to some length in the past to preserve higher education as a way for privileged social groups to consolidate status. Joseph Soares (2007) has documented the rise of the meritocracy at Oxford in the second half of the twentieth century. An Ivy selector recalled how his institution used to have this 'special rating system for prep school candidates'. Certain schools 'were pipelines for certain places, but that's changed a lot … that's part of a blatant way you can be more meritocratic in your process … a lot of schools don't have traditional feeder schools that way anymore'.

Similarly, in England, pipeline links between, for example, specific Oxbridge colleges and certain elite private schools are also a thing of the past. Only a small minority of respondents considered it 'not the role of universities to address wider inequalities' (academic selector England) or considered 'the primary aim of admission fairness to the institutional objectives rather than being fair to society' (US Ivy League selector) or being fair to individual, potentially disadvantaged, applicants.

The vast majority of selectors on both sides of the Atlantic are not only aware of the challenge of unequal prior schooling as we have seen in Chapter 1, many professionals have chosen to work in the admissions and outreach field with an intention to make a genuine difference to young people's lives.

Many selectors and, indeed, educational researchers and policy makers on both sides of the Atlantic note how the best way forward to change participation in elite higher education would be to 'fix the pipeline' (Russell Group admissions professional) and 'to change opportunities in the very early stages of schooling' (US selector) and that admission will be inevitably flawed 'as long as the link between schooling and property tax remains' (US selector): 'if we could, we would go back and change opportunities at 3rd grade, that's when opportunities are set' (Big Three selector).

As this pipeline is not easily fixable, admissions professionals and academic respondents in this project were keen for their own practice to be as fair as possible, although there was some disagreement as to what fairness meant in practice. The next section describes how selectors are rising to the challenge of addressing inequalities through outreach, making changes to the way they admit applicants, and changing the framework of admissions. The chapter then concludes with discussing some contested issues in admissions.

Widening the application pool: Outreach

You can't be admitted if you don't apply.

(Big Three selector)

We wish to increase the percentage of students from state schools and low higher education participation neighbourhoods.

(Russell Group admissions professional)

One aspect that makes elite universities 'elite' is the competitiveness of obtaining a place. Despite the already high competitiveness for gaining admission, 'barriers continue to exist in society and there is a need to cast our net widely' (Ivy League selector). While there are thus too many applicants in some ways, there are not enough applicants from groups that are under-represented in selective higher education.

Universities on both side of the Atlantic thus dedicate time and other resources to reaching out to schools and children from disadvantaged families or schools with little or no history of sending their graduates into higher education or selective higher education. These outreach or strategic recruitment operations often run alongside traditional recruitment activities that aim to maintain the steady stream of highly qualified applicants from more established pathways into higher education.

Examples of initiatives are the Princeton University Preparatory Program (PUPP), or Cambridge University's HE+ programme to support and encourage adolescents from non-traditional university backgrounds into higher education. Princeton works with twenty-five organizations that in turn work on the ground with kids from families of low income. Harvard's Financial Aid Initiative encourages students from families with below $80,000 to come to Harvard. There are also summer schools in the United States that offer, for example, AP courses or writing classes for students whose schools do not offer these. In the UK, Sutton Trust summer schools as well as those led by individual universities have been shown to be helpful in increasing preparedness and entry to selective higher education for participants. A recent addition to such schemes is the Sutton Trust-Fulbright Commission's programme of support for disadvantaged UK students to apply to selective US universities. If admitted, students can access the universities' generous international financial aid package to enable these UK students to study in the United States. These are all examples of initiatives that give bright, non-privileged students in publicly funded schools additional support, previews and tasters of higher education. Additional programmes in the

UK support and mentor disadvantaged students into specific careers such as law and medicine. Specific degree programmes such as the extended medicine and enhanced support dentistry programmes at King's College London allow disadvantaged students to take an additional year of study to complete their academic courses.

Some universities also run particular programmes for those giving information, advice and guidance to adolescents, such as US public school counsellors who are responsible for advising many more students than their counterparts in private schools. A non-Ivy selector observed, 'We might need a bit more outreach at public schools and public secondary counsellors, because they don't necessarily have the time or the resources dedicated to really focus on the college process.' English universities have also experimented with programmes for secondary school teachers to be part of outreach, for example, by being in residence at a university.

Outreach programmes tend to draw on knowledge about under-represented groups in higher education or in particular academic disciplines. Profiling software, family, school and postcode information can be used for identifying potential outreach students and to targeted school visits to help entice more higher education applications from disadvantaged groups. The aim is to make higher education more reflective of the general secondary school population in England and America respectively.

An example of strategic outreach or recruitment in the United States was recalled by this Ivy League selector:

> I was in Alaska, and McCormick County [South Carolina] on Native American reservations. Because we do feel that there is great perspective there to be represented ... that history, that voice, is an important part of what should be in our community. So we feel that we need to act affirmatively in trying to recruit qualified students who are from under-represented backgrounds.

Several US respondents also noted how recruiting athletes was considered part of their strategic recruitment. Some thought that recruiting athletes also helped with the socio-economic diversity of students. However, research does not support this link for the Ivy League institutions. Athletes here are less likely to come from families with income below $80,000 than applicants who are not recruited athletes.

There is evidence that private US colleges spend approximately two times as much as public colleges to recruit both applicants and admitted students, including outreach to previously under-served schools.

Even among those who strongly support outreach or strategic recruitment, there is acute awareness of some of the limitations of such initiatives even with the best intentions. For example, many universities rightly engage in a 'do it in your backyard' mantra and work with local schools and students. This can, however, lead to some areas like inner-city London being quite well served with outreach programmes whereas other, often rural or harder to reach areas, are not closely linked with universities. Some collaboration between universities is thus often desirable to achieve more equitable access to information for all young people. In England, collaborations between different universities tend to be least problematic when they concern early years interventions or aim to raise attainment for those participating in outreach schemes. In the final years of schooling, however, there can be more competition between universities as they compete for a potentially limited pool of high-achieving, disadvantaged young people.

The use of contextual or holistic admissions is a key strategy for converting outreach and strategic recruitment into admitted students.

Using Holistic and contextual admissions

> We use a lot of context. As a university, we have been very conscious of the need to engage with contextual information. Contextual information comes in many forms, some of it is actually bits of statistical information, some of it is what people read in the personal statement, and probably more important, in the references about an applicant's background. And, I think one of the other myths is that we do not care about this sort of thing. Actually, we do. (Nicholson 2013)

> We take into account the context within the school. If a kid is so much better than the rest of the school, that kid has a right to be at [this institution]. (Ivy League selector)

Holistic admissions in the United States or contextual admissions in England are a key strategy universities use for taking into account the social context of an applicant when making admissions decisions. In the United States, the approach means that each applicant is looked at individually in relation to all the information provided about or by them.

In England, contextual data flagging gives selectors at many Russell Group institutions, including Oxbridge, a quick view of a range of information about an applicant. A UK-wide review of contextual data in universities admission found that among eight case study universities a range of additional information about applicants was added to application files before final admissions decisions were made (Moore, Mountford-Zimdars and Wiggans 2013). The range of factors flagged for inclusion included school performance at age sixteen and eighteen, school progression rates, coming from a neighbourhood with low transitions into higher education or an area experiencing relative deprivation or other measures of neighbourhood disadvantage. Family information regarding whether the applicant was the first in family in higher education, had been in care or other individual circumstances such as forced migration background could also be taken into account. Some universities also used information as to whether an applicant had participated in an outreach scheme to flag disadvantaged applicants. Universities can decide how many of these measures, if any, they wish to use and how to use them – for example, whether an applicant needs to be in more than one disadvantage category before being flagged for particular consideration.

An Oxbridge admissions professional explained how:

> We evaluate these flags in terms of trying to make sure that everybody is conscious of them at the point of decision making ... and we also train the coordinators within a subject because we don't only moderate gathered fields within colleges, we also do it across the colleges, subject-by-subject, and in each admission subject there is a subjective convener and the part of the subject convener, while we train them annually, is 'remind everybody about the flags and what they mean' ... and the way [flags] are used, is then if there's someone with high scores and flags who's not being taken, someone's going to be put on the spot and then likely to be asked to justify that decision and if the justification is not a robust one ... that student is very likely then to be reassessed ... we are monitoring the difference it's making.

Academic selectors frequently use additional, more nuanced, ways to contextualize the academic profile of applicants. For example, one Oxbridge selector mentioned paying attention to whether the school offered advanced mathematics courses (further maths) as not to penalize applicants who had not taken it in the interview or noted that interviews themselves had to be contextualized as it would, for example, be 'quite unfair to expect to the same performance from someone who had done politics and someone who hadn't done politics at all'.

A Big Three selector also noted how the school context of curriculum offers was considered during the admissions process.

> This public school in Detroit – I know that they don't offer this advanced curriculum – but I would want to see that the student has made the most of

what has been made available to them. And the way we can see that is through a school profile. And the school will let us know the kind of courses that are offered, the way that they grade those courses, and how well they're doing, and that kind of thing.

Another Big Three selector echoed this description of holistic admissions practice by explaining:

> When we read students in context, we look at what they have done with what's been made available to them. So, for example, I know that the top private school in Michigan offers a huge number of advanced placement courses. ... I mean, the teaching is very, very good, and I would expect a student to be taking AP courses ... challenging themselves ... most high schools in the US will send us a school profile with the transcript ... some of the top schools will send us the profile of ... what kind of extracurriculars are offered, and how hard the students work.

For the United States, the annual 'national picture' report by NACAC shows that 'private college admission is more "holistic" than public college admission. Private selective universities considered a broader range of factors in the admission decision' (NACAC 2011). Contextual factors are considered alongside the other admissions factors discussed in Chapter 6 – grades in college, strength of curriculum, test scores, essay class rank, counsellor recommendation, demonstrated interest, teacher recommendation, interview, extra-curricular activities, subject tests and SAT subject scores.

For the United States, contextual factors or flags include race/ethnicity, gender, first-generation status, state or county of residence, high school attended and alumni relations. For example, a Big Three selector noted that while her institution did not have admissions targets by school, school information was 'definitely something we consider ... how many we're taking from private and from public schools.' Another Ivy League selector was keen to dispel the myth that some thought 'if you're from a high school where no one's ever applied to [this Ivy], you're at a disadvantage. And that's not the case at all. There are fewer applying from a smaller school in rural Indiana, for example, or inner-city Detroit. But, we'll want to see those students too.'

In both England and the United States, school recommendations are also contextualized. For example, there is knowledge that 'public secondary counsellors are very taxed ... whereas at a lot of private day schools and boarding schools, they have offices that are dedicated solely to college counselling' (Big Three selector).

Contextualizing applicants is not without its controversies. Criticisms come from two angles. First, there are those who are concerned about the impact on more privileged students who do not benefit from contextualization. Second, there are those who think contextualizing applicants is still not inclusive enough and can miss nuances of disadvantage and is open to being used to reproduce advantage as well as in the case of legacy admits.

A senior Russell Group strategist noted how contextual admission was 'politically the most contentious thing you do, and on my governing body it's a very difficult issue'. He elaborated that many of those who sit on the governing boards of selective English universities have children who are in private education and contextual admission is perceived as disadvantaging them and their peer group. Voices from the private school have also put forward that there is 'private school prejudice' and that they are being penalized for having graduates with high achievement. Universities also seek to balance the interest of outreach with maintaining their traditional parent and school support. One liberal arts college selector noted that his university did not wish to sever such ties by rejecting all applicants 'from traditional feeder schools'.

In England, an interesting area in which the focus of critics from the private school privilege position and those seeking more nuanced contextualization overlap is the issue of scholarships. The existence of a scholarship system within an otherwise elite private school system – indeed, as well as the existence of excellent state schools – means that the school an applicant applies from cannot always be equated with their families' socio-economic position. Not all applicants to university from prestigious secondary schools are affluent, and some applicants from state schools are as affluent or more affluent than some students whose parents pay for private schools.

Select applicants will have been to private schools because they won scholarships earlier on, others will have been in private education primarily because of their ability to pay or some lineage linking them with the school. One English selector stated that up to one-third of applicants to his university from private schools had been at the private school because of a scholarship.

While universities are matched against targets on the numbers of students they take by different school types, several Russell Group Institutions wish to present their intake statistics in a more nuanced way that takes into account the sometimes complex relationship between school type and socio-economic status as well as school moves during education between the private and the state school sector.

There are other voices arguing for enhancing the contextual data approach in admission. The question here is 'who is not flagged?' (Russell groups selector). Or, as this Oxbridge selector noted:

> I think it's [increasing access] a laudable goal ... but I feel strongly about rural working class white boys and why do they not get an extra chance to make themselves heard and then you got other people arguing for other groups and that I mean does seem to me completely fair.

This selector then perceived that there was an element of different groups being played out against each other with regard to whose context was judged worthy of a 'flag' or special consideration and who was not in this group. Indeed, there are some differences in what context Russell Group institutions flag. For example, refugee status was flagged by one institution but not systematically by others. Such detailed differences in what institutions might consider as part of their holistic evaluation may be unclear to applicants and potential applicants.

Another complexity in contextualizing applicants was pointed out by a Big Three selector in that certain disruptive or disadvantageous life events – she used the examples of parental divorce or death – can happen across social groups and are not exclusive to socio-economically disadvantaged applicants. This might explain why US selectors prefer a 'holistic' approach of seeking to understand each applicant and their particular circumstances to the 'contextual' approach of flagging or given special consideration to particular groups of applicants taken in England. Despite these conceptual differences in contextualization, however, in reality, there might not be a huge difference between the two approaches as long as they use individualized rather than formulaic cuts-offs for admitting students and extenuating individual circumstances are taken into account.

Finally, in the United States, special consideration does not necessarily occur only for outreach purposes. For example, US admissions offices might 'highlight' those from ethnic minority backgrounds, athletes and legacies. Such special consideration, on the one hand, serves the purpose of meeting institutional objectives in terms of having an athletic team and alumni giving. On the other hand, the ethnic diversity consideration serves the mission institution see for themselves in the wider world with regard to educating diverse students. This is somewhat different from flagging those who have been in care in England to acknowledge their particularly disadvantageous start in life.

The US legacy consideration in particular is also not designed to rectify inequalities and might indeed serve to reproduce advantage – indeed, this is a controversial aspect of admission for many US commentators. In the practical world of university admissions, one Ivy selector described some sort of horse trading of this controversial legacy consideration when explaining how he 'looked kindly' at applications from community colleges partly to 'counterbalance the effect of taking into account alumni connections'.

Changing the cost of higher education

The Ivies and other highly selective universities with large endowments have powerful policies in place to address the issue of the cost of higher education. The top tier of US institutions is needs-blind and can easily meet the financial cost of education for many of their undergraduates from endowment.

Indeed, this senior selector from a Big Three Ivy argued that the single greatest challenge in admission was.

> making the case that [Big Three Ivy] is open to talent, not to a special high degree of means either in intellectual capital at home or lots of money at home or privilege in other ways you want to define it but the talented people are the people who want to come here … and money is not a barrier.

She further elaborated how eliminating finances as a barrier was backed by strong institutional initiatives, saying:

> In the past ten years we have greatly upped the ante, greatly upped the level of support, especially targeting this support for students whose families are either very modestly compensated or positioned in American society which, by the way, is the bottom half of the United States … but we've also, … greatly enhanced the support to families who … have incomes of up to [figure close to $200,000] which sounds like a lot of money but living in America is really expensive. We began to see – and we looked at our data very closely, as you can imagine; we're obsessed with our data and that's why we have it – we were concerned that we were beginning again to not to attract the interest of students whose families were in that kind of middle income range and so we needed to reverse course. A lot of the most talented – academically talented – students come from those [middle income] families, as it happens.

This Big Three Ivy then has put into place specific policies to address the challenge of the 'squeezed middle' by extending financial aid up to those not living in financial hardship.

There is a 'run-away top of the super rich' (Ivy League selector) who can easily afford the cost of the sort of early education and life experience that enhance the chances of gaining admission to elite universities. Paying tuition fees and subsistence is also not a problem. At the other end of the wealth spectrum, for those with high demonstrated need, there has been a longer tradition of financial aid packages covering all the cost of higher education – although, as we have previously seen, young people in this group are generally less likely to have the grades required for admission. The concern is that those 'in the middle' who may have the academic credentials but are not so poor that they qualify for full aid struggle most with the costs of higher education. Indeed, one US selector reflected on his own experience of not enrolling at his first-choice university because 'I could not afford them [the fees at a university] and they could not afford me' meaning he had not qualified for financial aid nor did him and his family have sufficient disposable income to pay the fees. The shifting of financial aid to include greater fractions of the middle classes is a direct response to this challenge.

The impressive but costly financial aid initiatives of the Ivies are not always easily matched by institutions with smaller endowments. The issue of the 'squeezed middle' then is now perhaps a particular problem for those private institutions just below the top tier. Their smaller endowments, mean that there is a challenge when 'schools [meaning universities] can't give enough financial aid and students can't pay what is required' (Ivy League selector). A liberal arts college selector furthermore noted:

> I totally understand the reasoning for [scholarships] because you want to make college affordable and not just something for rich kids but it's very costly. If I get laid off from [my institution] because we don't have any money I'm going to be really pissed about it because I'm going to think well the $50,000 for the one kid that we take, that's my salary, you know, that's more than I get paid for one of these kids to come here for one year.

Having funding in place then is clearly key for supporting first-generation and poor as well as middle-class applicants in higher education. However, this observation is balanced against the observation that most US colleges – around 70 to 80 per cent – rely on student fee income to stay afloat.

In England, all higher education students are eligible for full loans to cover the costs of their tuition fees. In Russell Group universities, fees are generally set at £9,000 per year, this is the same for Oxbridge as for other institutions. Institutions are mandated to re-invest £1,000 of those fees into widening participation or financial support for students and the Russell Group universities have generous scholarship schemes for students from low-income backgrounds. For students entering higher education prior to 2016, those with a household income of £25,000 were eligible for a full maintenance grant from the government of £3,387 per year and partial maintenance grants were available for students with household incomes of up to £42,620, other students could obtain loans. However, matriculants from 2016 onwards, all these grants will be replaced by loans that are available to all students. Universities continue to offer their own grant schemes for students with low household incomes, although the amounts awarded vary by institution and available resources. The costs of higher education can still influence decision-making whether to continue into higher education at all, but there is support accessible by everyone regardless of where they study and additional support is available in particular at the universities with the largest endowments.

The main general difference between the costs of higher education in the United States and England is that default set up for government US student loans is beginning repayment just after graduation whereas the repayment for fees is linked to income in England meaning students only repay the loans once they start earning. However, the elite US institutions presented in this study offer bursaries rather than loans meaning that poor students can get a free education without having to pay back any of the costs of fees or living expenses. There are also some full fees bursaries and maintenance costs bursaries at Russell Group universities in England.

Changing how elite higher education is viewed

For many parents, where their kid ends up going to school [university] is like a report card on their parenting.

(US Big Three selector)

For some parents, university admission can be viewed the ultimate test of how well they had done in navigating the prior education system and bringing up their child.

One way of dealing with the challenge is questioning the reference point that following a particular trajectory and getting into a leading university in either England or the United States is indeed the report card or judgement day for their parenting. Perhaps surprisingly, selective institutions are the first to admit that there are other routes to a happy life than admission to a selective institution. Leading institutions speak highly and respectfully of their competitor institutions and convey that they consider an education at many other educational establishments as worthwhile. Selectors also value young people choosing to take time out or consciously choosing a different career path. In one instance, an English selector explained that he thought some students might find the environment, curricula and assessment systems at other institutions than his own more conducive for attaining highly.

One Big Three Ivy actively encourages students to take a gap year after school with the implicit aim to have time out of the pressured education system and to provide space to think. Another US selector encouraged students to view, 'Picking a college is like picking a spouse. You don't pick the "top ranked" one, because that has no meaning. You pick the one with the personality and character that complements your own.' Another US selector put it as 'finding the right fit, not the right sticker in the Volvo'.

Indeed, because well-informed parents and students can go to extra-ordinary lengths to gain a real or perceived advantage, educators are redesigning some education practices to prevent certain behaviour or playing excessive strategy games in education.

For example, some English private preparatory schools now split every month into three equal parts and select from births within each third to avoid a rush for being born on the first and an alleged rise in elected ceasarians on that day. The Independent School Admissions Association of Greater New York has been so concerned about the impact of coaching and the culture of anxiety the admissions test to private preparatory schools administered at age four creates that many of their consortia schools abolished the tests.

In England, some universities go to some length to establish the different types of school an applicant has attended for their GCSEs (usually taken at the age of sixteen) and for their A-level or equivalent qualification when they apply to higher education. This work is undertaken in particular to contextualise students' school changes between the state and private school sector in the final years of secondary education. A wealthy student who has been educated privately and only changes to a state school for the last two years will be reported as a state school admit. Some affluent parents strategically move their children into the state sector for this reason. Equally, a poor student with a scholarship to an elite private school would count as a private school admit. Some universities therefore think understanding school moves is important for genuinely spotting talent and for understanding applicants in context.

Overall, selectors themselves are a perhaps unlikely group of proponents for toning down the race to the top institutions they represent and calling for some measured approaches in thinking about the value and opportunities of elite and other forms of higher education.

Remaining challenges

In England, national and institutional policies to widen participation and financial support have increased the representation of those from less affluent families in higher education and in elite higher education. At Harvard, over 20 per cent of students do not pay anything for their education meaning their family income is below $65,000 (correct June 2015) with 70 per cent of students on some form of financial aid.[2]

While a lot of progress has been made to enhance the accessibility and affordability of higher education, several selectors also noted some limitations to how far their programmes went. As this Big Three selector noted:

> Occasionally you get kids that have, maybe a parent in jail, or ... You do see ... kids from families who are struggling, but really, like, real poverty is rare. They're just not ... I don't even know if those kids are applying to college, let alone [this Ivy]. So I mean, it happens, but it's very rare.

Similarly, in England, the representation of children who have been 'in-care' remains low in higher education and particularly in elite higher education.

Other remaining challenges include that the effect of a policy change can be unclear. As a result, different institutions can sometimes have different policies aimed at enhancing their admissions process. For example, some consider selection interviews as offering unique opportunities to shine regardless of background, others consider interviews as a barrier that leads to social reproduction. Thus, some universities strongly support interviews and others would like to see them abolished or have abolished them. Controversies also surround additional admissions tests in England: Oxford University has supported the development and conduct of a range of admissions tests to make selection fairer and to enable selectors to tap into potential that might not have shone through in standard school examinations. In contrast, Cambridge University has significantly fewer admissions tests and views as a strength of their admissions system that it is rooted in public examinations rather than additional tests. Indeed, a professional Russell Group selector observed how with additional tests 'you are doomed if you do [administer them] and you are doomed if you don't'.

In the United States, there are also controversies surrounding tests as barriers or enablers. In recent years, some less selective institutions have gone 'test optional' meaning that applicants do not have to submit SAT or ACT results. Such policies are designed to enable a wider range of students to apply. However, proponents of tests have also argued that tests allow applicants an opportunity to shine and offer additional information other than high school performance.

Chapter summary

Looking at societies through the lens of admission to higher education means trying to understand social inequality and the idea of education-based social mobility whereby those from modest social origins can be given an opportunity to develop their lives and employment prospects through education.

In the context of the constraints of their practice, many selectors sought of ways to support and admit students who had faced disadvantages. Perhaps ironically, the most selective and richest institutions are particularly well placed to offer bursaries to students who are high attaining but come from modest backgrounds. This is ironic in the sense that the majority of students from modest backgrounds either do not achieve the high grades necessary for filing a competitive application to the most selective universities or do not to apply even when they have such high grades. As a result, most disadvantaged students in higher education are in institutions that do not have generous institutional scholarships although they might be eligible for government-backed loans.

Nonetheless, significant changes have been made in higher education admissions over the past decades. Despite the fierce competition for places, admitted students are more diverse now in both England and the United States than they were in the past. Indeed, one selector reflected that:

> We're inclusive … we're more exclusive than we've ever been, and yet we're more inclusive than we've ever been. And it's really interesting to understand that and make sense of that at once. (Ivy League selector)

To conclude then, leading universities on both sides of the Atlantic understand the differential opportunities in early education and, by being mindful of such differences in admission and working to increase applications from disadvantaged students they avoid admitting only privileged students. In doing so, these universities are becoming more reflective of all high-attaining students, although they are some way off from being reflective of the profile of all school-leavers.

The next and final chapter then asks – does it actually make a difference to participate in elite higher education?

So What?

This chapter summarizes the key points from the previous chapters and debates questions that have not been raised previously but are relevant when considering the process of admission to elite higher education. It also offers some concluding observations.

Some things we have learnt about admission

The beginning of the book introduced Laura Spence, Barbara Grutter and Abigail Fisher. To recapitulate, in 1999, Oxford University rejected Laura Spence's application to study medicine, leading to national debates on the fairness of admission. Similarly, Grutter and Fisher's rejection by the University of Michigan Law School and the University of Texas sparked national debates. The preceding chapters have provided some answers as to the factors that came into play in the admissions decisions involving Spence, Grutter and Fisher – although we have to bear in mind that the US institutions that participated in this project are private institutions and not public ones like the ones subject to the Supreme Court rulings.

We have seen that while school performance is a key consideration in an Oxbridge application, in some subjects like medicine – the subject Laura Spence had applied to – admissions tests as well as interviews are held. All these aspects of an application are taken into account when making an admissions decision. While Spence's application from a low-performing state school may have signalled particular potential to succeed at university, there were other state school educated applicants with higher scores in other selection elements – indeed, Spence was beaten to her place by some other state-school applicants. Medicine also remains one of the most competitive subjects to apply for and it is possible that Spence would have succeeded in gaining a place in Oxford for a different subject. Some commentators have interpreted Spence's decision to study biochemistry at Harvard instead as indicating that she may not have been fully committed to studying medicine at that moment in time. However, she graduated from the graduate course in medicine at Cambridge in 2008 and she is now a practicing doctor in England.

The decisions regarding Grutter and Fisher are embedded in holistic admissions processes that consider individual applicants as well as the overall profile and characteristics of the admitted student cohort. There are no academic cut-offs or guarantees of admission as such. So, while Grutter and Fisher appear to have been solid and competitive applicants, there was nothing in their profiles that gave them an outstanding edge or 'hook' over other applicants that year. This means that while they were admissible, they were not part of the stellar pool of applicants.

Admissions processes in the United States and England have some similarities but also some differences. We have seen that admissions decisions in England are based primarily on applicants' demonstrated academic ability and academic potential. The assessment of ability and academic potential is fine-tuned by gathering information from a range of sources, including school performance and sometimes information from additional admissions tests and interviews. Contextual information about applicants' schools and personal information are also frequently used for enhancing the quality of decision-making in admissions. In England, a key consideration for selectors is applicants' expected ability and potential to achieve highly in their course at university.

In contrast, academic considerations were less important to the private elite universities in the United States researched here. While academic talent was necessary for gaining admission, on its own, this was not usually enough and needed to be complemented by having another hook in the application. Such hooks could relate to sporting prowess, race, musical talents, or having an existing link with the institution.

Table 9 summarizes key differences along a range of dimensions between the English and US institutions in this book.

Despite the differences, there were also a range of shared features and challenges in the two systems and some of the distinctions in the table are less black and white and more differences of degree. A shared feature in admission for both countries is some commitment among those working in admissions and outreach to increase the representation of students on campuses who come from less affluent backgrounds. Both admissions systems try making meaningful admissions decisions in a context of de facto unequal prior opportunities. There are shared challenges in selecting among very similar applicants and in finding valid and reliable ways to differentiate between applicants. Chapter 7 also highlighted shared challenges regarding incommensurability of different aspects of an application, the challenge of not being selective enough, drawing lines

Table 9 Similarities and differences in admission in the United States and England

Dimension of comparison	US private universities, highly selective	England public universities, highly selective
Goal of admissions	Crafting a class	Individual evaluation in context of school and circumstances
Learning at university	From diverse peers, outside classroom	Small tutorials and seminars (mainly Oxbridge only)
Fairness	To institution society and applicants	To applicants
Curriculum	Broad, for example, liberal arts, all-rounder	Specific, specialist
Stage in education	More 'penultimate' feel, specialist education at postgraduate level	More likely to be 'final stage' with postgraduate study for advanced specialization
Philosophical admission discourse	Using available opportunities and facilities Contribution to campus community	Developing academic potential and ability
Role of admission	Getting in as main hurdle, then about student experience	Getting in as starting point, then about academic achievement
Equity dimensions needing addressing	Race Individual extenuating circumstances	Schooling Social class Individual extenuating circumstances (see Equality Act 2010 for all protected characteristics)
Dominant rationale for equity discourse	Diversity as a valuable goal	Inequality can hide differences in potential to attain highly
Key stakeholders	Athletic Coaches Development Office Alumni office Admissions professionals PR office/media Academics Art & Music Societies Institutional strategy/mission	Academics Admissions professionals Institutional strategy/mission Media OFFA Recruitment/Marketing Planning

(Continued)

Table 9 Continued

Dimension of comparison	US private universities, highly selective	England public universities, highly selective
Success of admission	What graduates do with their lives, leadership at community, national and international level, contribution to university development	Graduation with a good degree and success in entering employment

where there are none, engaging with the media and being compliant or exceeding governance requirements of higher education.

Key differences in admission remain with regard to the emphasis in the United States on crafting a class as opposed to the emphasis on selecting individuals in England. Transatlantic differences also remain regarding the aim of admission, the undergraduate curriculum and learning model, and the main stakeholders in university admissions.

Some things we have not learnt about admissions

There are a range of things we have not learnt in this book. The preceding chapters have not investigated the experience of the admissions system from the students' point of view. They have not investigated the meaning of stratified higher education systems, the admission of students 'pre-qualification', what happens at universities once students arrive on campuses, and if it matters whether a student is admitted to elite higher education or whether the current model of elite higher education is the best possible way to serve local, national and international communities. Some of these questions are now considered. In some instances, features of the US and English system are compared with models used in other countries or with other models of learning.

What are the relative merits of pre-qualification systems?

Both the United States and England have pre-qualification systems: applicants apply to universities without having taken their final school examinations, although US applicants apply with their SAT or ACT results. This contrasts with other countries, for example, Ireland, where students apply to university only after their final school examination grades are known. The challenge of the pre-qualification system for selectors in England is that predictions about attainment can be inaccurate; while they are usually inflated, some students may suffer as their predicted grades may be lower than the grades they go on to actually achieve. Occasionally, students in England and the United States apply or reapply to university after having taken a year out following their school examinations. Indeed, selectors in England regarded those with known school examination results as particularly good choices because there was no uncertainty over whether their grades were above or below those required for matriculation. In the United States, too, there was an example of students being strongly encouraged to enrol after having taken a year off. However, the United States does not generally operate a conditional offer system.

The issue of whether a 'post-qualification' decision-making system would make the admissions process fairer and easier to conduct is debated occasionally in England. As this would entail changing the entire set-up of admissions cycles, there has not been much appetite for this change. The idiosyncratic feature of English admissions which requires applicants for Oxford and Cambridge and all applicants for medicine, dentistry and veterinary sciences to apply three months before the deadline for all other universities and courses also occasionally raises some eyebrows, but again without a strong call for change – perhaps because of the implications of re-organizing the admissions cycle.

This book has been silent on the relative merits of pre- and post-qualification systems. Indeed, whether applicants do better or worse under one or the other system is difficult to establish without having a randomized controlled trial or an experiment examining whether the profile of admitted students would change if all school attainment information was known at the point of admission.

Does it matter whether academics or professionals select students?

All the US interview respondents in this book were full-time admissions professionals. In England, some respondents were full-time professionals, others were academics who undertook admissions as part of their academic role. As discussed in Chapter 1, more and more admissions operations in England are being professionalized and centralized, and there are fewer examples of entire universities or individual departments within universities having academic-led admissions systems. However, notably, Oxford and Cambridge continue to have academic-led systems. In both the United States and England, academic-led systems are the norm for admission to postgraduate study.

Not all academics in the remaining academic-led undergraduate systems in England liked the idea of selecting their own students, although there were some who felt strongly that this was the right thing to do. One Oxbridge selector argued that the increasing complexity of the admissions system at Oxbridge required more professionalization. Another argument voiced against academic-led systems concerned the resources and time-investment required by having hundreds of academic staff involved in admissions processes. Whether a change to a professional system would be better was contemplated by an Oxbridge academic who noted 'I have no commitment to picking my own students … whether they [admissions professionals] would do a better job is a different question'. Other academics wished to see the academic-led systems continue. One proponent of academic selection observed that 'the current system is not cheap but it accomplishes the end goal to select the best people of a cohort that apply regardless of race or gender'; others liked the system because it was 'possible to see (potential) in the interview process which is not possible to see on paper or any other circumstance'.

So, is a professional-led or academic-led system for selecting students better? Part of the answer has to go back to the purpose of admission – one has to ask whether it is a decision that requires academic judgement on skills that a subject expert might be particularly well placed to assess or whether the purpose is to select people with a range of skills, or whether it is a matter of applying predetermined academic attainment criteria to application files.

Furthermore, the effectiveness and fairness of a system does not solely rest in the structure. For example, those working in academic-led systems value the debate and discussion around admissions criteria and standards and that new voices are continually heard when new academics enter the world of admissions for the first time with a fresh pair of eyes. A professional head of Oxbridge admissions noted how he was responsible to all academics and that this diversity and scrutiny was helpful and enhanced accountability.

Similarly, US admissions offices value not only diversity among their students but also among their staff as a way to continuously question, reflect upon and enhance their process. For example, a US admissions officer identified a risk in having admissions too professionalized. She noted a gap between what drives people to enter an admissions job 'valuing education, providing opportunities to others, lifting up other people to be successful' and 'the reality of aspects of the role where in the upper echelons of the admissions world it can be more about "what is best for the school and not what is best for the student"'. Having continued discussions and debating priorities has the potential to balance the interests of students and institutions in selection.

These observations highlight that there is consensus on both sides of the Atlantic that questioning how things are done and reflections are a good thing, however, neither a professional nor an academic-led system have a monopoly on being able to achieve this.

As a tentative conclusion then, academic-led systems are more resource-intensive but can generate insights perhaps not easily gained in a professional-led system. Professional systems might be better suited for crafting a class with characteristics at the group level and are arguably better suited to responding to the context of legal challenges and public scrutiny. Having a range of voices heard in a professional or academic-led admissions process seems most conducive to keeping alive debates about substantive as well as procedural fairness.

How does the implied student model affect admission?

The institutions that are part of this project also arguably have an implied student model of a student as someone who is able to live away from home, often in a residential or collegiate setting, studies full-time and probably goes to university straight after school or sometimes perhaps after one gap year. One Oxbridge selector actually remarked how the admissions system was 'not very well designed for anyone who is not a very standardized candidate, an 18-year-old'. Part-time and distance learners or those returning to education . later in life while managing jobs and families were not part of the key discussions with selectors for this project, although some of the universities have developed Massive Open Online Courses (MOOCs) and offer adult education courses.

The implied applicant can also be apparent in the way institutions publish statistics. For example, when looking for statistics on the ethnic profile of students, some US universities list the non-white students as 'diverse' students without actually mentioning the percentage of white/Caucasian students at the university. By implicitly using white as the comparator, the feeling that this is the norm might be – perhaps inadvertently – re-enforced. Other key parameters of the admissions systems, that is, SAT scores, school GPAs or A-levels and GCSEs, are geared towards younger applicants with uninterrupted education and standard educational credentials.

However, this implied student model is not shared across the US or English higher education sectors. Other university models exist. In England, the Open University, for example, operates a very different model of blended (online and face-to-face) learning designed to support part-time students, who often combine their studies with work or family responsibilities, who may not be able to travel or move away from where they live and who may not have undertaken standard school-leaving qualifications. Professional experience can replace standard credentials in this alternative model. Some US colleges are open access and others like the University of Southern New Hampshire are specifically designed for mature, part-time students.

The implied student model is part of the hidden assumptions of admission processes and it is only by seeing the familiar as strange through the eyes of other admissions models or other systems that those implied assumptions become apparent. Such implied assumptions make a difference as the profile of admitted students to the Open University is clearly different from the profile of students at Russell Group universities.

Are the current admissions procedures the best?

We have a 'no whining rule' here: don't just say you don't like it but come up with ideas of how to make it better.

(Harvard summer institute for admission)

Selectors within the admissions systems are probably one of the first people to point out minor or sometimes major areas that could be further improved in their systems. Indeed, one US Big Three dean of admission said how he knew 'all the problems there are with holistic admission' and how he had recently encountered a 'faked reference' and was aware that the college essays were of seminal importance, but at the same time, applicants could 'buy them from the internet'. Selectors on both side of the Atlantic saw a shortcoming in using tests and performance information which could be influenced by specially purchased preparation and coaching. The variation in who was reading application files or making decisions was also a point of concern although the joint decision and multiple readings of applications by different readers were thought to mediate against idiosyncratic decisions. Among English selectors, another concern regarded the relative weighting of different elements of the application, although there was not necessarily consensus what a universally acceptable way of weighting information would look like or whether such a universal or more formulaic way would indeed be desirable.

As the quotation above from the Harvard summer institute on admissions highlights, while some aspects of the admissions systems raise complex questions, the challenge is how to practically change and enhance systems. A Russell Group selector also said how he would be 'very receptive to suggestions for improvements'. Another English selector noted how while she was not saying the process was perfect, one had to acknowledge that 'you can go to any selection procedure in any institution, in any setting, not even in an academic institution' and find aspects of a selection process that could be improved.

Change in admissions systems in both the United States and England has happened over time, and the systems are in constant processes of development. For example, a retired US dean of admissions reflected on how emphases in what institutions were looking for had shifted over the last five decades with an increasing emphasis away from academic attainment. He considered this a positive development although he thought it possible that not all his colleagues would agree. US selectors also cited needs-blind admissions for US students and later needs-blind admission for international students as examples of key changes that had made admission fairer over time. In the English context, key changes to Oxbridge admissions have been changes in having or not having additional tests at admission, the introduction of 'college-blind' interviewing and more recently, the systematic introduction of contextual data in admission. Across the English higher education sector, the most significant shift is possibly the shift away from academic-led to professional, centralized admissions processes. These changes are themselves contextualized by changes in fees and student-funding regimes and the increasing complexity of admission.

Often, bigger changes are changes that happen over years rather than overnight. Such changes can be driven by a mixture of external pressures (media, government) as well as internal top-down institutional pushes or organizational requirements for change and bottom-up changes requested by academic and professional selectors. There are other changes or improvements that would be nice to have but are balanced against cost and resource implications.

Are the differences in admission to the elite universities represented in this book due to the US universities being private and the English universities being public universities?

It does seem to be the case that some of the differences in US and English admission are indeed due to the status of the universities. While the US institutions in this project are 'not-for-profit' organizations and use their endowment to further the mission of their institution, there are interesting similarities between the US private universities and private not-for-profit secondary schools in England.

For example, the most prestigious private schools in England – called public schools – consider fit, using opportunities and the ability to contribute as part of their selection process. Westminster School, for example, seeks applicants 'whose academic and other abilities appear to match the ethos and standards of the School and whose personal qualities suggest they have the potential to contribute sufficiently to the School community and benefit from the many opportunities that are offered here' (Westminster School 2013). Harrow school looks 'for boys who are enthusiastic; who will make the most of opportunities offered at Harrow; who are talented in their academic studies, or in sport, the arts or another activity; and who have the potential to show great leadership' (Harrow School 2015). Eton College also explains how they are not just looking for academic accomplishment 'There are lots of boys here who do very well academically at school and ultimately very well in exams, but we want young people who are eager to enjoy the other opportunities, sporting, cultural, social, that being at a school like this involves' (Eton 2015).

These statements taken from the websites of private secondary schools in England mirror conversations about using opportunities at the private US universities. So, privateness in itself might explain those similarities. Furthermore, policies like giving preferential admission to the children of alumni or donors are again found not only in US private universities but also in private schools in England.

Some public universities in the United States like the University of California system do not give admission preferences to alumni children and are thus more similar to the publicly funded – and, more importantly publicly accountable – universities in England. Many US public universities also operate numeric attainment cut-offs for admission which are more similar to practices in some Russell Group universities and universities just below the Russell Group.

So, the status of whether a university is publicly or privately funded does seem to play a role. Whether either system is better is a different question as there are different constraints and opportunities in the different models.

Does it make a difference whether the US or the English admissions system is used?

It depends. On the one hand, there are some students who gain admissions to the most selective English universities who would not gain admission to comparable universities in the United States. High academic achievers with little other interests or contributions might be in this group – perhaps with the exception of applying to specialist institutions for their talent in the United States. Inversely, some stellar athletes, development legacies or otherwise 'hooked' applicants might not be able to gain admission to the most elite sector of the English Russell Group but would succeed in the US competition for a place.

However, if one exchanged the US and English criteria for admissions, the result would be unlikely to be a landslide shift in the profile of admitted students. Affluent families with cultural, social and financial resources, who continue to be the core constituents for selective universities on both sides of the Atlantic, would be able to alter their support for their children in light of changing requirements and criteria. English parents and 'good' secondary schools would support students in building the profile of civic engagement and outstanding talents valued in the current US system. US parents would equally adapt to further increasing their focus on their children's attainment. This prediction is in line with sociological work from as early as the 1970s which argued that social stratification patterns will be the very similar in any advanced liberal democracy that has the family as the basic unit for organizing society (Featherman-Jones-Hauser hypothesis, 1975) regardless of the particular way in which organizations are structured.

Indeed, during this project, I participated in a simulated admissions exercise in the United States where we had to choose between several applicants for admission for a highly selective university. Most of the simulated 'admits' in this exercise would have fared well in a Russell Group university admissions process in England as well. There was only one applicant who had failed to gain admission in the US simulation exercise for being too 'geeky' and academic (see Chapter 3). This student was then admitted to Cambridge, England.

We have also seen that Laura Spence was unsuccessful in getting a place for medicine at Oxford but was admitted to Harvard and studied biochemistry and then Cambridge for Graduate Entry Medicine.

In the margins, it would make a difference if English institutions openly endorsed a diversity discourse as a goal in admissions. This would likely result in a greater number of black students being admitted to the most selective universities. However, as US research has also shown an 'Asian penalty,' the number of students from Chinese and other East Asian backgrounds would perhaps even go down – the impact on students from the Indian, Bangladeshi and Pakistani communities is difficult to predict as this is a proportionately smaller group in the United States. They might experience a slight increase in representation if they were treated akin to Hispanic applicants in the United States.

Conversely, US institutions would be less ethnically diverse if they adopted an English-style admissions system and East Asian and white students would probably increase their representation on campuses in a purely academically focused system. The quality of the athletics teams would also suffer with fewer athletes among the admitted students as their sporting prowess would not compensate for lower grades. Orchestras and drama societies might remain relatively unchanged.

Some things we have not learnt – beyond admissions

There are a range of questions that are relevant to admission and elite higher education that this book has not answered. The reason is that the sort of research that would allow us to answer some questions can be difficult and resource-intensive. At the core of a lot of the unanswered questions is a counterfactual: would students who have gone to elite universities fared differently in life and employment had they not gone? Would those who did not attend an elite university fared differently if they had gone? There are ways to try and match students who participate in selective higher education and those who do not as closely as possible. However, the challenge remains that the two groups are still somewhat different. Unlike some natural science or psychological experiments were we have 'randomized controlled trials', this is often not possible in educational research.

Finally, a lot of the questions that remain unanswered cannot be answered by simply asking one person one question at one moment in time. Instead, we are interested in what happens to students months, years, even decades after graduation – how are they doing? And how does this relate to the sort of higher education experience they had? Some studies ask adults retrospectively about their experiences and some cohort studies track students over many years to find answers to these questions.

A final challenge, which indeed applies to this book, is how to generalize from conversations with some people, in the case of this book, admissions professionals and academic selectors, especially when different people say different things. It can be challenging to establish whether one person holds a very atypical view or whether a range of different views is indeed representative. Talking to a range of different people helps mitigating against this challenge.

Bearing those limitations to what we can know in mind, the next sections consider specific questions regarding what we have not learnt from this book.

Are stratified higher education systems better than non-stratified systems?

> I mean there's a particular aspect of this system in Britain which distinguishes it from other places … this whole thing is really about a prize – a prize is getting a place at a top university and that prize is something that we [selectors] are distributing. If it were the case that, there was not much difference between Oxford and Cambridge on the one hand, and everyone else on the other, then this wouldn't matter very much. But there is a sense in which it does matter a lot and that the prize is very valuable, and therefore we should distribute it in a way which is fair. … One way of unpacking that is actually to make the prize less valuable, you could just have a university system which was less differentiated in which case it didn't matter who won the prize but of course we're not going to move in that direction and so if we're going to have this as a prize then we have to make it fair. (Oxbridge selector)

A larger issue when looking at England and the United States in comparative perspective is that both countries have highly stratified higher education systems with the sorts of highly selective and sought-after prestigious institutions studied in this book only educating a small minority of all higher education students. The majority of higher education happens elsewhere, in other institutions with often less competitive entrance requirements. Overall, there is a relationship between the structure of higher education and the structure of society, with the more disadvantaged students disproportionately clustering within the less prestigious tiers of stratified higher education systems. From within the stratified higher education systems, this can easily seem like just an inevitably way systems are. However, many other countries have more equal status among different universities. This can mean that competition for places at particular universities is less fierce than in the Anglo–Saxon world. Broadly speaking, in most continental European countries, it matters more what subject students study at university rather than at which institution they study. Admission to university in some other European countries is also more akin to a matriculation process of students exercising their democratic entitlement to participate in higher education rather than a competitive process of being selected and chosen among peers for participation in a particularly desirable tier of higher education. Indeed, in some Nordic countries such as Denmark, students are paid to go to university regardless of family income. Many other countries have no or very modest fees for higher education. These differences highlight different models regarding the purpose, role and function of higher education in different countries and the different relationship between higher education and the common good or development of citizens, societies and their economies.

A paradox is that while the less prestigious institutions in stratified higher education systems educate many more of the disadvantaged students than the prestigious institutions, the financial support and opportunities available for those select students who are admitted to the top tier institutions in stratified higher education systems are much more generous than in the less prestigious institutions and can dwarf the support students in non-stratified systems can access.

Overall, we do not fully understand the impact of having stratified or non-stratified higher education systems or full-funding for everyone or high fees in higher education on the pattern of who can access higher education. Even countries with much more equal university and funding systems like Denmark show that students from more affluent families and those from poorer families still choose different subjects and institutions when they progress into higher education. However, as a minimum, considering the context of other countries shows that there is nothing inevitable about the stratification of higher education or fees and financial support regimes.

What happens at university after admission?

Getting into higher education is just a first step on the road to completing a degree. Elite higher education institutions in both England and the United States have exceptionally high completion rates with more than nine out of ten students who start their degree completing it – this compares with a national average of only one in two students completing their university studies in the United States at the university they started and one in three not completing their studies across English higher education.

These high completion rates in elite universities are the convergence of a lot of things. Students at risk of dropping out might find it easier to access hardship funds or financial aid at wealthy elite institutions than at other universities. There is some consensus that students from poorer families or families without a history of higher education have a higher chance of graduating if they attend an elite compared with attending a non-elite university. The residential set-up and the feeling of belonging and connectedness this fosters seem key in supporting students to graduation.

However, Denmark, as an example of a country with high support for students across all institutions, has a national completion rate coming close to the most selective US and English universities, fewer than one in seven students dropping out. While the elite universities studied in this book thus achieve exceptional completion rates within their national context, there are other national university and funding models that can also facilitate high completion across an even wider range of institutions and diverse students.

There is currently growing interest in both the United States and England regarding the 'learning gains' at university (Arum and Roska 2011; HEFCE 2015). In other words, what have students learnt that they did not know before they entered higher education? And, are different institutions better or worse at 'adding value' to the knowledge and skills that students already have when they enter higher education? There are already some 'learning gains' or 'added value' comparisons available for secondary education, but higher education evaluations are not at this stage yet. It is possible that 'learning gains' might indeed be higher for institutions that have traditionally been regarded as less prestigious.

The question of curricula is key for thinking about what happens to students once they are admitted and enrolled in higher education. In previous chapters, discussions have linked some differences in admissions to differences in the purpose of undergraduate higher education and the curricula in the United States and England. English students choose a subject for study at the point of application and many US students only decide once they are within higher education which majors they wish to pursue. There is an implicit expectation in the United States that students will continue into 'graduate school' to specialize, although postgraduate education is also becoming increasingly important in England for gaining 'graduate-level' employment after university. These differences in specialism highlight quite different purposes for undergraduate higher education and go some way to explaining the different selection criteria in the two countries.

A further consideration regarding the curriculum in higher education is what skills are honed and rewarded. This is of interest because of the linkage between elite higher education and positions of power in key public spheres such as politics, law and the media. For example, the Oxbridge education system and the one-to-one tutorials it provides are often considered as a particularly good preparation for succeeding in robust debates and arguing a point of view. The system might, however, be less good at developing team players or arriving at compromises. This contrasts with the discourse of learning from diverse peers used in the US context where peer-learning is a clearly articulated aim of the curriculum. Further research could investigate whether these different philosophical approaches regarding the curriculum actually make a difference to the lived experience at university and result in elite graduates in England and the United States having distinct skills.

The role of extra-curricular activities might partly mitigate the differences in emphases in the core academic curriculum. Both, the US and the English elite education systems offer huge opportunities for involvement in sports, clubs, societies and charitable activities alongside the core academic curriculum. Participation in extra-curricular team sports can, for example, complement the skills acquired in a more individualistic academic education system. Indeed, as even elite higher education is something more students participate in than there are 'elite' graduate jobs, extra-curricular activities and internships are increasingly important for employment or further study outcomes after graduation. Again, more research would be needed to fully understand how the purpose of the curriculum in England and the United States, extra-curricular activities and opportunities relate to transitions into employment after university.

For England, it matters not only to participate and graduate from higher education but also the grade with which students graduate is crucial. Selectors voiced concerns about the employment prospects for their graduates where they thought having any degree from a good university was not enough for getting a good job, it needed to be a good degree. One Oxbridge selector remarked how not getting a high grade

> is much more of a black mark against somebody than it would have been, say ten or fifteen year ago. And when everybody is succeeding, then the penalties for failure are that much higher.

There seemed to be slightly less concern about the detailed degree classification of graduates in the US system. This could be because applications to graduate school also rely on elements other than using university degree results such as additional standardized tests.

Although there has been a rise in focus on student satisfaction and happiness, there is also some evidence that unhappiness and pressure can contribute to higher attainment for some students perhaps at the cost of quality of life. The impact of pressures to succeed, whether or not this includes pressures to attain the highest academic degree class possible, is again apparent on both sides of the Atlantic. A Big Three selector noted that 'students are coming to campuses with a lot more mental health issues than a generation ago'. He noted that there were various theories why this was the case, although the primary task for the university was to support the students thus affected. Similar alarms have been raised in UK universities where universities note higher demands from students to access counselling services and how these are – in the words of one Russell Group admissions professional – 'over-stretched and understaffed'. Indeed, he noted an eight-week waiting list for a first appointment at his institution. Elite higher education then is clearly not plain sailing and a happy experience for everyone who has chosen and is chosen to participate in it.

What is the longer-term impact of elite higher education on students?

The ceremony at the end of an undergraduate degree is called graduation in England. While Americans understand this term, they also know this ceremony by the more popular name 'commencement'. This terminology highlights how, in the American context, this event marks the beginning of the true purpose of admission and higher education: how will the class of graduating students fare in their lives in the real world? What will they choose to do – and how big and extensive will their reunion files be after twenty-five years? And, what will be their ability to support the university financially in the future?

English graduations are still formal and celebratory occasions, especially compared with the often understated or non-existent ceremonies in some continental European countries. However, their purpose is largely restricted to celebrating accomplishments at university and thanking families and friends for supporting the graduates through their studies. Alumni networks and events as well as fundraising are growing post-graduation phenomena in England but have not reached the sophisticated levels and scale of US networks and fundraising: graduation is still an occasion at which the key remit of the English undergraduate university is largely accomplished whereas it is the beginning of someone being an alumnus or an alumna of a US university for the rest of their lives.

The question of what graduates do with their lives has received more attention in US than in English universities. Outcomes in the United States are broadly conceived and do not only include how much money graduates earn – although this is of interest on both sides of the Atlantic – but also whether they are happy with their lives and contribute to the communities in which they live. For example, the seminal work by William Bowen and Derek Bok *The Shape of the River* (1999) showed how non-white graduates from across all universities participated disproportionately more in the civic lives of their communities than their white counterparts. There is also research showing that graduates increasingly marry other graduates and often those who graduated from the same institution they did, so university attendance can have significant effects on some of the most personal aspects of peoples' lives.

US selectors were also aware of how the cost of college impacted on life decisions, such as moving back home – the 'bomerang generation' as well as marrying later, buying houses later and having kids later and one selector observed how 'in doing so, they [graduates] are no helping the economy as they are not buying washers and cars' (Ivy League selector).

'To be happy'. This is usually the first answer any parent gives when asked what they wish for their children. So, does elite higher education make those who had the opportunity to participate in it happier in the long term? The evidence here suggests that selective universities do not help create happier or more productive people. Indeed, a perhaps unlikely team of observers, admissions staff and one academic at Harvard noted:

> It is common to encounter even the most successful students, who have won all the 'prizes', stepping back and wondering if it was all worth it. Professionals in their thirties and forties – physicians, lawyers, academics, business people and others – sometimes give the impression that they are dazed survivors of some bewildering life-long boot-camp. Some say they ended up in their profession because of someone else's expectations, or that they simply drifted into it without pausing to think whether they really loved their work. Often they say they missed their youth entirely, never living in the present, always pursuing some ill-defined future goal. (Fitzsimmons, McGrath and Ducey 2011)

This observation is not saying that elite higher education is not worth it, but it is observing that some students experience or use it not as an enabling opportunity to live the life they want but as a step onto a conveyor belt to something that they may not have wished or chosen had they reflected upon it. There are also psychological reasons why struggles for happiness might not be alleviated or perhaps even intensified when everyone with whom one compares oneself is so highly accomplished. The good news then is that the vast majority of graduates who do not participate in the top tiers of higher education – indeed, as well as those who do participate – can pursue happiness as it is not determined by whether or not someone participates in elite higher education.

Overall, there is still a lot we could explore in future research about the detailed ways in which participating in a particular form of higher education impacts on a range of life outcomes and how universities support their students.

A further question that directly links the admissions debates presented in this book with the question of added value is to what extent universities simply select those who already have the attributes they seek to develop or to what extent they actually tap into potential that is distinct from demonstrated ability and then develop it.

As a thought experiment, one can think of this difference as the difference between a modelling agency and a training camp. A modelling agency will only recruit people who already have the looks they are looking for. In contrast, a training camp or military or aviation academy will not select those who are already proficient in what they are meant to learn, students cannot usually drive tanks or fly commercial aircrafts before they start their training. Instead, training camps are looking for potential that indicates that a person can learn those skills within a given time frame.

The discourse of selection on potential is strong in both the US and England. In the United States, potential was frequently framed in terms of potential to benefit from the university experience on offer and potential to contribute to the campus community and other communities later in life. In England, potential was framed more in academic terms as potential to achieve and succeed in the course of study. However, at closer inspection, the discourses of potential are very closely related to discourses of ability. For example, the Law Aptitude test taken by many applicants for law in England tests the skills that students will need to do well in legal education. Potential to contribute to life on a US campus is derived from statements about previous contributions applicants have made to their school and wider communities.

The tendency then is for actual admissions decisions to lean more towards the 'modelling agency' way of selecting even if a strong discourse of trying to select like an academy is used. This, in turn, may mean that the universities dominating international League tables might also not provide the highest 'value added' or transformation for their students simply because so many of their enrolled students are already very high achieving before their university experience and already demonstrate at least part of the key skills that the degree programmes seek to develop.

A related question about added value concerns whether it matters for outcomes post higher education where one went to university. Here, there is some perhaps surprising research by Stacey Dale and Alan Krueger in the United States which indicates that those good enough to get into elite higher education institutions 'need not bother going' as their life outcomes are similar whether or not they actually went to those prestigious universities. According to this work, the only group for whom elite higher education genuinely makes a difference are those who were from disadvantaged backgrounds and for whom elite higher education unlocked access to networks and ways of being in the world that they would have not been able to access otherwise. This group was described by one Ivy League selector as 'the student who did not know before going to [this institution] that "to summer" is a verb for some people'. However, other work suggests that it is white men who are better at reaping the labour market rewards of elite higher education.

Work in England is currently ongoing to see whether social background has a stronger influence on employment outcomes than university attended. This work seems to indicate that those from the most privileged social backgrounds benefit most from elite higher education. There is some indication from German research that even among those who graduate from good universities with the highest academic credentials – a doctorate – those who came from more privileged families do better in the labour market than those from less advantaged backgrounds.

These observations raise wider questions about the effect of elite higher education on different students and also again about the 'added value' of elite higher education compared with other forms of education and compared with the direct impact of social background. In a risk-averse social context where many middle-class families in the United States, England and elsewhere start competing for good schooling and opportunities early on (see Chapter 8), it is unlikely that any research showing that students who did not attend the most selective universities can do well in life will lessen the pressure on places for the most select forms of education – however, it will be interesting for more research to investigate the question of the added value of elite education.

Does elite higher education serve the public good?

The philosopher John Rawls has invited anyone thinking about social justice to take part in a thought experiment (1971): if we were all born behind a 'veil of ignorance' where we did not know which position in life and which characteristics we would have once we entered the world, what sort of society would we design? Rawls argues that we would choose a society that was fair and not too unequal. There would still be some inequalities. For example, we might still choose to have a stratified system of higher education which some can and some can't participate in.

However, in this thought experiment, the purpose of elite higher education clearly has to be to benefit the many. Graduates should not merely add to their personal well-being or economic resources but should contribute to society – this would be the condition under which those behind a veil of ignorance would agree to offer special opportunities for some because everyone benefits. So, does elite higher education serve the public good?

Many of the professionals we rely on in health, education, law, media, politics and the civil service are graduates. In the highest echelons of the professions, many – but not all – have graduated from prestigious universities. While there are 'private returns' to these individuals in being successful in their chosen career, the hope is that there are also public benefits to society at large from their leadership and thus from elite higher education. However, some recent US work by Steven Brint questions the link between elite higher education and positions of power as it shows how there is no relationship between university attended and the top professional jobs in some fields (2014). This is not to deny the historic and contemporary role of elite universities in creating new knowledge and innovation.

Moreover, the psychologist and US university leader, Robert Sternberg recently challenged the public benefit argument of especially elite but also other higher education (2012). He observed that the people who had brought about the financial crisis in the 2000s, people who had gambled the houses and life-time savings of many, were often graduates from the most prestigious higher education institutions. Sternberg concludes this observation with calling for changing university admission from admitting applicants who fit into a particular model of high grades and the parameters of sport and participation to trying to find young minds who are innovative and will bring a new angle to debates. A related point that goes back to what happens within higher education is that elite universities either do not prioritize or develop fundamental ethical behaviour in their graduates or such training does not always sustainably translate into ethical practices once students graduate.

The answer to the question of whether elite higher education serves the public good then seems to be that sometimes, but not always, it does. Elite higher education has no exclusive hold but makes a contribution to serving the public good. Perhaps more could be done so that people behind a veil of ignorance would opt to keep elite higher education for everyone's benefit. Indeed, it is also not clear whether elite higher education is necessary for public benefits or whether having a less differentiated higher education system is equally well placed to meeting those public good and public service aspirations. Tentatively it seems that just as the fairness of an admissions system does not always follow from its format (academic or professional-led) the eliteness or non-eliteness of a university system does not necessarily in itself say something about the system's ability to enhance the lives of the communities the system serves.

Conclusion

England and the United States have stratified higher education systems with fierce competition for places at prestigious Russell Group and Ivy League universities as well as selected other institutions and courses. By looking at university admissions, much more becomes apparent than who is selected to study at a certain institution for a few years. The values underlying admission show how English and American societies construct the deserving person who is chosen to enjoy the opportunities elite education offers.

There are differences in what institutions are looking for in selection and also differences in who does the selecting. The private US universities are crafting classes that meet the requirements of a range of stakeholders from within the university, graduates and society at large. Classes then are crafted to have demonstrated academic ability as well as sporting abilities, a range of other talents including music, artistic and charitable, alumni or development relations, and diversity in terms of their ethnic, regional and social origin. English selectors are primarily interested in academic attainment and potential but also closely look at the context in which this attainment is achieved. Both countries face challenges regarding how to select fairly in a context of unequal opportunities related to family contexts and prior schooling.

The systems are designed to achieve somewhat different aims. Overall, there is support that the systems are largely working in achieving these aims – however, it is also fair to note that there is little 'counterfactual' research that would show who would be selected and what the results would be if a completely different admissions system was used. The two admissions systems constantly evolve to keep up with social, legal, technological and other developments.

The evidence on whether elite higher education matters, perhaps surprisingly, seems to indicate that elite higher education is neither sufficient nor necessary for leading happy lives and has a link, but no exclusive link, to desirable employment. Elite higher education might make most of a difference to those who would not have had access to opportunities and networks without it. There are currently vivid debates about what students learn when in higher education, what the long-term effects of elite higher education are and how to increase the diversity of talent coming through higher education to perhaps more creatively face the challenges of constantly evolving global economies and societies.

Higher education admission is a high-stakes selection context that is also a spectator sport for the national media and those following it. This fascination is unlikely to go away, indeed, the most recent application figures for the most prestigious universities show significant year-on-year growth. The yield figures for the Big Three US institutions are at a historic high, showing that – perhaps heightened by the context of economic uncertainty – students and those advising and supporting them are looking to the best-known institutions for their higher education. The curious world of university admissions will continue to evolve and adapt to changing contexts when deciding who, among the many potentially eligible applicants, should be offered a place.

Further Reading and Resources

This section provides an overview of selective further readings and resources for those wishing to find out more about university admissions. The section also contains links to practical resources for anyone wishing to apply for an undergraduate degree in England or the United States.

United States

The individual websites of universities and colleges describe in detail what is required for applying to their institution and the financial aids available.

Good all-round introductions to college admission

There are some good general books about college admissions. Based on over a year of working in the admissions office of a liberal arts college in Northeastern United States, Mitchell Stevens describes the admissions process from an insider's perspective. Jean Fetter, originally from Wales, UK and an Oxford graduate herself, provides an insightful overview of seven years as dean of admissions at Stanford University. A more recent analysis of admissions is provided by a former admissions officer at Dartmouth College, Michele Hernandez.

Fetter, J. H. (1995). *Questions and Admissions: Reflections on 100,000 Admissions Decisions at Stanford.* Stanford, CA: Stanford University Press.
Stevens, M. (2007). *Creating a Class: College Admissions and the Education of Elites.* Cambridge, MA: Harvard University Press.

Other general texts include Douthat's reflection on his time as an undergraduate at Harvard, the film in 500 words or less which follows four high school students through their college application process, Amy Chua's account of what it takes for an Ivy law professor 'tigermum' to start her daughters' college game early and Schoenstein's reflection on twenty-first century parenting.

Chua, A. (2011). *Battle Hymn of the Tiger Mother.* New York: Penguin.

Douthat, R. G. (2006). *Privilege: Harvard and the Education of the Ruling Class.* New York: Hyperion.

Schoenstein, R. (2002). *Toilet Trained for Yale: Adventures in 21st-Century Parenting.* Boston: Da Capo Press.

The seminal book by William Bowen and Derek Bok evaluates the effects of college on students' post-graduation lives. The book looks at civic participation and well-being as part of the outcomes of college.

Bowen, W. G. and Bok, D. C. (1998). *The Shape of the River: Long-term Consequences of Considering Race in College and University Admissions.* Princeton, NJ: Princeton University Press.

Introductions to particular aspects of college admission

Race

Bowen, W. G. and Bok, D. C. (1998). *The Shape of the River: Long-term Consequences of Considering Race in College and University Admissions.* Princeton, NJ: Princeton University Press.

Written by Bowen and Bok, the former presidents of Princeton and Harvard, this book looks at what college graduates are doing with their lives decades after graduating. Graduates admitted under affirmative action policies contribute significantly to public life.

Karabel, J. (2005). *The Chosen: The Hidden History of Admission and Exclusion at Harvard, Yale, and Princeton.* Boston: Houghton Mifflin.

The result of decades of scholarly and archival research, this book is a detailed overview of admissions policies and their origins at the Big Three Ivies.

Warikoo, N. K. (2016). *The Diversity Bargain: And Other Dilemmas of Race, Admissions, and Meritocracy at Elite Universities.* Chicago: University of Chicago Press.

This book explores how undergraduate students at elite UK and US universities think about the meaning of race and merit.

Socio-economic

Espenshade, T. J. and Radford, A. W. (2009). *No Longer Separate, Not Yet Equal: Race and Class in Elite College Admission and Campus Life.* Princeton, NJ: Princeton University Press.

Empirical research in this book shows that racial diversity has been increasing on US campuses. However, not all non-white groups receive beneficial special consideration in admissions. Racial diversity can also hide a lack of socio-economic diversity on campus.

Legacies

Golden, D. (2006). *The Price of Admission: How America's Ruling Class Buys Its Way into Elite Colleges – and Who Gets Left Outside the Gates.* New York: Random House.

As the title suggests, this is an investigation into the relationship between money and admissions and the idea of 'legacy admits'.

Athletics

Lincoln, C. (2004). *Playing the Game: Inside Athletic Recruiting in the Ivy League.* Chicago: Nomad Press.

This book explains how athletic recruitment and admissions work in the Ivy League.

Tier One Athletic Resources (2010). The Essential Guide to Ivy League Athletic Recruiting, available online.

This is a 'how to get recruited' guide for anyone wishing to gain admission to the Ivy League based on athletic talent.

Steinberg, J. (2002). *The Gatekeepers: Inside the Admissions Process of a Premier College.* New York: Viking.

There are several websites for those interested in athletic admission:

The National Collegiate Athletic Association can be found at http://www.ncaa.com.

There is also a special website for Ivy League sports – http://www.IvyLeague.com.

There are also two Athletic Associations that are not part of NCAA and which cater to community colleges and small private colleges respectively. The National Junior College Athletic Association can be found at http://www.njcaa.org and the National Association of Intercollegiate Athletics is hosted at http://www.naia.org.

Practical resources

For those thinking about applying for undergraduate study in the United States, the admissions sections of individual institutional websites have detailed information. In addition, general resources about a range of institutions are available. Examples include the *US News* college rankings http://colleges. usnews.rankingsandreviews.com/best-colleges, and the *Forbes* college ranking http://www.forbes.com/top-colleges/list/.

The following websites offer general information and guidance on the application process:

Testing: The SAT and ACT websites offer detailed information on the tests they offer: http://sat.collegeboard.org and http://www.actstudent.org.

The Common application and Universal application websites also provide detailed information about the process of applying to US institutions: https://www.commonapp.org and https://www.universalcollegeapp.com.

NACAC: The National Association for College Admission Counseling http://www.nacacnet.org, an organization with nearly 13,000 professionals dedicated to serving students as they make choices about pursuing post-secondary education. The website offers extensive resources for students and parents. NACAC conducts an annual survey about the state of college admission, including factors universities and colleges consider in admissions decisions: www.nacacnet.org/soca.

College Navigator: http://nces.ed.gov/collegenavigator/

A resource of the US Department of Education. College Navigator gathers admission, retention, graduation and financial aid data for every college in the country.

Know How 2 Go: http://www.knowhow2go.org/

A public service initiative that helps middle and high school students prepare, apply and pay for college. Sponsored by The American Council on Education, the Lumina Foundation and the Ad Council.

England

Academic writing and policy reports

In England, the US genre of admissions books does not have an equivalent. The closest to this genre is Joseph Soares' book on changes at Oxford University. Perhaps it is unsurprising to learn that Soares himself is an American who briefly stayed in Oxford, England for a research visit.

Soares, J. A. (1999). *The Decline of Privilege: The Modernization of Oxford, University*. Stanford, CA: Stanford University Press.

In addition, there are two academic books that tackle social class and race in higher education:

Archer, L., Hutchings, M. and Ross, A. (2002). *Higher Education and Social Class: Issues of Exclusion and Inclusion*. London: Routledge.

Reay, D., David, M. and Ball, S. (2005). *Degrees of Choice: Social Class, Race and Gender in Higher Education*. Stoke-on-Trent: Trentham Books.

A lot of scholarly work in England on admission to higher education is in the form of academic journal articles which are usually only accessible freely in subscribing libraries or on a pay-per-article basis for non-subscribers. The style of these pieces can be less accessible for general readers than books; on the upside, they are based on rigorous and scholarly investigations. The topics in the English literature focus more on the students than the selectors and focus on social class, type of secondary schooling and race in admission and progression at university. Key articles here include:

Boliver, V. (2013). 'How fair is access to more prestigious UK Universities?' *British Journal of Sociology*, 64 (2): 344–64.

Hoare, A. and Johnston, R. (2011). 'Widening participation through admissions policy – a British case study of school and university performance', *Studies in Higher Education*, 36 (1): 21–41.

Linda Croxford, L. and Raffe, D. (2013). 'Differentiation and social segregation of UK higher education, 1996–2010', *Oxford Review of Education*, 39 (2): 172–92.

Ogg, T., Zimdars, A. and Heath, A. (2009). 'Schooling effects on degree performance: A comparison of the predictive validity of aptitude testing and secondary school grades at Oxford University', *British Educational Research Journal*, 35 (5): 781–80766.

The following article looks particularly at the impact of type of school and the writing of personal statements:

Jones, S. (2013). 'Ensure that you stand out from the crowd: A corpus-based analysis of personal statements according to applicants' school type', *Comparative Education Review*, 57 (3): 397–423.

Overall, key resources for finding out about admission and thinking about admission in England are policy reports, legislation and practical resources.

One key resource are the reports published by the Higher Education Funding Council for England on a range of aspects of higher education, including admission and student experiences, freely available at: http://www.hefce.ac.uk/pubs/. The Higher Education Statistical Agency also publishes freely available reports on participation patterns in higher education https://www.hesa.ac.uk/pis.

In addition, the charity the Sutton Trust has a range of research report relevant to higher education admission freely available at: http://www.suttontrust.com/research-category/university/.

Practical resources

Applications for undergraduate study in the UK are processed through a central clearinghouse, UCAS. UCAS stands for the 'Universities and Colleges Admissions Service'. UCAS processes over 2.5 million applications every year, for some 650,000 prospective students across the UK and beyond: helping them gain access to more than 340 UK universities and colleges. www.ucas.com.

Supporting Professionalism in Admissions (SPA) was set up after the 2004 Higher Education Review led by Steven Schwartz (http://www.admissions-review.org.uk/). SPA offers a number of policy and good practice guides as well as research reports. Material is freely available at www.spa.ac.uk. Of particular interest are the reports into contextual admissions www.spa.ac.uk/information/contextualdata/spasworkoncontextual/, Equitable admission for under-represented groups (with the Equality Challenge Unit), www.spa.ac.uk/support/goodpractice/equality/equitableadmissions and SPA's good practice statement of Admissions Policies 2014 www.spa.ac.uk/support/goodpractice/admissionspolicies.

Individual institutions maintain websites containing all relevant information for applying to their undergraduate programmes. A list of all UK universities with weblinks to the institution's homepage is available here: www.universitiesuk.ac.uk/aboutus/members/Pages/default.aspx. A list of Russell Group universities is available here www.russellgroup.ac.uk/our-universities. Those interested in applying for Oxford and Cambridge might be interested in the sample interview questions published by Oxford University: http://www.ox.ac.uk/admissions/undergraduate/applying-to-oxford/interviews/sample-interview-questions.

Two of the big newspapers in the UK, *The Times* and *The Sunday Times* as well as the *Guardian* publish annual 'university guides' that are popular with prospective students, parents and university administrators. www.the sundaytimes.co.uk/sto/University_Guide/ and www.theguardian.com/education/ universityguide.

There are also consultancies operating in the admissions sector and there are commercial guidebooks. Social media sites such as Twitter, Facebook, The Student Room and Mumsnet also offer discussions regarding higher education.

Notes

Chapter 1

1   Mike Nicholson was the Director of Director of Undergraduate Admissions at the University of Oxford for eight years from 2006 to 2014.

Chapter 2

1   The respondent was referring to the US policy to aim and admit students from all US states.
2   The respondent referred particularly to the differences between state-funded and privately funded secondary schools.
3   The numbers presented here were last checked in July 2014.

Chapter 3

1   Research has found the SAT to be a valid predictor of retention at university and, jointly with GPA, a strong predictor of performance at university. All US institutions in this project required applicants to have sat the SAT although some less selective institutions have gone 'SAT optional' in recent years.
2   The SAT is marked in three parts out of 800 each, thus allowing for a total of 2,400 points.
3   The Fields medal is the International Medal for Outstanding Discoveries in mathematics and awarded every four years. It is often viewed as the greatest honour a mathematician can receive and considered on par with the Nobel Prize available in other disciplines.
4   A2-level and AS-level and equivalent qualifications are key considerations in all admissions decisions and, for a few years, universities were allowed to recruit unlimited number of students with grades AAB (and later ABB) or higher while there were restrictions on the number of students universities could recruit with lower grades. Since 2013, the government has lifted any constraints in terms

of student number controls and universities can decide themselves how many students they wish to recruit regardless of grades.

5 The data above is based on the best three A-levels completed by candidates during 2012 and 2013. Candidates may have taken more than three A-levels but the table shows only the best three A-levels. Applicants with A-level grades below AAA may have achieved additional Pre-U qualifications or A-levels prior to 2012. In some circumstances candidates who miss their conditional offer may still be accepted if there are extenuating circumstances such as illness. Source: University of Oxford Admissions Statistics 2013, Cambridge University admissions statistics 2013.

6 For example, multiple mini interviews, that is several short interviews, are used in admission to medicine.

Chapter 4

1 Indeed, the second in line to the throne had achieved an A, B and a C at A-level from Eton College when he gained admission for History of Art. These are not stellar grades from what is perhaps the best-known English private secondary school. His family background may have played a role in admissions. The University of St Andrews has not commented on the matter or responded to a specific request to clarify.

2 More detailed arguments and discussions about the role of race in college admissions and the historic and legal context in the United States are available elsewhere. Interested readers are pointed to the further readings contained in the Further Reading and Resources section of this book.

3 All Supreme Court rulings have focused on public universities (University of California (1978), University of Michigan (2003), University of Texas (2013). Only some of the rulings have concerned admissions to undergraduate programmes (Jennifer Gratz and Patrick Hamacher, University of Michigan, (2003 ruling), Abigail Fisher, University of Texas at Austin (2013 ruling) with other rulings concerning professional postgraduate programmes (Alan Bakke, Medical school (1978 ruling), Barbara Grutter, Law school (2003 ruling)).

4 Both Oxford and Cambridge have a way to compare how students from different colleges perform academically. These tables are called the Norrington Table in Oxford and the Tompkins Table for Cambridge. Points are awarded for the degree class achieved by a final year student with a First class degree gaining the highest points. The reference to 'losing points' implicitly refers to this table as the respondent relates students' extra-curricular involvement to not fulfilling their

academic potential and achieving an Upper Second rather than the First they might have been capable of.

Chapter 5

1 The University of California system is an example of a state system that does not have teacher recommendation.
2 Correct as checked in June 2014.

Chapter 7

1 In the particular instance I observed, the selectors decided that this applicant did not make the cut-off for their college but the applicant was 'exported', that is passed on for consideration for admission to another college and ultimately gained admission there.
2 The liberal arts colleges represented in this project were all part of the NCAA Division III grouping.
3 This context might have changed by the time this book appears in print. The Green Paper – Higher education: teaching excellence, social mobility and student choice, published November 2015 set out draft plans to remove universities from the list of institutions that have to answer to Freedom of Information requests.

Chapter 8

1 In addition, two state Sixth Form Centres in England, serving students for the last two years of their schooling, have emerged as pipelines for selective higher education (Hills Road Cambridge and Peter Symonds in Winchester). Admission to these schools depends on good performance in prior education, prior school attended and locality.
2 In contrast to England where bursary recipients do not have to undertake particular roles, US universities often offer a combined study-work programme so that bursary recipients can contribute to the cost of their education through term time work at the university.

References

Admissions Consultants (2013), Figures are for the Fall 2013 entering class. Admissions Consultants. Available at: http://www.admissionsconsultants.com/college/Ivy_League_table.asp.

Admissions to Higher Education Steering Group ('Schwartz Report') (2004), *Fair Admissions to Higher Education: Recommendations for Good Practice*, Nottingham: Department for Education and Skills Publications.

Amici Curiae (1978), Brief for Columbia University, Harvard University, Stanford University, and the University of Pennsylvania, Regents of the University of California v. Bakke, Brief at 14, 438 U.S. 265 (1978), No. 76–811.

Arum, R. and Roksa, J. (2011), *Academically Adrift: Limited Learning on College*, Chicago: University of Chicago Press.

BBC (2000), Chancellor attacks Oxford admissions, 26 May 2000.

Bernstein, B. (1971), *Class, Codes and Control Basil Bernstein Volume I Theoretical Studies towards a Sociology of Languag*, London: Routledge.

Bourdieu, P. (1986), 'The Forms of Capital', in *Handbook of Theory and Research for the Sociology of Capital*, edited by J. G. Richardson, 241–58, New York: Greenwood Press.

Bowen, W. and Bok, D. (2000), *The Shape of the River Paperback*, Princeton, NJ: Princeton University Press.

Brint, S. (2014), *Conference Presentation, Knowledge Status and Power: Elite Education, Training and Expertise*, Paris: Sciences Po, 23–24 October 2014.

Chapman, K. (2013), Dartmouth Admits 2,252 Students to the Class of 2017, Dartmouth Now, 29 March 2013.

Chua, A. (2011), *Battle Hymn of the Tiger Mother*, New York: Penguin.

CMA (2015), UK higher education providers – advice on consumer protection law Helping you comply with your obligations, CMA briefing paper 33, published 12 March 2015.

Douthat, R. G. (2006), *Privilege: Harvard and the Education of the Ruling Class*, New York: Hyperion.

Equality Act (2010), chapter 15. London: Stationery Office.

Espenshade, T. J. and Radford, A. W. (2009), *No Longer Separate, Not Yet Equal: Race and Class in Elite College Admission and Campus Life*, Princeton, NJ: Princeton University Press.

Eton College (2015), Entry to Eton- Registration, Selection and House Placement (videoclip) available at: http://www.etoncollege.com/Registration.aspx?nid=6070d702-c6ca-4ca1-bbe2-6df39809078c.

Featherman, D. L., Jones, F. L. and Hauser R. M. (1975), 'Assumptions of Social Mobility Research in the US: The Case of Occupational Status', *Social Science Research* 4, no. 4: 329–60.

Fisher v. University of Texas at Austin et al. (2013), No. 11–345.

Fitzsimmons, W., McGrath, M. E. and Ducey, C. (2011), Time Out or Burn Out for the Next Generation (2000, revised 2011) available at: https://college.harvard.edu/admissions/preparing-college/should-i-take-time.

Grutter v. Bollinger (2003), 539 U.S. 306 (2003) 288 F.3d 732.

Harrow School (2015), *Admissions*, Harrow: Harrow School.

Harvard (2013), *Harvard Summer Institute on College Admissions*, Cambridge, MA, June.

Harvard College (2015), *A Brief Profile of the Admitted Class of 2019*, Cambridge, MA: Harvard College.

Higher Education Act (2004), chapter 8. London: The Stationery Office.

Higher Education Funding Council for England (2015), *Invitation to Submit Expressions of Interest in Piloting and Evaluating Measures of Learning Gain*, Bristol: HEFCE.

Higher Education Statistics Agency (2015), *Destinations of Leavers from Higher Education in the United Kingdom for the Academic Year 2013/2014*, Cheltenham: Higher Education Statistical Agency.

Hughes, R. (2013), Oxbridge applications: Five things you might not know. Which university. Available at: http://university.which.co.uk/advice/ucas-application/oxbridge-applications-five-things-you-might-not-know.

Jones, S. (2013), 'Ensure that you stand out from the crowd: A corpus-based analysis of personal statements according to applicants' school type', *Comparative Education Review* 57, no. 3: 397–423.

Karabel, J. (2005), *The Chosen: The Hidden History of Admission and Exclusion at Harvard, Yale, and Princeton*, Boston: Houghton Mifflin.

Laneri, R. (2010), America's Best Prep Schools, 29 April 2010, Forbes.

Lareau, A. (2011), *Unequal Childhoods: Class, Race, and Family Life, 2nd Edition with an Update a Decade Later Second Edition, With an Update a Decade Later Edition*, Berkeley: University of California Press.

Moore, J., Mountford-Zimdars, A. and Wiggans, J. (2013), Contextualised admissions: Examining the evidence Report of research into the evidence base for the use of contextual information and data in admissions of UK students to undergraduate courses in the UK, Report to Supporting Professionalism in Admissions August 2013.

National Association for College Admission Counseling (NACAC) (2011), State of College Admission Report. NACAC. Available for purchase at: http://www.nacacnet.org/research/PublicationsResources/Marketplace/research/Pages/StateofCollegeAdmission.aspx.

National Association of College and University Business Officers and Commonfund Institute (2014), U.S. and Canadian Institutions Listed by Fiscal Year 2013

Endowment Market Value and Change in Endowment Market Value from FY 2012 to FY 2013, Revised 2014. Available at: http://uk.reuters.com/article/2011/11/01/uk-cambridge-endowment-idUKTRE7A05IR20111101.

Nicholson, M. (2011), Director of Admissions Oxford University, *BBC Magazine*, 31 January 2011.

Nicholson, M. (2013), What Are Universities Selecting For? Conference Speech, Sutton Trust Advancing Access and Admissions Summit recording on, 25 November 2013. Available from the Sutton Trust website and from YouTube at: https://www.youtube.com/watch?v=sj8oS01pGT4.

Phillips Exeter Academy (2007), Major Financial Aid Initiative Announced Today: A Free Exeter Education to Those With Need, News and Events, Phillips Exeter Academy, 7 November 2007.

Quinn, K. (2005), *The Ivy Chronicles*, London: Pocket Books.

Rawls, J. (1971), *A Theory of Justice*, Cambridge, MA: Belknap Press.

Reay, D., David, M. and Ball, S. (2005), *Degrees of Choice: Social Class, Race and Gender in Higher Education*, Stoke-on-Trent: Trentham Books.

Soares, J. (2007), *The Power of Privilege*, Stanford: Stanford University Press.

Spencer, T. (2011), *Harvard Summer School Admission 2011*, Ted Spencer, Conference presentation at the Harvard Summer School, Cambridge, MA.

Sternberg, R. (2012), *Conference Presentation. Undergraduate Admissions for the 21st Century.* 18th May 2012 in Trinity College Dublin. Available from youtube https://www.youtube.com/watch?v=yha1D6ZrO_0.

Stevens, M. (2007), *Creating a Class: College Admissions and the Education of Elites*, Cambridge, MA: Harvard University Press.

St Paul's Girls' School (2015), *University Destinations 2014*. Available at: http://spgs.org/academic/university-destinations.

Supporting Professionalism in Admissions (2014), *Newsletter*, autumn 2014, Cheltenham: SPA.

Sutton Trust (2008), *University Admissions by Individual School*, London: Sutton Trust.

Sutton Trust (2013), *Advancing Access and Admissions Summit*, London, 13 and 14 November 2013.

The Wall Street Journal (2007), High Schools How the Schools Stack Up, 28 December 2007.

Tier One Athletics (2012), *The Essential Guide to Ivy League Athletic Recruiting*, Kindle Edition, available to preview at: http://www.tier1athletics.org/.

UCAS (2015), *Fraud and Similarity – Guidance for Applicants*, Cheltenham: UCAS.

University of California Regents v Bakke (1978), no. 76–811.

University of Cambridge (2013), Undergraduate Admissions Statistics 2013. University of Cambridge. Available at: http://www.undergraduate.study.cam.ac.uk/sites/www.undergraduate.study.cam.ac.uk/files/publications/undergrad_admissions_statistics_2013_cycle.pdf.

University of Oxford (2013), *Admissions Statistics 2013*, Oxford: University of Oxford.

Vasagar, J. (10 January 2012), So who is good enough to get into Cambridge?, *Guardian*. Retrieved from www.guardian.com.

Waters, M. C., Heath, A., Tran. V. C. and Boliver, V. (2013), 'Second Generation Attainment and Inequality: Primary and Secondary Effects on Educational Outcomes in Britain and the U.S.', in *The Children of Immigrants at School: A Comparative Look at Integration in the United States and Western Europe*, edited by Richard Alba and Jennifer Holdaway, 120–59, New York: New York University Press.

Westminster School (2013a), *Destinations of 2013 Leavers*. Available at: https://www.westminster.org.uk/life-at-westminster/academic-life/results.

Westminster School (2013b), *Policy on Admissions*, London: Westminster School.

Wetherby School (2015), *Admissions Policy Admissions Policy*, London: Wetherby's Pre-Preparatory school Notting Hill.

Glossary

This glossary provides an alphabetical list of terminology and their definitions used in university admissions. Each term is categorized as belonging to US or English admissions discussions or to both.

ACT, US

The ACT (pronounced A, C, T) is a standardized admissions tests used as part of the admissions process of many US universities and colleges. All institutions represented in this book require either SAT (see definition) or ACT scores. The ACT asks questions directly related to what students have learnt in high school courses and is therefore an achievement test designed to measure 'readiness for college'. The standard ACT is a multiple choice test with sections in English, mathematics, reading and science. Institutions in this project tended to require the ACT plus writing test which contained a 30-minute pen and paper writing section. The cost is $52.50 for taking the test plus writing and releasing the test results to up to four colleges.

Admissions tests, England

Applicants for some subjects for undergraduate study in England have to complete additional admissions test. Examples include the BioMedical Admissions Test (BMAT) for medicine and related degree programmes and the Law National Aptitude Test, the LNAT. In contrast to the United States, both medicine and law can be studied as undergraduate degrees (see definition) and do not have to be taken as postgraduate degrees. In addition to such national tests, some universities, notably Oxford University, use tests that applicants have to take to be eligible for application to a particular course at this university. An example here is the HAT (Oxford History Aptitude test).

The tests in England are different from the SAT or ACT (see definitions) tests in the United States in that they are usually directly related to the skills a successful student for a particular degree subject requires. The US admissions tests focus on more generic ability, aptitude or specific prior knowledge.

A-levels, England

This is an abbreviation for the 'General Certificate of Education Advanced Level'. It is an academic qualification taken in England, Wales and Northern Ireland. Many students take A-levels through following a two-year course of study after they have completed their GCSEs. Most students are aged seventeen or eighteen when they take their A-levels. The first year of the A-level course ends with the award of Advanced Subsidiary (AS) qualifications, equivalent to half an A-level.

Alumni, US, England

Alumni are all graduates, that is successful former pupils or students, of a seat of learning. The singular of this Latin word is alumnus for male graduates and alumna for female graduates. The term alumn is sometimes used as a gender neutral singular reference. Interviews with alumni are frequently used by US universities as part of their admissions process.

Big Three (see also Ivy League), US

This term refers to the Big Three Ivy League universities, Harvard, Yale and Princeton. Sometimes these schools are also referred to as HYP. In this book, quotations are attributed to a Big Three selector if the respondent works or worked at Harvard, Yale or Princeton.

Blue-chip athlete, US

'Blue Chips' are high performers in high school athletics in the United States. These athletes are expected to have an immediate impact on any college team that recruits them. They are sought after by recruiters for college. The private US universities in this book all had special admissions routes for blue-chip athletes; usually entailing lower academic admissions requirements.

College/University, England, US

A university is always an institution of higher education. In this book, the term college is used only in the context of liberal arts colleges (see definition) in the United States and colleges at Oxbridge (see definition). Strictly speaking, undergraduates at institutions like Harvard and Yale are admitted to Harvard college and Yale college that are part of the larger Harvard and Yale universities. Here, the college is the part of the university that educates undergraduate students. In England, a college can also mean a constituting part of a collegiate university (see definition Oxbridge); or a college can be a place of learning in secondary education (see definition) or for vocational education. In this book, the term university is used wherever possible to avoid any confusion regarding the wide range of meanings the term college can have.

Common application, US

The common application can be used by applicants to apply for undergraduate study at over 500 US higher education institutions. As the name suggests, applicants complete a 'common' part of the application that can be passed on to a range of institutions. In addition, some institutions require applicants to complete a 'supplementary part' to the application. Membership in the common application scheme is voluntary and not all US institutions are part of it (see also: Universal Application).

Contextualized admissions, England

This means evaluating applicant's prior attainment and potential to succeed in higher education in the context of the circumstances in which their attainment has been obtained. Specifically, contextual information such as personal circumstances and contextual data such as school performance information are used.

Degree classification, England

The grading for undergraduate degrees at English universities consists of five categories. From highest to lowest, these categories are: First-class honours (1st);

Second-class honours, upper division (2:1, pronounced two-one); Second-class honours, lower division (2:2, pronounced two-two); Third-class honours (3rd); and Ordinary degree (pass).

First-generation student, US

First generation or first in family describes those who are the first in their family to participate in higher education. This means that the parents of those students do not hold any qualifications at degree level or higher. In England, the term 'no history of higher education' is sometimes used.

General Certificate of Secondary Education (GCSE), England

The vast majority of English school children, including all children in state schools, take GCSE examinations. The grades capture the academic accomplishment over two years with the final examinations usually taken at age sixteen. Students then receive an individual grade for each subject for which they took the GCSE examination. GCSEs are graded from A* (pronounced A-star), the highest possible grade, to G as the lowest pass grade and the fail grade U (ungraded). Applicants for the most selective universities usually apply with a string of A*, A and perhaps some B qualifications in their GCSEs and have taken the examination in ten or more subjects. The examinations are overseen by individual exam boards and thus standardized across different schools.

Grade Point Average (GPA), US

The GPA is a measure of attainment used in secondary schools and colleges and universities. The GPA is calculated by taking the number of grade points a student earned in a given period of time of middle school through high school. A conversion table is used to translate A to F grades into numerical scores. GPAs are on a scale from four (highest) to zero (lowest). Universities consider high school GPA in admission although some admissions offices calculate their own average (based on only selected subjects) and do not simply use the GPA provided by the school. While GPAs can be used to compare students within the same school, they are not standardized across schools. This makes them different from the school-leaving examinations in England and partially explains the existence of additional standardized tests (SAT and ACT) in the US system.

Graduate study, US, England

Graduate study is further study in higher education after students have completed their undergraduate studies (see glossary). Typically, in England, taught graduate study entails taking a one- or two-year long master's programme. Some degree subjects in the United States can only be studied as taught graduate programmes with law typically taking three years and medicine four. Graduate research degrees leading to PhDs/doctorates are also available.

Graduation, US, England

This is a ceremony to mark that an undergraduate (see glossary) or graduate student has passed his or her examinations. At a graduation, degrees are formally awarded.

Higher education, US, England

Education systems are usually split into three tiers: Primary education, secondary education and tertiary, third level or higher education. The term post-secondary education can also be used to include all sorts of education happening after secondary school. The higher education institutions in this book are all universities, colleges or institutes of technology. While higher education includes undergraduate and postgraduate or professional studies, this book only focuses on admission to undergraduate study.

High school (US)/secondary school (England), see also private school, public school

A high school or secondary school is a school which provides education for children after primary school and before higher education.

Holistic admission, US

The holistic review of applications in admission is an individualized way of considering academic factors such as grades as well as the applicant's individual context, their experiences and other skills and attributes.

Ivy League, US

This term originally referred to the athletic conference comprising sports teams from eight private universities in Northeastern United States. The term is now used more generally to describe this group of eight universities. The eight institutions are Brown University, Columbia University, Cornell University, Dartmouth College, Harvard University, Princeton University, the University of Pennsylvania and Yale University.

Harvard, Yale and Princeton are sometimes referred to as 'HYP' or the 'Big Three Ivies'. This shorthand description is also used in the current book.

Ivy League schools are ranked among the best universities in the United States and worldwide. There are other highly ranked private universities – like Stanford, Caltech and MIT and public universities like the University of California, Berkeley or the University of Michigan that are not part of the Ivy League.

Liberal arts college, US

Liberal arts colleges in the United States emphasize undergraduate teaching and study in the liberal arts (humanities) and sciences. Liberal arts colleges tend to have fewer, if any, graduate programmes and have lower student numbers than Ivy League universities.

Matriculation, England, US

When students start their study at university, they enrol at the institution. Another term used for enrolment is matriculation.

Music scholar, England

Colleges in Oxford and Cambridge as well as some other English universities including Durham and Bristol offer music scholarships. Musicians, organists and sometimes choristers receive payment and/or benefits in return for contributing or leading services and other aspects of music provision. The competition for music scholarships at Oxbridge precedes the standard admissions round for academic subjects, it is a rare occasion where potential organ scholars can compete for places at both Oxford and Cambridge colleges. Music scholar need to succeed in both the music competition and the academic competition for a place at university.

Oxbridge, England

This term is used to refer simultaneously to the universities of Oxford and Cambridge in England. Applicants for undergraduate admissions are only allowed to apply to either Oxford or Cambridge in any given application year (but see music scholars).

Oxford and Cambridge have a college system. Each college is an independent institution. Jointly, all colleges constitute the universities of Oxford or Cambridge respectively. There are some similarities between such 'constituting' colleges and the residential house system found at some US universities.

Private school, US or independent school/public school, England

These are schools that require payment of tuition fees. The schools are 'independent' from the state and private – usually not for profit – organizations. Confusingly for international observers, the most prestigious and often academically selective private schools in England are called public schools. In contrast to US free public schools, English public schools charge some of the highest fees within the secondary education system.

Public school (US)/state school (England)

Most English and US students attend a secondary school funded by the state and/or local taxation. These schools are called 'state schools' in England and 'public schools' in the United States.

Russell Group, England

The Russell Group, named after the hotel where the first meeting took place, is an association of 24 British public research universities. All the internationally highly ranked institutions like Oxford, Cambridge, Imperial College London and University College London are members of the Russell Group. The universities of Oxford and Cambridge are sometimes referred to separately as Oxbridge.

SAT, US

The SAT (pronounced S, A, T) is a standardized admissions tests used as part of the admissions process of many US universities and colleges. All institutions represented in this book required either SAT or ACT (see definition) scores. The SAT contains sections on evidence-based reading and writing and mathematics. In addition, some institutions in this study required results from SAT subject tests. Subject tests are available for natural sciences, foreign languages, history and literature.

School counsellor, US

High school guidance counsellors help students with their college applications and choices and their references. Counselling professionals evaluate students through counselling sessions, interviews and aptitude tests. The ratio of students per counsellor is significantly higher in large public schools than in private or magnet schools.

UCAS, England

UCAS is the Universities and Colleges Admissions Service. UCAS provides a central place for the undergraduate application process for almost all British universities. Applicants submit a single application through UCAS for a maximum of five different courses (four choices if applying to medicine, veterinary medicine/science or dentistry) at up to five different universities. Universities do not see which other courses or universities an applicant has applied to. Applicants cannot usually apply to both Oxford and Cambridge in the same year. Some subjects at some universities require additional test results from, for example, medicine or law admissions tests. UCAS manages the offers from universities to applicants and gives applicants a choice to accept one offer as their 'firm' offer and one offer as their 'insurance' offer.

Undergraduate, England, US

This book is about admission to undergraduate study. Undergraduates are those studying for their first degree in higher education (see definition). Typically, undergraduate study at the universities represented in this book leads to the award of a Bachelor degree. Undergraduate admission thus contrasts with postgraduate study where those applying to study in higher education often already have an undergraduate degree or a professional qualification and now study towards a master or doctorate.

Universal application, US

The universal application is similar to the Common Application. It is a voluntary scheme that universities can choose to adopt in admissions for receiving applications for undergraduate study. The scheme has fewer members than the common application form.

Index

Lightning Source UK Ltd.
Milton Keynes UK
UKOW06n0640210716

278906UK00011B/326/P